CONTRACTOR'S PLAIN-ENGLISH LEGAL GUIDE

Quenda Behler Story

Craftsman Book Company
6058 Corte del Cedro / P.O. Box 6500 / Carlsbad, CA 92018

I wish to thank my husband, Donn, for all his invaluable support and assistance.
Quenda Behler Story

A Word of Caution

The information contained in this book, including the material on the CD-ROM in the back, has been written as general information, and may not comply exactly with the laws in your state. Your best source of advice on the law as it applies to you will always be legal counsel familiar with the law in the communities where you do business.

Looking for other construction reference manuals?

Craftsman has the books to fill your needs. **Call toll-free 1-800-829-8123** or write to Craftsman Book Company, P.O. Box 6500, Carlsbad, CA 92018 for a **FREE CATALOG** of over 100 books, including how-to manuals, annual cost books, and estimating software.
Visit our Web site: http://www.craftsman-book.com

Library of Congress Cataloging-in-Publication Data

Story, Quenda Behler, 1941-
    Contractor's plain-English legal guide   /   by Quenda Behler Story
        p.   cm.
    Includes index.
    ISBN 1-57218-106-0
    1. Construction industry—Law and legislation—United States—Popular works. 2. Construction contracts--United States--Popular works. I. Title.
    KF1950.Z9 S76 2001
                                        2001055514

Contents

Part One: Startup Legal Problems 5

1. **What Do You Need to Start a Construction Business?** 7
   Can You Work Out of Your Home? 8
   What Do You Need from the IRS? 10
   What Do You Need from the State? 12
   What Records Should You Keep — and Why? 20

2. **Sole Proprietor, Partnership or Corporation?** 25
   When Does It Make a Difference? 25
   What Is a Sole Proprietorship? 27
   What Is a Partnership? 30
   What Is a Corporation? 42

Part Two: Construction Contracts 51

3. **What Does Every Contract Have to Have?** 53
   The Four Requirements for a Contract 53
   A Contract Starts With an Offer 55
   A Contract Must Benefit Both Parties 60
   An Offer Has to Be Accepted 62
   Consumer Protection Notices 63
   If the Contract Doesn't Have Everything 64

4. **Contract Terms: Filling In the Blanks** .. 67
   Who Are the Parties? 67
   Scope of the Work Clauses 76
   The Payment Amount 80
   The Payment Terms 82

Work Schedules 86
Change Orders 88
Indemnity Clauses 90
Settling Disputes 93
Warranty Clauses 93
Consumer Clauses 94

Part Three: Legal Guidelines for Running a Business   97

5. **What If You Hire Someone?** 99
   Employee or Independent Contractor? 100
   Taxes and Social Security Payments 101
   Unlawful Discrimination in Hiring 102
   Protecting Others from
    Employee Negligence 107
   Employee Handbooks 109
   Affirmative Action Programs 112

6. **What Do You Have to Do for the IRS?** . 113
   The Self-Employed and the IRS 113
   Your Employees and the IRS 121
   What If You're Audited? 122
   What If You Haven't Filed Tax Returns? 123

7. **How Do You Collect What's Owed You?** 125
   Small Claims Court 127
   What Is a Construction Lien? 128
   Lien Waivers 138
   What Is a Stop Notice? 142
   Payment and Performance Bonds 143

Part Four: Legal Problems on the Job Site   145

8. **What Laws Affect the Building Site?** . . 147
   - Building Codes 147
   - The Zoning Laws 151
   - The Accessibility Laws 159
   - Other Permits You Must Get 161

9. **How Is Safety Regulated on the Job Site?** 163
   - OSHA Job Site Safety Requirements 163
   - Employers' Obligations Under OSHA 164
   - Employees' Rights Under OSHA 167
   - OSHA Inspections 170

10. **What If Someone Is Injured on the Job Site?** 171
    - When Your Employee Is Injured 171
    - When a Sub or Sub's Employee Is Injured . . 174
    - When an Owner or Visitor Is Injured 175
    - If a Trespasser Is Injured 177
    - If the Contractor Is Sued for Negligence 177

11. **What If You Use Subcontractors Instead of Employees?** 179
    - What Is a Subcontract? 179
    - Employee or an Independent Contractor? . . 181
    - If an Independent Is Injured on the Job 183
    - Trouble Between the General and the Owner. 186

12. **What Contract Problems Do Subcontractors Have?** 189
    - Between the General and the Customer 190
    - Between the General and Subs 193
    - Solution — The Subcontractor's Addendum 201

Part Five: Legal Issues in the Construction Industry   209

13. **What Warranties Affect the Construction Industry?** 211
    - Express Warranties 212
    - Implied Warranties 214
    - Disclaimer of Warranties 216

14. **What Consumer Protection Laws Affect Your Business?** 221
    - State Consumer Protection Laws 221
    - The Federal Consumer Protection Laws 228

15. **What Legal Protection Is Available for a Company in Financial Trouble?** 235
    - Protecting Your Personal Assets 236
    - When Your Business Is in Trouble 239
    - Save Your Business Without Bankruptcy . . . 240
    - Bankruptcy the Only Solution 241

16. **What About Retirement, Disability or Death?** 245
    - Retirement Plans 245
    - Health and Disability 248
    - Death 250

17. **A Few Last Words About You and Your Lawyer** 253
    - How to Choose a Lawyer 253
    - When to Call a Lawyer 253
    - When to Call Another Professional 254
    - What to Expect 257

Glossary 259

Index 266

What's on the CD? 269

Part One:
Startup Legal Problems

Chapter 1

What Do You Need to Start a Construction Business?

Chapter 2

Sole Proprietor, Partnership or Corporation?

What Do You Need to Start a Construction Business?

The construction industry is filled with small builders, remodelers, and subcontractors — businesses that can't easily afford $100 to $200 an hour to hire a lawyer to help them start up or to handle their day-to-day legal problems. But in modern America, legal problems are like snakes in the swamp — you might not see them, but you know they're there.

This book is intended to help you get through the swamp without having to hire a $100-an-hour guide. It's written to help small builders, subcontractors, and remodelers recognize and manage the legal tasks, which, with a reasonable amount of time and thought, they can do for themselves. Some of those legal tasks aren't as difficult as you might think. In many cases, they are tasks a lawyer would simply hand off to his secretary. However, it won't be the secretary's hourly rate you'll be paying. If you can read and understand the material for a contractor's licensing test, you can certainly read and understand this book — and you can probably do all the tasks the lawyer's secretary can do.

Another, equally-important purpose of this book is as a "heads-up" for those situations where you *do* need a lawyer — or some other kind of professional, like an accountant, an insurance specialist, or a financial advisor. When you need a professional, you need to get one *before* it's too late. It's a lot easier to pull someone out of a swamp when he's only ankle-deep. When he's in up to his neck, it's a major job, if not impossible. Wait too long and sometimes all that a professional can do for you is collect a big fee.

Although, by using the Contents and the Index, you can find answers to your questions in this book without reading the entire book, I hope you do read it all. The book will give you a lot of general information that should help you stay out of lawyers' offices as much as possible — not just by telling you what you can do yourself, but by telling you *where the snakes in the swamp are hiding*. Forewarned is forearmed. If it's something that can happen to you, it's probably already happened to someone else. If you know how it happened to them, you can make sure you don't go there. Why learn the expensive way?

And when a particular problem comes up in the course of your business, before you call your lawyer, check first to see if it's covered in this book. I've tried to cover most areas of trouble. There's a good chance I've covered that one. If so, maybe I've saved you a lawyer's bill!

And now on to the subject of this chapter.

You want to start up your own construction business. You want to be the one who calls the shots and who makes the money. But even though you might not choose it, you're in a partnership. Your partner is the government. It doesn't pound nails for you, it doesn't sell jobs for you, it doesn't do any of the worrying or suffer headaches for you — but if you ever make any money, the government will be right there to share with you. Sometimes you can get a government agency to help you out, and we'll cover that later in the book. But at startup time, you have to consider and follow their rules.

There are many requirements for a startup contracting business, and they come from several different levels of government. In this chapter we'll cover the most important ones, whether you're starting out alone at your kitchen table or setting up a corporation.

Can You Work Out of Your Home?

There's one major advantage small construction companies have over the larger companies: It's easier for a smaller company to keep its overhead costs low by not doing things like renting office space and hiring a lot of office staff. Many small construction businesses start out in a workshop behind the garage, in the garage itself, in an extra bedroom, or off the kitchen table.

By using modern technology, a small construction company can do without all kinds of office help like receptionists, accounting clerks, and even salespeople and secretaries. Instead, you can use a telephone answering machine with voice mail, a pager, and a computer with spreadsheets and word processing programs.

Possible Zoning Problems

One possible problem with working out of your home is your local zoning code. Some communities restrict what kind of business (or how large a business) can be operated in a home or in a residential area. Remember that the zoning definition of "home" includes the barn and the garage and any other kind of outbuilding.

It's how the property is zoned, not whether or not anybody is actually living in it, that makes the difference. You could have a vacant lot, but if that lot is zoned as residential, it's intended to be used as somebody's home. So whether you could put a trailer or a tool crib on that lot and use it as your permanent office would depend on what the local zoning laws say about what can be done in a home besides living in it.

Most zoning codes *do* allow some in-home businesses, but restrict the kind of business. The goal of these restrictions is to avoid the kind of traffic coming into residential neighborhoods that businesses, such as retail services or a business with several employees, would generate. The zoning laws especially want to keep businesses out of residential neighborhoods that use heavy, noisy equipment — such as construction businesses — that would disturb people in their homes.

The zoning laws also often restrict the kind of advertising a home business can do to indicate its presence. The idea is that commercial advertising in a residential area lowers property values. That's why zoning laws typically either limit the size of a business sign or don't allow one at all.

So before you set up shop in your home, you should check with your local municipality to see if it's lawful to run your kind of business there. You should also plan on being discreet. Many communities don't enforce their rules until the neighbors complain. If all you're doing in your business-in-your-home office is making and receiving phone calls and sending and receiving mail, chances are there won't be complaints. But if you have lumber delivery trucks rolling in and a steady flow of clients parking on the street, chances are you'll be hearing from city hall.

What About Deducting the Home Office?

Until 1999, the IRS had a nasty little surprise for contractors who worked out of their home. The IRS said that if the office located in your home wasn't your principal place of business, you couldn't deduct it as a home office. What, you ask, is your principal place of business if you're in the construction industry? The job site, the IRS answered.

One of the things that made this principal place of business rule so illogical was that if you went out and rented an office, you could deduct it even though you were doing most of your business at job sites, not at your office.

Under pressure from small businesses, the IRS changed its rule, and, starting in 1999, the principal place of business rule was changed to allow a home office deduction if the business's principal administrative and management tasks took place there.

Even under the new rules, you need a place dedicated to the business before you can deduct a home office. That has to be absolutely the *only thing* you do there. If you work off your kitchen table, that table will never qualify for a deduction. Also, you can't use your home office to create a business loss. In other words, you can only write off home office expenses *against profits.*

If you're a sole proprietor and you want to write off a home office, you must fill out and file a Form 8829 along with your Schedule C. It's a complicated form. If you use it, first ask for IRS Publication 586: *Business Use of Your Home.*

What Do You Need From the IRS?

There are as many horror stories about dealing with the IRS as there are about going to the dentist. I think that's a shame, for two reasons. First, those stories can scare people out of doing some really easy things that they need to do, because they think they will be too complicated to handle on their own. Second, when people get into trouble, they think they're doomed. They often become paralyzed with fear and don't deal with the situation. Now, sure, I know some people have had some genuinely nightmarish experiences with the IRS, but I think those are statistically rare. I also think that, in some of these horror stories, the person telling the story doesn't always include every single fact. Sometimes the situation wasn't quite as one-sided as their story suggests.

My experience with the IRS (knock on wood) is that mostly the agents want to help you work out your problem.

There's a very useful publication, available free from the IRS, that you should get right away. It's Publication 334: *Tax Guide for Small Businesses.* It's available at IRS offices, or they'll mail one to you if you ask for it. You can also phone them at 1-800-829-3676 to ask for the publication.

What About a Taxpayer Identification Number?

The first thing you need from the IRS is a number, although you may already have it. You'll have lots of forms to file with the IRS — and the IRS keeps track of those forms with numbers, not names, so it's important to get the right number to put on your tax forms. You'll need some kind of taxpayer identification number — what they call a *TIN* — to put on your forms so those forms don't get lost. The phrase taxpayer identification number includes several different kinds of numbers. You may already have all the taxpayer identification you need: your social security number. Depending on your situation, you may not need anything else. Here's how to tell if you can use your social security number, or if you need to apply for a TIN.

For a Sole Proprietorship

If you're not a partnership or a corporation, and if you have no employees, you can simply write your social security number on those lines on your 1040 form, Schedule C and on your quarterly self-employment income reports that ask for your EIN (Employer Identification Number).

For a Partnership

Partnerships don't have social security numbers, so your partnership will need the kind of taxpayer identification number called an EIN (Employer Identification Number). Your partnership TIN is an EIN. Got that? All joking aside, you'll need an EIN for your partnership even if you don't have any employees.

Without an EIN, all the income the partnership earned would be credited to whichever partner used his or her social security number on the partnership reporting forms. That partner could owe a lot of extra tax to the IRS, while the other partners get a free ride!

To get an EIN, fill out an IRS Form SS-4 and mail it to the IRS. The IRS will assign a number to the partnership and mail it back.

For a Corporation

Corporations must have an EIN even if they don't have employees. Fill out the SS-4 form, send it to the IRS, and the IRS will assign an EIN number to your corporation and mail it to you. This number will be only for the corporation, not for the shareholders — even if there's only one shareholder.

For Any Business That Has Employees

If your business has employees, it'll need an EIN even if the business is a sole proprietorship. To be sure your reports and payments get credited at the right places, you'll also need your employees' social security numbers. You get those by asking your employees to fill out W-4 forms for you. The IRS will mail all of these forms to you if you just call and ask. Their phone number is 800-829-3676.

There's more information on these topics in Chapters 5 and 6. Also, the IRS publishes a free publication, which is surprisingly clear and readable, called Circular E, *Employer's Tax Guide.* When the IRS mails you your EIN, it sends along a copy of Circular E.

What Do You Need From the State?

The state regulates your business names, your license requirements and may impose some additional tax requirements. Your state may or may not have an income tax. It may charge sales tax on some of your installation activity. Contact your state treasury and find out what you have to do to satisfy your state tax requirements.

You Probably Need a License

Most states don't allow anyone without a contractor's license to do business in the construction trade. The penalty for doing business without a license is usually that any contractor who's not properly licensed can't sue to collect payment for completed work. So if you're unlicensed and your customer stiffs you, there's not much you can do about it. The customer may get the work for nothing. More about this later in the chapter.

The licensing requirement is meant to protect consumers. The idea is that by requiring a license, the state can set some minimum standards. That's not a bad idea in an industry where anyone who owns a hammer thinks he's a carpenter. By preventing an unlicensed contractor from collecting for his work, the state motivates contractors to get their licenses — and does it without spending a lot of money on investigators and enforcement.

There's another way the licensing laws protect consumers. If the customers of a licensed contractor believe that the contractor has cheated them, they can make a complaint against that contractor's license. If the state then determines that it's a valid complaint, the state can fine the contractor, or even cancel that contractor's license. Generally speaking, the state won't usually pull a contractor's license just for complaints about bad workmanship, unless the contractor's work has actually caused a dangerous situation. In circumstances involving bad workmanship, the state usually just leaves the customer to his or her warranty rights.

But usually the state *does* act against the contractor's license in cases where the contractor has accepted money, then either didn't start the work, or didn't finish it.

Taking away a license is an administrative procedure. A contractor whose license is threatened can, and probably should, seek the help of a lawyer.

A contractor's license can also be revoked for failure to pay the mandatory annual licensing fee. That's usually automatic.

How to Get a License

State licensing requirements vary widely. Not every state requires a license for every construction activity. Some states issue a one-size-fits-all sort of license, which lets the person with the license do everything. Other states break down their licenses into specialties such as general contractor, and specific trades, such as electrician, plumber, and so forth. The license may also act to regulate activities such as advertising, selling, and some aspects of the contracts between customers and contractors. Craftsman Book Company, the publisher of this book, has a Web site called Contractors-License.org that details the licensing requirements in each state. It has frequently-updated information on states' requirements, and links to each state's contractor's license Web site, where you can find out if a contractor has a license and if it's current, and learn other useful information.

Before issuing a license, most states require applicants to demonstrate that they have some experience in construction, and that they're credit-worthy. Some states make the applicant pass a test. And some, my home state of Michigan, for example, require all three: experience, creditworthiness, and an examination.

Who Must Be Licensed?

In Michigan, anyone who is self-employed and works in the construction trade has to have an appropriate license. Michigan has different levels of construction licenses. A general contractor's license is available for builders or remodelers. There's a residential maintenance and alteration contractor's license (you have to pass a trade test for your particular trade), and separate licenses for electrical, plumbing and mechanical contractors. Also, anyone selling remodeling or building projects has to be licensed as a salesperson and work under a builder or contractor who is also licensed.

But there are some exceptions to the requirement for licenses. In some states, a construction worker doesn't need a license to perform work for less than $600 compensation. There are some other exceptions, too. Be sure to check in your state before you start working as a contractor.

Some states, Kansas for example, don't license contractors at all. But cities or counties in those states might. So if you find you're in a state that doesn't require a license, don't assume that you're off the hook and can start building. You might be in for an unpleasant and expensive surprise!

Homeowners — A homeowner or a landlord doesn't need a license to build anything on their own property (although they'll probably need a building permit).

Developers — In a state that requires builders to be licensed, any land developer, subdivider, or real estate agent who owns the property and intends to sell it, must have a construction license or use a licensed contractor in order to build on the property. They don't get the homeowner's exemption because they don't intend to make their home on the property — they're holding that property for resale.

Subcontractors — Most states require that anyone doing business in the construction trade get a license. "Doing business" includes subcontracting for other contractors.

Partnerships — Different states have different rules about partnerships. Some states allow a partnership to use the license of one of the partners. However, the partner who has obtained the license must be a managing partner, or the partnership cannot legally use his or her license.

States such as Michigan require a partnership to have a license in the partnership's name, even though one or more of the partners is already individually licensed. When the partnership applies for the license, one of the partners (it must be a managing partner), takes the test. The license is then issued in the name of the partnership and it becomes a partnership asset.

Joint ventures — A joint venture is a kind of partnership, so most states require a joint venture to do whatever partnerships are required to do. If the state requires a partnership to obtain its own license, a joint venture must also obtain its own contractor's license. That's true even if the joint venture has only been set up for a limited project such as building a single mall, one building, or an apartment building. The requirement applies even if the joint venture is set up by two or more partnerships that have their own licenses.

Corporations — Some states won't license corporations. They only license individuals. So in those states, an individual in the corporation must get a license in the company name. The person who takes the tests and qualifies for the license on behalf of the corporation must hold a managing position in that corporation.

A few states won't let construction companies incorporate at all. The states that do allow construction companies to incorporate generally require those corporations to get their own license, even though one or more of the individual shareholders in the corporation may already hold a license.

Are There Penalties for Not Having a License?

There are criminal penalties for engaging in the construction business without a license. It's a misdemeanor that's punishable by a fine or imprisonment — or both. However, the public prosecutor is the one who decides whether or not to enforce criminal penalties. Usually the public prosecutor isn't interested in putting unlicensed contractors in prison, *unless* they've been cheating their customers.

The real penalty for contracting without a license is that a contractor without the proper license can't sue a customer. That means he can't sue for nonpayment or enforce a construction lien, because a contractor has to go to court to foreclose on a lien. For more information about construction liens, see Chapter 7.

The license requirement gives consumers a powerful way of protecting themselves from the dishonest or unskilled contractors (who tend to be the ones without a license). Consumers dealing with an unlicensed contractor may not have to pay for the work the unlicensed contractor did for them. They may even be able to get any money back that they've already paid to the unlicensed contractor. In some states, this is true even if the customer actually *knew* the contractor was unlicensed and lured him into doing the work, knowing that the contractor wouldn't be able to collect.

This can be hard on contractors who weren't acting in bad faith. There are cases where the contractor was unlicensed only because of a technicality or a failure to promptly pay a license renewal fee, but still wasn't allowed to sue to collect payment. It sounds harsh, but the courts rigorously enforce the rule against letting an unlicensed contractor sue a customer. After all, it's an effective way to enforce the state's licensing laws. It gives the contractor a powerful motive to make the effort to get that license.

Exceptions to the rule — Some states will allow a contractor some recovery (on an unjust enrichment, or *quantum meruit* theory) if the contractor can demonstrate that the failure to have a license was only a technical error. For example, unlicensed contractors have been allowed to sue their customers for payment in the following cases based on these facts:

- Two licensed contractors had set up a joint venture partnership. They were both properly licensed, but didn't realize that their joint venture was supposed to have its own license.

- Another contractor had a license for the bulk of the time that the work was being done, but had failed to renew it promptly. He was only unlicensed for a brief period of time.

However, no unlicensed contractor should count on this relief. There's at least one case on record where the court refused to let a contractor collect from a customer where the contractor worked on the project for several months and was unlicensed for only ten days because he had failed to make his annual license payment.

This is an area in which the law varies from state to state. If you're involved in this kind of problem, you should get help from a lawyer who knows exactly what your local laws are. Your lawyer may tell you that you're in a state that closes the courthouse doors to an unlicensed contractor — period. You might as well not bother trying. Just write it off to the high cost of experience. However, you may be in one of those states where, in certain situations, unlicensed contractors can sue for unjust enrichment, or *quantum meruit.*

Impact on the property owner — The penalty for not having a license doesn't have any impact on the property owner. The law is only intended as a hammer to force unlicensed contractors to get licenses. It's not intended to punish anybody else. Even though the courts are closed to an unlicensed contractor, a property owner could sue his unlicensed contractor for breach of warranty and even for breach of contract.

Let's look at an imaginary example: Harry Homeowner hired Contractor Cal to build a room addition. The contract price was $15,000. When Contractor Cal was two-thirds done (and Harry had paid him $10,000), Harry learned that Cal had no license. He immediately told Cal to stop work, and hired a licensed contractor to finish the job. This second contractor charged Harry $9,000 for the balance of the job — $4,000 more than he would have had to pay Cal.

Even though it was he who stopped Cal from finishing, Harry can now sue Cal for breach of contract. Cal could be made to reimburse Harry the $4,000 difference. In a few states, Harry could even get back the $10,000 he's already paid Cal as well.

A homeowner could also sue an unlicensed contractor who has violated his warranties of good workmanship or fitness of purpose. For example, suppose an unlicensed contractor installed a deck without proper footings and in the first winter, the deck heaved and racked out of square. The homeowner could sue the unlicensed contractor for breach of warranty.

The one thing that a property owner can't do, however, is sue for specific performance. A lawsuit for specific performance is one that demands that the court order the defendant to complete his contract. A contract with an unlicensed contractor, in a state that requires a license, isn't enforceable. It would be an illegal contract, and the court won't order anyone to perform an illegal contract.

Suppliers to an unlicensed contractor — A supplier to an unlicensed contractor doesn't lose the right to sue the unlicensed contractor. But in most states, a supplier to an unlicensed contractor does lose his right to a construction lien on the building site. Since the unlicensed contractor couldn't enforce a lien against the property owner, the supplier can't either.

In order to get compensated for materials already supplied to a job, most states will allow the supplier to sue the homeowner directly for unjust enrichment. After all, Bigger Lumbers didn't intend to donate the materials to Harry the homeowner, and Harry surely expected to pay somebody at some time for materials. Unfortunately, the damages on an unjust enrichment lawsuit can present a further problem for Bigger Lumbers. What you win in an unjust enrichment lawsuit is supposed to reflect the value of the goods, which may not be the same as the cost of the goods.

And, in most states, Bigger Lumbers won't be able to get paid if Harry has already paid Cal, the unlicensed contractor, for the materials. They won't make Harry pay twice for the construction materials used on his job. In many states, this is true even when Cal does have a license.

Subcontractors to an unlicensed contractor — Suppose the subcontractor has a license, but the contractor doesn't. If the contractor doesn't pay the subcontractor, the subcontractor can sue the unlicensed contractor for payment. In fact, the subcontractor could sue the contractor for payment even if the subcontractor didn't have a license, either. It's only the homeowner who can't be sued. Licensed or not, the subcontractor can't sue the homeowner if the general contractor didn't have a license. The subcontractor doesn't have any rights against the homeowner that the general contractor didn't have. That's because the subcontractor's rights are derivative. That means the subcontractor gets (derives) his rights from the contract between the homeowner and the general contractor. If the general contractor can't sue the property owner, neither can the subcontractor.

In Michigan, a licensed subcontractor who was working with an unlicensed contractor wasn't even allowed to collect against the Builders Fund when the unlicensed contractor didn't pay him. The court ruled that the contractor couldn't have collected from the Builders Fund, so his subcontractor couldn't collect either. That's in spite of the fact the fund was established to protect (among other people) subcontractors from property owners who don't pay.

Another contractor — The legislation barring unlicensed contractors from suing property owners for collection is only intended to protect the property owner. It has no effect on another contractor doing business with the unlicensed contractor. Other contractors or suppliers can sue the unlicensed contractor, or the unlicensed contractor can sue them. In fact, they can sue each other even if none of them is properly licensed.

For example, suppose an unlicensed contractor hired a properly-licensed subcontractor to pour a foundation, and a big crack opened up because the cement was improperly cured. The unlicensed contractor can sue the subcontractor for the money it cost to repair the crack and for any money that the delay cost the contractor.

What About Design and Build Contracts?

Some states require design professionals to be licensed by the state. In those states, a construction contract that includes design functions that aren't performed by a licensed engineer or architect may not be enforceable by the contractor against the homeowner, because of the lack of a proper license. However, most states that require a separate design license have held that a contractor without a design license is permitted to do design work under the supervision of a licensed design professional, like an architect or engineer.

What About Federal Projects?

Federal law, not state law, applies to federal projects. Federal agencies have their own rules and regulations about which contractors can do federal work. If a contractor or a subcontractor working on a federal project meets the federal requirements, it won't matter if that contractor isn't licensed by the state the project is in. And any contractor, licensed or not, can sue if he doesn't get paid for work done on a federal project.

The Name of Your Business

Even if you're running an unincorporated business all by yourself off your kitchen table, that business is still separate from you in some sense. Customers or suppliers may not realize that you are John's Better Roofs, so most states require you to file the name of your business with some local agency.

Assumed Names

In most states, unincorporated businesses must register their business name in what's usually called a fictitious or an assumed name registry. There's nothing sinister about that — it just means you're doing business under a name that's not exactly your own. That business name must be registered even though it includes your name.

For example, John Smith can advertise himself as John Smith, Master Carpenter. Even though that business name includes his own actual name, it's also the name of his business. Most states will require it to be registered as an assumed name.

The law in some states doesn't use the terms "assumed name" or "fictitious name." Instead, those states may describe you as a company "Doing Business As . . ." or even just as a "d.b.a." The term is different, but the intent is the same.

In Michigan, you have to register with the Assumed Names Index, located in the county clerk's office. Some states require a filing at the state level and publication in a legal newspaper along with the registration. That gives someone who's already using that name an opportunity to object.

Selecting a Business Name

Before you chose a business name, try to make sure no one else is using that name, because it's against the law to use a business name that already belongs to someone else. While it's not actually a crime unless you do it with intent to deceive, if someone else is already using that name, they could sue you for trademark infringement. They could collect damages from you, and force you to stop using that name, even if you've built up a business under that name.

If there's a business already registered under that name in the Assumed Names Index, the county won't accept your registration. But you can't assume that just because they do accept the registration, there's no one in the next county or somewhere else in the state using that name. When you're choosing a business name, take reasonable precautions, like first checking phone books and directories to see if someone else is already doing business under that name. Nowadays you'd better check on the Internet too!

If your name is John McDonald and you want to call your company McDonald's Construction Company, will there be a problem with that? Probably not — for two reasons. First, because you're using the word construction as part of the name. That means people hearing your company name won't assume you're selling hamburgers. If you were, or if you were a restaurant or some kind of food supply company, you'd be hearing from McDonald's expensive attorneys. The second reason it's probably all right to use McDonald's Construction Company is that McDonald's most likely hasn't registered that name as a trademark in conjunction with construction. If they have, you'll be hearing from their attack-attorneys.

Corporation Names

Corporations aren't usually required to file assumed or fictitious names or d.b.a. certificates with the county agencies. The name of the corporation and its official address is already on record with the agency in the state that regulates corporations. But the corporation will have to register if it's doing business under a name other than its corporate name. Like individuals, corporate names can't infringe on someone else's trademark.

In addition to trademark restraints, most states regulate what a corporation can call itself. That's to protect people who may not realize that they're doing business with a corporation, and therefore can't sue the individual they're doing business with for nonpayment or breach of contract. They can only sue the corporation.

State laws have strict rules about what can be put into a corporation name, and they'll review the name of a corporation to see if it meets their standards before accepting the incorporation papers. What the state wants is something in the business name that makes it clear to people doing business with that company that it is a corporation. The name has to include words like Incorporated, Corporation, Company or Limited. Usually, an abbreviation like Inc. or Ltd. is also okay. Corporations do have to file an assumed names certificate if they're using one. If the corporation chooses to do business under an assumed name, even that assumed name has to meet the state corporate naming standards.

What Records Should You Keep — and Why?

Personally, I don't think you should ever throw away business records. You might not agree, especially if you can't put your car in the garage because of all the banker boxes full of records you have stored in there. So, what I'm going to do here is talk about the minimum time you should keep your records for legal purposes. There are four legal reasons, besides business reasons, you should plan to keep your records.

You Might Need Your Records for Tax Audits

The IRS regulations say you should keep your receipts, canceled checks, and other financial records for whichever is longer: either three years from the due date for filing your return, or two years from the date the tax was paid. If you have employees, you must keep your employee withholding records for at least four years.

That's what IRS regulations say, but believe me, the real number is six years. That's because the IRS has six years to assess you if you failed to report gross income 25 percent greater than what's shown on your income report. So, just in case you're accused of that, you'd better keep the records to prove you didn't — or at least, didn't do it intentionally — for six years.

If you aren't filing tax returns at all, then just keep everything forever. If you're caught, at least you'll have some evidence refuting the Rockefeller-like income that the IRS could decide you had.

Your Insurance Company Might Audit You

You should keep copies of your contracts with subcontractors and copies of their certificates of insurance on file for at least three years, because your workers' compensation insurance company might audit your records. If they do audit you, and if they find that you don't have copies on file of your subcontractors' insurance certificates, the insurance company may assume that's because your subcontractors weren't insured. What's your insurance company likely to do about that? They'll hit you with a nasty surcharge, because you've exposed them to more liability than they'd agreed to accept. Insurance companies hate that.

You Might Be Sued

Another good reason to keep your records is because somebody might sue you. It could be a breach of contract lawsuit, a warranty lawsuit, or a problem with an employee (like a workers' compensation claim for an injury you say never happened).

Your testimony in a lawsuit is more convincing if you have business records that support it. Even if these are records you prepared yourself, they're admissible in court if you prepared them in the ordinary course of business. As long as you wrote it down at the time of the event (and you typically do write down that kind of event), written evidence is more convincing than anybody's memory — and a darn sight more likely to be accurate.

For legal purposes, I recommend keeping copies of all your business contracts, purchase receipts, punch lists, employee injury records, and a daily phone log that includes all phone contacts with your business customers and the job site. Even if you don't actually use these records in court, it's important to have them to jog your memory. You'd be surprised how easy it is to forget the details of even the most difficult and contentious situation.

Statute of Limitations

You don't have to live in fear of a lawsuit for the rest of your life. People can't wait forever before they decide to sue. It's simply not reasonable to let a potential lawsuit hang over someone's head indefinitely. So, if someone has the right to sue you for some reason, the law requires that they do so within a reasonable period of time — before all the witnesses die and everyone has forgotten what the fuss was about in the first place.

The law that says the right to sue expires after a certain number of years is called the Statute of Limitations. Different states use different periods of time for their Statute of Limitations. If you're in a situation where you need to be concerned about that, you should check with your attorney.

The Statute of Limitations varies for different kinds of lawsuits, and for different states. But for most kinds of civil (noncriminal) actions, the average limitation is three years. I suggest keeping your records for six years, however, because there are situations in which the plaintiff could get extra time to bring a lawsuit.

For example, if the plaintiff is a minor, the Statute of Limitations won't even start expiring until the plaintiff becomes an adult. That means that if a child trespassing on your job site was injured, that child could possibly wait until he or she was 18 to sue you. In a situation like that, I'd advise getting some legal advice about what you might be able to do to keep this from hanging over your head for years. Your liability insurance carrier may also have some legal assistance to offer you in this situation.

Keep All Employee Records

When you're deciding what records to save, don't forget to keep all of your employee records for at least three years. You should keep their personnel files, including all applications, evaluations, injury reports, W-4s and INS I-9 forms, as well as any complaints about them. Workers' compensation claims have very short notice requirements, but other kinds of claims, like discrimination or ADA issues, have different standards.

The IRS requires that all new employees fill out W-4 forms, which include their social security numbers and how many dependants they want to deduct. The employers don't have to file these forms with the IRS in most situations, but they must keep their employees' W-4s in their office files.

When you hire someone who's not a citizen, you must fill out and keep an INS Form I-9, which you can get from the Immigration and Naturalization Service. In the I-9 form you swear that you believe that your employee isn't an illegal alien, because you took reasonable steps to check his or her status. Those reasonable steps include checking immigration papers. You should make copies of the papers you examined and keep those copies with the I-9 form in your office files for at least three years after hiring or for at least one year after terminating that employee.

Summary

In this chapter we've covered most of the issues you'll have to consider when you start your business. Remember, some of them depend on what kind of business you set up — sole proprietorship, partnership or corporation. But how do you decide which is best for your business? That's the subject of the next chapter.

2

Sole Proprietor, Partnership or Corporation?

Sole proprietor, partnership or corporation? Those are the three broad categories of business structures. But what difference does it make? Why does your business have to be anything?

The answer is simple: Your business doesn't have the option of being nothing. Under the law, if you don't choose a business structure, the law will choose one for you. Think of it as the law's default programming. The law says that if you're the only owner of an unincorporated business, then you're a sole proprietor. If there's more than one person involved, you're a partnership. If you want to be something else, or if you want to do things a bit differently than the law's structure for a partnership or sole proprietorship, there are some specific hoops you have to jump through.

This chapter will describe the differences between those business structures. But first, we'll describe the situations where those differences are important.

When Does It Make a Difference?

How your business is structured makes a difference when major life changes occur: death, divorce, debt, retirement, or the selling of the business. It also makes a difference in how your business is taxed. We'll start by explaining what the critical life changes *are* that impact your business. In the next section we'll look at how those changes are affected by the business structure you choose.

When the Business Owner Dies

When you die, the law needs to know about your business structure so it will know how to pass the title to your business on to your heirs. The business structure will not only determine how to do that, it'll determine if it's even possible. In some types of business structure, death ends the business — period.

Business Taxes

All businesses are not treated the same in the Internal Revenue Code. Different kinds of business structures are taxed in different ways. Except for Subchapter S corporations, corporations are taxed very differently than sole proprietorships and partnerships. While partnerships and sole proprietorships are taxed in pretty much the same way, the IRS *reporting requirements* for partnerships are very different from the requirements for sole proprietorships.

Also, there are fringe benefits you can arrange in the corporate structure that will benefit an owner/corporate employee. They're not available for a partnership or sole proprietorship. A corporation can deduct the cost of some kinds of fringe benefits from its taxes, like certain kinds of health insurance, pension plans, or other employee benefits. Sole proprietorships or partnerships can have these benefits, too, but they generally can't deduct them from their taxes.

When the Business Is Sold

If you decide to sell your business, your business structure governs that procedure. Selling a business is more complicated than, for example, selling your car, where you just sign over the title. It's more complicated because parts of your business are intangible. You can't reach out and touch things like your contract rights, your company goodwill, your insurance rights, your company logo, your reputation, your accounts receivable, and so forth. You can't just point to your company intangibles and say, "There they are, take them away" — unless the business is incorporated.

However, if the business is incorporated, it's sort of like selling your car. You can just sign over the stock and hand it to someone.

Business Debts

A compelling reason for incorporating is that when a business is incorporated, the business debts are only collectible out of the business assets. Unless there's been some sort of serious fraud, business creditors can't reach the personal assets of the shareholders. For example, suppose you inherit $10,000 from your Aunt Matilda, while your incorporated business is unable to pay its debts. However much your business creditors would like to get their hands on that $10,000, they can't — unless you voluntarily give it to them

That's not true of sole proprietorships or partnerships. Business creditors *can* reach the personal assets of the business owners to pay off business debts. The reverse is also true. Personal creditors can reach business assets to satisfy personal debts. For example, the bank that financed your partner's car could seize his share of partnership property to pay off the car note.

If There's a Lawsuit

The law wants to know the business structure so people will know how — and who — to sue.

In a partnership or a sole proprietorship, the business owners are sued as individuals. Their personal and business assets will be at risk. Say you're a sole proprietor. The pitch on the roof you built on someone's garage was too low and caused the whole thing to collapse when the first snow came. The homeowner is after you for $30,000. You personally will be the defendant in the lawsuit. You could lose your house, car, savings, kids' college fund, or whatever it needs to pay that $30,000.

However, if the business is incorporated, only the business can be sued, not the individual shareholders. If you're the owner of *Roofs Incorporated*, even if you're the only shareholder, anyone with a complaint against the company has to sue *Roofs Incorporated*. You won't be the proper defendant, and if you're named in a lawsuit, your attorney can get your name taken off the suit. If the corporation has no assets, the plaintiffs can't get anything. No one can come after your personal property.

What Is a Sole Proprietorship?

A sole proprietor is what you are when you don't have a partner and you're not incorporated. That kind of business structure is called a *sole proprietorship*.

Simplicity is the big advantage of sole proprietorship. It has the least amount of paperwork, the least regulation, and the simplest form of tax reporting requirements. You don't have to file anything or do anything to be a sole proprietor, because that's what you are when you aren't anything else.

However, there are disadvantages to being a sole proprietor:

▌ It's difficult to pass on a business to your heirs in an orderly way.

▌ Selling the business is complicated.

▌ It's nearly impossible to protect the business assets from the sole proprietor's personal creditors, and vice versa. Your business creditors can reach your personal assets. Your personal creditors can reach your business assets. For example, suppose you're an unincorporated roofer who owes money for roofing shingles that you ordered and used, but didn't pay for. If you were to win the lottery, the supplier can sue you and collect his money out of your lottery winnings. Whether this is good or bad depends on whether you're you, or you're the roofing supplier.

A Sole Proprietorship and Taxes

A business that's a sole proprietorship doesn't pay federal income taxes on its profits. Instead, the business owner pays the taxes.

If you're the sole proprietor of an unincorporated business without employees, your business doesn't have to file or pay anything. At tax time, you fill out a Form 1040, Schedule C, showing if your roofing business made a profit or loss in the previous year. Then you write the amount of the profit or loss on the front page of your individual 1040 Income Tax Return form just as if the profit or loss was a salary (but on a different line than the salary line). Then you mail your 1040 form and Schedule C (together with your self-employment tax form and any other forms you may need — see Chapter 6) to the IRS. Then you can sit down and relax. Your taxes are done.

When a Sole Proprietor Dies

When a sole proprietor dies, that's the end of the business — instantly. If you own a roofing business, that roofing business ceases to exist at the moment of your death. All that's left is to pay off your bills, and settle the claims against your estate (like any unfinished roofing jobs). Death doesn't cancel those contracts, by the way. The property owner can sue your estate for breach of contract. When the bills and claims are settled, whatever assets are left in the business can be passed to the heirs. Those assets include tools, vehicles, any money in the bank, and accounts receivable. This usually results in the heirs inheriting something that's worth considerably less than what it was worth when you were alive.

The problems that occur when a sole proprietor dies are among the most compelling reasons to incorporate.

Buying or Selling a Sole Proprietorship

If you want to sell a business that's a sole proprietorship, what you're really selling is a package of business assets that you own. Because the business is a sole proprietorship, the business itself has no life of its own. It can't own anything — not tools, accounts receivable, contracts, or anything else — even though these things are an inherent part of the business. You, the proprietor, own those assets.

It's possible to put the package of assets together in such a way that the practical effect is that the business continues without a break. But it has to be done carefully. Whether you're the seller or the buyer of a sole proprietorship, you should get the advice of an attorney so you'll get the outcome you want.

If you're selling or buying a business, here's something else you have to worry about: If you're the buyer, you don't want to buy someone else's debts. If you're the seller, you don't want to owe the debts of a business you no longer own.

The complexity in buying and selling small businesses is one of the reasons so many small businesses incorporate.

The Debts of a Sole Proprietorship

If you're a sole proprietor, you're personally responsible for the business's debts. Whatever money you have — no matter where it came from — can be reached to satisfy your company's debts. Your business creditors can come into your home and seize the chair you're sitting on, or the $5,000 your Aunt Matilda left you in her will. (If things actually get this bad, remember that there is some protection from creditors. See Chapter 15.)

It works the other way around too. Your personal creditors can reach your business assets to satisfy debts, even debts that had nothing to do with the business.

For example, suppose you make the mistake of co-signing on your teenage son's car. Then your son loses his job at McDonald's and can't pay off the car loan. The car dealer can sue you and attach money in your business account to pay off the loan. This is going to be a particularly difficult problem for you if you had that money in the account to pay for materials on a job you're supposed to start. If you'd been incorporated, this wouldn't have happened.

If There's a Divorce

If a sole proprietor is involved in a divorce, his or her business, like the rest of his property, is a marital asset that the court can divide between the parties. With a small, solely-owned business, often the only way to do that is to sell the business and divide the proceeds.

If There's a Lawsuit

If your company is sued, that means you're being sued, because in a sole proprietorship, legally you are your company, and vice versa.

Partnership planning checklist
1. What kind of business is your partnership? What will it do? Remember that some states require a very specific statement of purpose.
2. Where will the money to start the partnership come from? From the partners? Who pays in how much?
3. Are the partners all equal partners or does one partner own more than another?
4. Which partner will keep the business records? Run the business? Sign contracts or checks?
5. How will the profits be shared? Equally? What if one partner does more work than the other?
6. What will happen if one partner wants to withdraw? Or dies? Consider buy-out provisions funded with term life insurance policies.
7. What if one partner becomes ill or disabled? Consider health and disability insurance.

Figure 2-1 *Partnership planning checklist*

For example, suppose while installing a roof, your employee dropped a hammer on Sam the homeowner's head. If Sam sues for negligence and wins, that judgment is a kind of debt that lets Sam collect money from you as an individual. Like all your other creditors, he's not limited to the assets of the business even though the accident was a business incident. If you win the lottery, Sam can attach your lottery winnings to pay off his lawsuit.

That's only true if Sam actually wins the lawsuit, of course. If he loses, he gets nothing, but these days most negligence lawsuits never get to the point of winning or losing. Right or wrong isn't the question anymore, not when jury verdicts in negligence lawsuits can sometimes be for millions of dollars. Even if you win and the judgment is zero, your legal fees to defend your case can be thousands of dollars. The stakes are so high, the parties usually settle out of court. They often can't afford to do anything else.

What Is a Partnership?

When two or more people own an unincorporated business that's run for the purpose of making a profit (even if it doesn't), which the partners intend to share, equally or unequally, that's a partnership.

The partners don't even have to be human beings. A partner can be another business or even a corporation. However, having a corporation for a partner doesn't change the partnership into a corporation.

Partnership planning checklist

8. What if one partner decides to sell his or her share in the partnership? Or is sued for divorce? Will that end the partnership? If there's a buy-out agreement, how is it funded? How will the value of an individual partner's share be calculated?

9. What if the partners decide to sell the business?

10. If the partnership is dissolved, how will the assets be distributed?

11. What will be the name of the partnership? Check with your county clerk or state agency — probably the Secretary of State's office — to find out if a name is available. If someone else is using it, you can't. Some states require the name of at least one of the partners to be in the business name.

12. What licenses are required? In some states, even though an individual partner has a contractor's license, that license can't be transferred to the partnership. The partnership has to get its own license. The person getting the license must be a managing partner. Don't forget that your county and city may also require permits or licenses.

Figure 2-1 *Partnership planning checklist (cont.)*

Partnership Agreements

It's not necessary to have a formal agreement to establish a partnership, but it's better if there is one. What happens if the partners don't have an agreement setting out the terms of their partnership? Then the Uniform Partnership Act, which every state except Louisiana has adopted, will make the decisions the partners should have made when they established their partnership, even if those decisions aren't what the partners actually intended or wanted.

In a partnership agreement, the partners can agree to put one or more partners in charge. They can agree to unequal shares of the business profits. They can also agree, in advance, how to settle disputes and how to deal with the death or divorce of one of the partners, usually through some sort of buyout arrangement. They can agree to limit the authority of the other partners to make contracts or to incur debts that the partnership will have to pay.

Figure 2-1 is a partnership planning checklist that shows the types of questions you should consider in your agreement. Figure 2-2 is a sample partnership agreement. (There is a blank copy of this agreement on the disk in the back of the book.)

Bigger Builders Inc.
22 Commerce Drive •Lansing, MI 55555
Phone (555)555-1234 • Fax (555)555-6789
Website: www.biggerbuildersinc.com

GENERAL PARTNERSHIP AGREEMENT

This Agreement is made on the __21__ day of <u>August</u> in the year <u>2000</u> between <u>Ron Klick</u> and <u>Sam Klack</u> , hereinafter referred to as Partners. *(Any number of people may set up a partnership.)*

Partnership Name

1. The name of the Partnership is <u>Klick & Klack</u> . *(Remember to check the local authorities, probably the Secretary of State, to confirm that the name is not being used by some other company.)*

Partnership Purpose

2. The Partnership is formed for the purpose of engaging in the business of <u>constructing, remodeling, and restoring residential and commercial buildings</u>. *(Some states require a very specific statement of purpose.)*

Duration of Partnership

3. This Partnership will begin on the date of this Agreement and will continue until <u>2020</u> , or until such time as one Partner gives <u>30</u> days written notice by certified mail of his or her intention to dissolve the Partnership, whereupon the process of Partnership dissolution described in this Agreement shall begin. *(Fill in the life of the partnership and however many days of required notice that the partners agree upon.)*

Place of Business

4. The Partnership's principal place of business shall be located at <u>55 West Office Drive, Lansing, MI</u> . All Partnership books and records shall be kept at the principal place of business. The principal place of business may be changed and other places of business may be established by written agreement of the Partners.

Capital Contributions

5. The Partnership's initial capital shall consist of cash to be contributed by the Partners in the following amounts: *(Capital contributions do not have to be in cash.*

Figure 2-2 *Sample partnership agreement*

It's possible for a partner to make his or her contribution in services or goods if the other partners agree. The other partners have to agree upon the value of those contributions. Necessary capital contributions could be calculated, for example, on the basis of one year's overhead costs plus the cost of necessary tools, business equipment and business vehicles.)

Name <u>Ron Klick</u>   Amount $ <u>25,000</u>

Name <u>Sam Klack</u>   Amount $ <u>25,000</u>

Each Partner's contribution shall be paid in full within <u>60</u> days after the date of this Agreement. If any Partner fails to make their contribution in full in a timely fashion, the Partnership shall be immediately dissolved, and each Partner will be entitled to the return of such amounts as they have contributed. *(Unless the partners agree otherwise, capital contributions are what determine the percentage of the partnership each partner owns.)*

Voluntary Capital Contributions or Capital Withdrawals

6. No Partner shall make a voluntary contribution or a withdrawal of capital without the written consent of all the Partners. *(A change in the contribution of capital could change the percentage of the partnership which that partner owns.)*

Division of Profits and Losses

7. Profits and losses shall be divided equally among the Partners unless all the Partners agree in writing to a different allocation of profits and losses. Within <u>30</u> *(enter the number)* days of the end of the Partnership's fiscal year, there shall be distributed in cash to each Partner an amount equal to his or her proportionate share of the Partnership's profits less any amounts drawn in advance against profits. *(If there is a profit, the money does not actually have to be distributed. The partners could agree instead to retain some for operating capital, but the taxable effect is still that each partner has received taxable income.)*

Partnership Funds

8. All Partnership funds shall be deposited in the Partnership's name. The Partners will select in writing who shall have signatory authority for withdrawals or checks. *(Most modern banking practices exclude the option of requiring multiple signatures on a check.)*

Partnership Drawing Account

9. Each Partner shall be entitled to draw against his or her share of the profits in such amounts and at such time as shall be agreed in writing by the Partners. *(This clause is so that partners do not have to wait until the end of the year to benefit from earnings.)*

Figure 2-2 *Sample partnership agreement (continued)*

Partnership's Fiscal Year and Accounting Method

10. The Partnership's fiscal year shall end on <u>December</u> of each year. The Partnership's books shall be maintained on a fiscal year basis and on a <u>cash</u> *(cash or accrual)* basis.

Accountings to the Partners

11. Within <u>30</u> days after the end of each fiscal year, the Partnership shall furnish to each Partner a copy of the Partnership's income tax returns for the fiscal year together with a profit and loss statement, and a balance sheet showing the Partnership's financial position at the end of the fiscal year.

Partnership Management

12. Each Partner shall have an equal right in the management of the Partnership except as otherwise agreed upon in writing by the other Partners. Each Partner shall devote full time and attention to the conduct of the business except as otherwise agreed in writing by the other Partners. *(If one of the partners will be contributing less than a full-time effort, that should be agreed upon in advance.)*

Partnership Authority

13. Each Partner shall have authority to bind the Partnership in making contracts. Each Partner shall have the authority to incur debts in the Partnership name or on its credit, but this authority is subject to a limit of $<u>50,000</u> . No Partner shall incur debts in excess of this amount without the prior written consent of the other Partners. *(Note that this limitation is not a defense against a creditor who did not have notice of that limitation. The effect of this clause is to require a partner who exceeds this limit to reimburse his partners for money they may have to pay out to creditors.)*

Employment and Dismissal

14. No Partner shall hire or fire any employee without the consent of the other Partners, except in the case of gross misconduct which exposes the Partnership to possible liability. *(This is not a necessary clause unless the partners want it. The partners can give this authority to every partner, or just to particular partners.)*

Partnership Vacation and Sick Time

15. Each Partner shall be entitled to <u>10</u> days of vacation and <u>10</u> days of sick time. Those days of vacation and sick time shall not result in a proportionate reduction of that Partner's share of profits for that fiscal year. *(The partnership should consider obtaining disability insurance for the protection of a partner who falls ill or becomes disabled.)*

Figure 2-2 *Sample partnership agreement (continued)*

New Partners

16. New Partners may be admitted to the Partnership with the written consent of all of the existing Partners. In the absence of a written agreement to the contrary by the Partners, each new Partner shall be required to match the original contribution of capital. Each new Partner shall agree to the terms of this Agreement and shall execute it accordingly. Admission of a new Partner shall not cause a dissolution of the Partnership.

Dissolution

17. The Partnership shall dissolve and terminate upon any Partner's death, permanent physical or mental disability, or becoming a party to a divorce action, or a voluntary withdrawal, which shall include intent to sell that Partner's interest, unless within <u>90</u> days after the Partnership received notice of any of these events, the Partnership elects in writing with the written consent of the remaining Partners, to buy the withdrawing Partner's interest. The purchase price of the withdrawing Partner's interest shall be calculated in accordance with clause number 19. *(The partnership should consider the purchase of a term life insurance policy on each partner to fund the purchase of a deceased or disabled partner's interest.)*

Transfer of Partnership Interest

18. A Partner's interest may not be transferred or sold in whole or in part without the written consent of the remaining Partners. *(Bear in mind that refusing such transfer and also not purchasing the withdrawing partner's interest triggers automatic dissolution.)*

Valuation of Partnership's Share

19. For purposes of purchase, and in the absence of a written agreement setting a value, the value of the Partnership shall be determined by the independent accounting firm of `Pencil Pushers, Inc.` in accordance with generally accepted accounting procedures. *(Consider using an appraiser instead. It's always a good idea to agree on an accounting firm or an appraiser before there's a problem.)*

Payment Terms for the Purchase of a Partner's Share

20. If the Partnership is obligated to purchase a Partner's interest because of the death or disability of that Partner, the Partnership shall pay for that interest in cash within <u>180</u> days after the date upon which the Partner's right or obligation to purchase became fixed. *(If there is life insurance available, this language requires the payout of those insurance proceeds promptly.)*

Figure 2-2 *Sample partnership agreement (continued)*

Otherwise, in the event of a Partner withdrawing, the other Partners shall purchase his or her share of the Partnership through a down payment of <u>twenty percent</u> of the value of that Partnership which shall be due within <u>sixty days</u> of notice of intent to withdraw. The remaining Partners shall then execute a promissory note for the balance of the withdrawing Partner's share which shall be payable <u>in five equal amounts in each of the following years</u>. *(The buyout agreement doesn't have to be like this one. It can be whatever buyout arrangement the partners agree to. The important thing is to have one.)*

Non-competition Clause

21. Following withdrawal from the Partnership, the withdrawing Partner shall not carry on a business similar to the business of the Partnership within the area of <u>Ingham County</u>. *(Describe the area where the partner is prohibited from competing: a state, county, city, neighborhood or whatever.)*

Arbitration Clause

22. It is hereby agreed that all disputes arising out of this Agreement shall be submitted to binding arbitration in accordance with the rules of the American Arbitration Association.

Amendment of the Partnership Agreement

23. This Agreement may be amended by the written consent of all the Partners.

Entire Agreement

24. This instrument contains the entire Agreement of the parties. Any prior agreements, oral representations, or modifications shall be of no force or effect.

Severability

25. If any term, provision, covenant, or condition of this Agreement is held by a court of competent jurisdiction or by an Arbitrator to be invalid, void, or unenforceable, the rest of the Agreement shall in no way be affected, impaired or invalidated.

Signatures

In witness whereof, the Partners have executed this Agreement on the <u>21</u> day of <u>August</u>, in the year of <u>2000</u>.

Signatures: Residence addresses:

_____   1450 Noith Road Lansing MI

_____   1020 Smith Road Lansing MI

Figure 2-2 *Sample partnership agreement (continued)*

Blank Copy on CD-ROM

There's a blank copy of Figure 2-2 included on the disk in the back of the book.

However, there's a glitch to watch out for. Each partner is, in effect, an agent for all the other partners. So suppose the partners agree to limit which one of them can sign a contract that will bind the business and the other partners. Another partner could still sign contracts that bind the other partners, even if that particular partner didn't have the actual authority to sign contracts.

For example, if John and Sam set up the Weather-Tight Roofs Partnership, and they agree that John is the only partner who can sign contracts, that agreement is enforceable between John and Sam. Then, if Sam signs a contract with Harry that John objects to, John can sue Sam for reimbursement or resort to a prearranged penalty against Sam that's laid out in the partnership agreement. But Harry can still enforce that contract. People doing business with John and Sam have the right to assume that John and Sam have the same authority and powers. The exception to this would be if Harry actually knew better. If Harry knew, or had reason to know, that Sam didn't have the authority to sign this contract, then Harry wouldn't be able to enforce it against the partnership.

In short, if Sam signs a contract for fancy new office furniture for the partnership, John can't cancel the contract. But John may be able to force Sam to reimburse him for his (John's) share of the cost.

Who Controls a Partnership?

The Uniform Partnership Act says that the partners share control and make decisions equally. If a situation or a problem arises that they can't agree on, the partnership comes grinding to an end. That's the only solution the Uniform Partnership Act offers: the automatic dissolution of the partnership when the partners disagree. If Sam and John can't agree about what to do about that new office furniture, the Uniform Partnership Act says that's the end of their partnership. Unless, of course, they have an agreement with a mechanism in it to settle their disputes when they can't agree.

If the partners discuss and agree in advance about what they'll do if they can't agree, that agreement will control what happens, not the Uniform Partnership Act. They might agree to arbitration by a third party, or maybe to flip a coin. It really doesn't matter. What does matter is that they have a provision to cover disputes written into their partnership agreement.

Partnership Taxes

At the end of the taxable year, the partnership has to file Form 1065, U.S. Partnership Return of Income, showing how much money the business made or lost. These are net figures. Partnership expenses are deducted and reported on Form 1065, not on the individual partner's Form 1099. The partnership gets the deductions, not the partners.

At the same time as the partnership files its Form 1065, the partnership also gives each partner a Schedule K-1. The Schedule K-1 shows how much profit or loss was distributed to each partner. Just remember that how much profit or loss doesn't mean how much money the partners actually took home. It means how did the partners agree to share those profits or losses: equally? 60/40? or some other split of the profits and losses?

For example, suppose John and Sam agreed to a 60/40 split because John put in more time with the partnership. If the partnership made $100,000 in profits, then John gets a K-1 that shows an income of $60,000 and Sam gets a schedule K-1 that shows an income of $40,000. That's true even if the partnership kept $25,000 in the bank to buy a new dump truck next year.

The partners report as income on their individual 1040s their share of the money (or their share of the losses) that's shown on their Schedule K-1.

What If a Partner Dies?

The Uniform Partnership Act says that when one partner dies, the partnership is instantly over unless there's an existing agreement between the partners that says otherwise. That's true even if there were more than two partners. Without the protection of an agreement that provides for the continued life of the partnership, the unexpected death of a partner will put the remaining partners immediately out of business.

That's one of the reasons a partnership agreement is so important. Even if the surviving partners want to end the partnership upon the death of a partner, it's easier and less likely to be a financial disaster if there's a dissolution procedure in place. The agreement should provide a way of keeping the partnership alive until an orderly settlement of the partnership can take place.

Usually the partnership agreement provides that if one of the partners dies, the surviving partners can buy his or her share of the business. An agreement like that is often funded by a life insurance policy. The policy pays the heirs for what would have been their share of the business. In other words, the insurance funds the buyout. That guarantees something for the heirs that represents the value of the business, and it protects the surviving business partners from having to scramble around for money to buy the deceased partner's share.

If guaranteeing an inheritance isn't a problem, the partners could simply agree to write mutual wills naming each other as the business's heirs. But if one of the partners has a wife and/or children, then the partnership should consult an estate lawyer for assistance in drawing up this agreement. That partner's family may have certain statutory rights that could defeat this arrangement.

What If a Partner Divorces?

In a divorce, the courts can redistribute marital assets, which include partnership shares. The court may require the divorcing partner to sell his share of the business or to distribute his share to his or her spouse. That means the partners could find themselves with the estranged spouse as their new partner.

The best way of avoiding this is to have a divorce action trigger a clause in the partnership agreement that says if one partner is involved in a divorce, the other partners have the right to buy out the divorcing partner's shares. They don't have to, but they can if that's the only way the other partners can protect themselves.

For example, suppose Sam and John were partners, and Sam's wife sued him for divorce. The best thing for John would be if the partnership agreement provided in advance that the partner who wasn't being divorced had the right to purchase the other partner's share of the partnership in the event of a divorce action. Then the divorce court could divide up the proceeds from John's purchase of Sam's share between Sam and his wife. That way, Sam's divorce wouldn't put John out of business.

Who Has to Pay Partnership Debts?

Every partner is responsible for all of the debts of the partnership. The legal phrase is that each partner is "jointly and severally liable" for the obligations of the partnership. That means creditors can try to collect from all the partners, or they can zero in on just one partner who may look more collectable than the other partners. The partner who pays more than his share of the debts can sue the other partners for reimbursement of the amount that was more than his share, but the creditors don't have to worry about that. It's not their problem.

Creditors aren't limited to collecting their money from partnership or business assets either. A partner could wind up paying partnership debts out of the money from Aunt Matilda's will.

If a Partner Has to Pay More Than His Share of Partnership Debts

If there's no formal agreement, the Uniform Partnership Act provides that a partner who has to pay more than his share of partnership debts is entitled to reimbursement from the other partners for the money that exceeded his share of the debt (assuming they have anything to collect).

If a Partner Has Debts Outside the Partnership

A partner's share of the business can be reached by his creditors, no matter how they got to be his creditors. If Sam co-signs on his son's car loan and can't pay off the loan, the financing company can come after Sam's share of the partnership.

The basic rule is that non-business creditors can't reach beyond the partner's share into the shares of the other partners. That sounds good. But it doesn't always work that smoothly in reality. The problem is figuring out exactly which part of the business is that particular partner's share. What do you use as the divider? The amount of money that each partner contributed toward startup costs? A percentage of the profits? Part of the fair market value of the business?

The partnership agreement can say that if partnership assets are used to pay off one partner's personal debts, then that partner must reimburse the other partners. And the partnership agreement can, and should, provide a method of calculating the value of each partner's share.

If There's a Lawsuit

If you want to sue a partnership, you don't actually sue the partnership; you sue one or more of the partners. For example, you could sue Sam Smith and John Doe doing business as Weather-Tight Roofs, but you don't have to sue both if you don't want to. You could just sue Sam, and let him worry about John. If Sam loses the lawsuit, he could sue John for reimbursement of John's share of the judgment and legal costs. However, Sam doesn't actually have to wait that long. He can, if he wants to, ask the judge to bring John into the lawsuit while it's still going on, because John is required by law to "contribute" to the costs of a judgment.

Selling a Partnership

When all the partners consent, selling a partnership is much like selling a sole proprietorship.

If All the Partners Don't Agree to Sell

If one of the partners wants to sell the business, but the others don't, this disagreement has the effect of automatically dissolving the partnership under the Uniform Partnership Act. You can't have a valid partnership with people who don't want to be partners. This is one of the problems that the partnership agreement should address before it happens.

If the partners don't have a partnership agreement that provides another means of solving this problem, then the partners only have two choices. First, they can agree on how to split up the partnership assets. Second, if they can't agree, they can go to court and ask a judge to decide how to split up the partnership assets. Obviously the partnership assets will be worth less in their component parts than they were worth as an on-going business. Think of the dissolution process as a kind of a business divorce (and it's often as nasty as a divorce). Under those circumstances, you can then think of the partnership agreement as a sort of prenuptial agreement that solves some of the property settlement problems in advance, while all the parties are still speaking to each other.

If Only One Partner Wants to Sell His Share

You can have a similar problem when one partner wants to sell his partnership share to someone else. If a partner wishes to sell his or her share and the other partners agree, that's easy. But if one of the other partners doesn't consent (and there's no existing agreement about how to deal with a partner's withdrawal), the partner's effort to sell his share of the business has the effect of dissolving the partnership. The partners will have to divide up the assets and go their separate ways. If the separating partners can't agree on how to divide up the assets, then a court must be asked to do it.

Obviously, planning in advance about how to handle these problems avoids some enormous headaches. After all, partners do drop out along the way for a variety of reasons: personality conflicts, divorces, death, or maybe they just plain don't want to do it anymore. So, your partnership agreement should include:

- A method for allowing a partner to sell or transfer his/her interest.
- A method for valuing each partner's share at the time of withdrawal.

Often, the other partners will want the opportunity to buy the departing partner's share, rather than accepting a new partner into the business that they may not know (or even worse — not like). The partnership agreement should include this option.

Limited Partnerships and Joint Ventures

It's possible in some states to set up a limited partnership, or a joint venture where one or more of the partners are different from the general partners. That limited partner has only invested in the partnership. He's not liable for the debts of the partnership, and doesn't participate in management. This arrangement isn't available in every state — and it's very regulated where it *is* available. There are also a lot of pitfalls, especially in tax issues. Before you get involved in a limited partnership, *always* consult your attorney.

What Is a Corporation?

A corporation is a legal fiction — a kind of pretend-person that the law creates. It's owned by its shareholders, who may number anywhere from one person to millions of stockholders. The corporation, not the shareholders, is responsible for its own debts, its own contracts, and its own wrongdoing. The corporation also pays its own taxes, unless it's set up as a Subchapter S corporation (we'll discuss that a little later).

The corporation can keep its money, or distribute it to shareholders as dividends after paying corporate taxes on its earnings. Then, if and when it does pay dividends to the shareholders, those shareholders pay income tax on that money. It's earned income to them, so they report it on their 1040 tax returns, and it's taxed at the usual individual rates. So the corporate profits get taxed twice, once in the hands of the corporation, and then a second time in the hands of the shareholders.

It's possible for a corporation to avoid the problem of double taxation. It can choose to be taxed under a section of the Internal Revenue Code called Subchapter S. That option is explained in the next section.

Here's something you should consider if you're thinking about incorporating. Unless the corporation is a Subchapter S corporation, the person running the corporation, even if he or she is the only shareholder, can only get money out of the corporation in the form of dividends or salary. If the shareholder is paid a salary (which is usually the best way to do it), that salary must be reported on a W-2 in the same way that any other employee's earnings would be reported.

Blank Copy on CD-ROM

There's a blank copy of Figure 2-3 included on the disk in the back of the book.

Despite the double taxation, there are several things about incorporation that make it attractive to business owners. Incorporation provides a quick and easy way to pass the business on to heirs, or sell it to people who want to buy the business. It also provides some protection to the business owners if something goes wrong. If the corporation has business debts or has to pay for breach of contract or warranty problems, only the assets of the corporation can be reached for those payments. The shareholders don't have to pay those debts out of their pockets. Figure 2-3 is a sample Articles of Incorporation. (There is also a blank copy of this form on the disk in the back of the book that you can use. Remember that state requirements vary. Review your state requirements before filing your Articles of Incorporation.)

There Are Different Kinds of Corporations

The broadest difference in corporations is between "publicly-held" corporations and the more common "closely-held" corporations. Both kinds of corporation start out in the same way: Their incorporators set them up

ARTICLES OF INCORPORATION

I. The name of this corporation is <u>Klick Klack Inc.</u>

II. The purpose of this corporation is <u>the construction, remodeling, and restoration of residential and commercial buildings.</u>

III. The name and address in this state of the corporation's initial agent to accept service of process is <u>Ron Klick 55 North Road Lansing MI</u> .

IV. This corporation is authorized to issue only one class of shares of stock, which shall be designated as common stock. The total number of shares it is authorized to issue is <u>10,000</u> shares. *(The number of shares issued depends on what you might want to do with them in the future. For example: bring in more shareholders, sell some of the stock and so forth. If you wish to have more than one class of stock, consult your attorney.)*

V. The names and addresses of the persons who are appointed to act as initial directors of this corporation are:
1. <u>Ron Klick 1050 North Road Lansing MI</u>
2. <u>Valerie Klick 1050 North Road Lansing MI</u>
3. <u>Sam Klack 1020 South Road Lansing MI</u>

VI. The corporation is authorized to indemnify the directors and officers of this corporation to the fullest extent permissible under state law.

VII. IN WITNESS WHEREOF, the undersigned being the persons named above, have executed these Articles of Incorporation.

[signatures: Ron Klick, Valerie Klick, Sam Klack]

Date: *8-21-00*

(If you want this to be treated as a Subchapter S Corporation, you have to file Form 2553, Election by a Small Business Corporation with the IRS. Remember that corporate form and required documents are regulated by state law, and you should review your state requirements before filing your Articles of Incorporation.)

Figure 2-3 *Articles of Incorporation*

Not Every State Allows
Construction Companies to Incorporate

One of the big attractions of incorporating is that the individuals who own the corporation can't be made to personally pay the debts of the corporations (unless there's fraud going on). Nor do they personally have to pay the damages when a corporation is responsible for a breach of contract or warranty. This allows a contractor to protect his own savings from angry customers or unpaid creditors.

However, in some states, the consumer protection laws don't allow the owners of a construction company to avoid personal liability by incorporating. So if you're thinking of incorporating, first check with your state authorities about the rules in your state. In most states, that's either the Secretary of State or the Commerce Department. If you're not going to get the benefit you're looking for by incorporating, maybe incorporating isn't the way you should go.

under the laws of their state. The difference between closely-held and publicly-held corporations lies in the number of shareholders they have, and how they sell their stock.

By incorporating, a company divides itself up into shares of stock, which it can then sell or distribute as the company chooses. Selling its stock is simply a way for the company to raise money from investors. However, selling stock is a highly regulated activity. What usually triggers those regulations is the number of people being offered the stock, not where that stock is sold. How the company chooses to sell those shares of stock, and how many people they sell their stock to is what makes the difference between "closely-held" and "publicly-held."

Publicly-Held Corporations

Publicly-held corporations sell their stock to the public. Anyone can buy that stock. A publicly-held corporation can be sold on the big exchanges like the NYSE (if it meets the standards of that exchange) or it can be sold like Tupperware. But no matter how it's sold, it must meet the federal and state standards of disclosure.

You don't see a lot of publicly-held construction companies. For one thing, that's not how building projects are typically financed. Also, the need to raise money usually isn't so urgent that it offsets the control the company founders lose when they sell stock to the public at large.

Issuing and selling shares of stock is a way to raise extra money for the corporation. But if you plan to raise capital that way, you'll need the advice of an attorney, an accountant, and probably a financial planner.

Closely-Held Corporations

Closely-held corporations are owned by only a few stockholders, some-times only one, and the company's stock isn't sold in the open market. It's a privately-owned business. Because the corporation isn't public, the corporation's business isn't subject to the disclosure requirements of a publicly-held corporation. In fact, it's almost impossible to find out what's going on in a closely-held corporation unless the owners want to tell you.

Shareholders in a closely-held corporation can sell their stock, but they may be required by the corporate by-laws to first offer their shares to other shareholders or to the corporation itself before they can sell it to outsiders.

Closely-held corporations are taxed as either a standard corporation (sometimes called a C corporation) or as a Subchapter S corporation. The C and S initials refer to sections of the tax code.

Subchapter S Corporations

Although Subchapter S corporations are corporations, they're taxed in much the same way as partnerships. This kind of corporation gives small business owners the advantages of incorporation, but without some of the complex paperwork. Also, Subchapter S eliminates, for a small business, one of the big disadvantages of incorporation: the double taxation. Remember, in a standard C corporation, the company's earnings are taxed, then its dividends are taxed again when they're issued to shareholders.

Qualifying As a Subchapter S Corporation

A corporation qualifies for Subchapter S treatment by the Internal Revenue Service if it has no more than 75 stockholders, is a U.S. corporation, all the stockholders are U.S. citizens or estates, and it has only one class of stock.

Subchapter S corporations don't pay corporate taxes. Instead, the taxable earnings or deductible losses go straight through to the shareholders. They pay individual taxes on the corporate profits, just as if the business were a partnership or sole proprietorship. This pre-vents the business profits from being taxed twice in the way that other corporations are.

However, all the profits and losses are credited to the stockholders in the year that they're earned. If the Subchapter S corporation keeps some of its earnings for reinvestment, the shareholders have to pay income tax on that money in the year it was earned, even though they don't actually receive it.

Some states don't recognize the S classification for the purposes of state taxes. In those states, you'd have to report and pay the state corporate taxes (if you're in a state that has that kind of tax) in the same way that a standard corporation does. To elect to be treated as a Subchapter S corporation, the corporation must file IRS Form 2553 by the 15th day of the third month from the beginning of their taxable year.

A Subchapter S corporation, instead of filing a corporate tax return and paying a tax on its profits, simply reports its income to the IRS. Then each shareholder pays income tax on his or her share of these profits. A Subchapter S corporation's taxable income and losses are simply "passed through" the corporation straight to the shareholders without corporate tax payments. For more information, see Chapter 6.

How Do Corporations Work?

Running a corporation, even a Subchapter S corporation, is more complicated than a sole proprietorship or a partnership. There are meetings that the corporation is required to hold and document. The image of a corporation's sole shareholder sitting down to a meeting with himself is good for a snicker, but nonetheless, it's a meeting he'd better not miss. The corporation also has to file forms with the state and with the IRS that other types of businesses do not.

Who's in Charge of a Corporation?

The Board of Directors is in charge of a corporation. They're elected by the shareholders and stay in place until they are voted out by the shareholders. Every year, the shareholders elect a Board of Directors, who in turn choose officers to manage the corporation. In small companies, the shareholders, the board of directors, and the officers may be all the same people. There's nothing illegal or unusual about this.

How Are Corporations Taxed?

Corporate profits are taxed twice: once as corporate profits and then again as dividend distributions to the shareholders. The exception to this is a corporation that qualifies for Subchapter S treatment.

In addition to federal corporate taxes, most states also impose a corporate tax on corporations bases in that state. In some states, a corporation that qualifies for Subchapter S treatment under the Internal Revenue Code may also receive similar treatment under state law — but don't count on it. Check with your state Department of Treasury to see if your state allows this extra benefit.

Are There Other Tax Benefits?

Corporations can treat certain employee benefits, like health plans and life insurance packages, as deductible expenses even if the corporate employee is the business owner.

For example, if Sam the roofer is incorporated, his corporation can fully deduct the cost of the corporation's employee health plan, even if it only covers Sam. If Sam isn't incorporated, he can only deduct a limited amount of his insurance costs and health costs on his itemized Form 1040 as an individual.

Sam would be better off with a corporate health policy, but he should first consult with an insurance specialist to be sure his corporate health plan meets the IRS standards. Fortunately, health insurance companies have lots of specialists who would be happy to help Sam with that.

Most corporate benefits (like health plans or pension plans) that qualify as tax deductible expenses must be extended to employees, whether they're shareholders or not.

The Debts of a Corporation

Shareholders aren't personally responsible for the corporation's debts. That's the best part of being incorporated, as far as many people are concerned. No matter how bad the business gets, the shareholders can't lose more than their actual investment. It works the other way around, too. The assets of the corporation can't be used to satisfy the debts of its share-holder/owners. Otherwise, if I owned ten shares of IBM stock, and I defaulted on my mortgage or car payments, IBM assets could be used to pay my debts. This might be okay with me, but IBM might not like it when my creditors seized some of their inventory.

Of course, lenders know this, too. When they're approached for a loan by a small business that's incorporated, they often ask the owners to co-sign the debt with the corporation. If you co-sign, you've just lost your protection from company debts that being a corporation provides.

If the Corporation Is Involved in a Lawsuit

If the business does something wrong, only the corporation can be sued, not the shareholders. Shareholders can't be sued as individuals when the corporation is guilty. There's an important exception to this rule, however, called "piercing the veil." It happens when there's some sort of intentional and serious fraud, almost criminal activity. However these "piercing the veil" situations are rare.

A corporation can also sue people, just as if it were a real person. If the corporation is the plaintiff, it will sue in its own name. The plaintiff in the lawsuit will be, for example, Weather-Tight Roofs, Inc, not Sam the owner and sole stockholder of Weather-Tight Roofs.

If the Corporation Is Sold

It's easy to sell a business that's incorporated. You don't have to worry about the title to assets or who is supposed to pay the business debts. All of those things stay with the corporation and don't change. The only thing that happens is that title to the corporate shares passes to someone new. That's true whether all of the shares are being sold or just one of them. The corporation isn't affected, only the shares.

If a Shareholder Dies

The corporation doesn't die just because an owner dies. Unlike a sole proprietorship or a partnership, the corporation keeps on ticking. Now granted, if a key person like the only shareholder dies, it's not good for the long-term business prospects. But at least the corporation doesn't legally fall apart.

Disadvantages of Being Incorporated

We've discussed how a corporation works — and most of the points we've made are advantages of the corporate structure. Aren't there any disadvantages? Well, yes.

There's More Paperwork

It takes more paperwork to set up a corporation (we lawyers like to call it *incorporating*), and it takes more paperwork to keep it going. The IRS has lots of extra forms for corporations to file, and almost every state requires annual filings to keep the business incorporated. The corporation type that takes the least amount of paperwork is a Subchapter S corporation.

Corporations also have to have officers and a Board of Directors who must meet at least once a year. They've got to keep careful records of those meetings. Office supply stores carry incorporation kits that include forms that explain how to run the meetings and what to put in the minutes.

A Corporation Is More Expensive

Although all the expenses are tax-deductible, incorporating your business will cost more. I'm a great believer in buying those do-it-yourself incorporation kits for a one-man operation, or a husband and wife setting up a company. I think those kits are often a useful alternative to a $150-an-hour lawyer.

	Sole Proprietorships	Partnerships	Corporations
Startup	Not difficult at all. Get the necessary licenses. File the Assumed Name Certificate (may be called something else in your state, like a Doing Business As . . . Certificate). The business owner can use his own social security number as a federal ID number unless the business has employees.	A formal agreement is a good idea, but not mandatory. Get the necessary licenses. File an Assumed Name Certificate (may be called something else in your state, like a Doing Business As . . . Certificate). Get an Employer Identification Number to use as your federal ID number.	You must file Articles of Incorporation with the state. Annual meetings and filings are also required. The corporation has to obtain licenses and a federal ID number.
Running the Business	The owner is in complete control.	Control is by the unanimous agreement of the partners unless the partners agree differently.	Shareholders give control to the officers and business managers. In small corporations, these are often the shareholders themselves.
Owner's Liability	The owner is responsible for all the debts of the business and for anything that goes wrong.	The general partners are responsible for the debts of the business and for anything that goes wrong.	The shareholders are not responsible for the company debts or the actions of the company unless there's been serious fraud.
Taxes	The owner reports and pays all taxes on business profits on his own Form 1040.	The partnership has to report its income, losses, and deductions, but it doesn't pay income taxes. It passes income and losses through to the partners as individuals.	Except for Subchapter S corporations, the corporation pays taxes on the business profits. Shareholders also pay taxes on their dividends, if and when dividends are distributed.
Dissolving the Business	The owner can wind up his debts and contracts and sell the business or just quit doing business anytime.	The business is automatically dissolved by the death, disability or withdrawal of a partner unless there's an agreement to the contrary. A well-planned partnership agreement will have a buy-out plan for the remaining partners if one or more partners wishes to quit or dies.	Corporations exist in perpetuity unless the shareholders vote to go out of business or unless the required annual reports aren't filed with the state.

Figure 2-4 *Quick list for comparing sole proprietorships, partnerships and corporations*

It's another story, however, if you're incorporating an existing business instead of setting up a new one. That can be tricky, and you'd better be prepared to write that check for legal fees. Also, while you may not absolutely need an accountant, your life will be so much less complicated if you consult one. You don't have to actually hire an accountant. They're like lawyers — they work by the hour. Just find one who will give you the level of service you need. That will leave you lots more time to actually run your business instead of filling out confusing records and forms.

I hope this chapter has helped you weigh the pros and cons, and decide what kind of business structure works best for you. (If you need to refresh your memory, Figure 2-4 is a concise summary of the three kinds of business structures.) Now, when you've got your construction business up and running, what's the first thing you're going to face? Writing contracts. That's what we'll cover in the next chapter.

Part Two:
Construction Contracts

Chapter 3

What Does Every Contract Have to Have?

Chapter 4

Contract Terms: Filling in the Blanks

What Does Every Contract Have to Have?

Contracts are like houses: every house has to have a certain structure — the foundation and the framing. Without that foundation and framing, the house will collapse. After the foundation and framing are installed, you can do those things that have everything to do with what the house looks like, and nothing to do with keeping it from falling down around your ears.

This chapter is going to look at the contract structure: the foundation and the framing of contracts. These are the elements that a contract must have to make it enforceable. In other words, the things that keep a contract from collapsing into an unenforceable piece of paper. In the next chapter we'll discuss the details that vary from contract to contract depending on the job — the scope of the work, exactly how much it will cost, how and when payments will be made.

The Four Requirements for a Contract

Contract structure is simple. To have an enforceable contract, you need:

1. Parties

2. An offer

3. Consideration

4. Acceptance

Take this example. Cal the carpenter and Harry the homeowner are talking about Harry's floor. Harry and Cal are the *parties*. When Cal the carpenter says to Harry the homeowner, "I'll fix your floor for $500," that's an *offer*. Fixing the floor and paying $500 for the work is the *consideration* for the contract — what each party is going to do in the contract. When Harry says "Fine. Do it," that's an *acceptance*. Harry's acceptance makes it into an enforceable contract.

If one of the parties doesn't pay or doesn't do the work, that party is guilty of *breach of contract.* The other party can sue and collect whatever damages he or she has suffered. If Cal doesn't fix the floor, Harry can sue him. If Cal does the work and Harry won't pay him, Cal can sue Harry.

Easy, right? That's what every law student learns the first day in contracts class. So how come when you go to write a contract with your customer, it doesn't turn out to be that easy?

It isn't that easy because modern law has layered this simple contract between Harry and Cal with additional rules and requirements. First we'll take a closer look at the basic contract structure. Then, in the following sections of this chapter, we'll look at the 20th century additions that are necessary for a binding contract.

Does a Contract Have to Be Called a "Contract"?

No, the law doesn't require that an agreement be labeled "contract." The parties can call it an agreement, a contract, a subcontract, or anything else that makes it clear that the parties are making enforceable promises to each other. What makes it a contract isn't the title. What's important is that it's clear the parties intended to agree about something that has an offer, consideration and an acceptance in it, and that the parties all basically understood what they were doing.

Does a Contract Have to Be in Writing?

No, not every contract has to be in writing to be enforceable, but lots of them do. Because state laws vary so much, there's no one single answer to that question. However, there's one thing that is absolutely clear: No matter what state you're in, or what your local laws are, you can avoid a potentially huge amount of trouble by putting your contracts in writing. All of them. Every single one, including the change orders. The days of the handshake contract are over.

Does a written contract have to be long and hard to read? No, not at all. A simple job can be done with a simple contract. Even a handwritten note that contains the necessary terms could be a contract. There are several supply companies that sell short preprinted contracts that are just fine for most uncomplicated jobs.

There are also longer forms for more complicated jobs. Several are available on computer disks that you can buy from a variety of sources. There are some sample contracts on the CD in the back of this book.

With some careful thought and good forms as a guideline, a small contractor can prepare many of his or her less complex contracts. It has to be done carefully, but it isn't rocket science. Take the time to understand

Why Do Contracts Need to Be in Writing?

Even contracts that aren't required by law to be in writing *should* be in writing — and that includes change orders. Otherwise, it might not be possible to enforce them "exactly as intended." Here are four reasons to put your contracts in writing:

1. The first reason, of course, is that the law in your state may require that certain types of contracts be in writing. If you get *all* of your contracts in writing, then you don't have to worry about which contract has to be in writing and which contract doesn't.

2. The most important reason to put it in writing isn't about the law at all. It's about *understanding* the agreement. We tend to hear and absorb what we expect and want. And so do our customers. In a verbal contract, they might not think they're agreeing to what *you* think they're agreeing to. And when they don't get what they expected to get, you might not get the payment that you expect. When the contract is in writing, it's still possible to disagree about the meaning of words, but there's much less chance of a mistake or misunderstanding between the parties. It's the best way possible to be sure that everybody is talking about the same thing.

3. A written contract, even if it's not required by local law, will put you in a much better position if you actually do wind up in court for some reason. Your written contract immediately proves that you did actually have a contract, so your attorney won't have to waste time (especially at $200 an hour) proving that there was a contract between the plaintiff and defendant. Instead, your attorney can get immediately to the important stuff like getting you your money for the work that you did — or would have done if the defendant hadn't breached the contract.

4. And, if you do go into court and win, the court will have a much clearer idea of what to give you if there's a written contract in place. Putting it in writing means you have a better chance of actually getting what's due you, and what you had hoped for if you did win.

what you're putting into your contract and why. Books like this one can answer your questions, and there are also many conferences and seminars you can attend that are sponsored by schools, industry publications like the *Journal of Light Construction* or *Remodeling* magazine, or industry associations like NARI or the Home Builders Association.

A Contract Starts With an Offer

The property owner can make an offer to a builder or remodeler, which the builder or remodeler can turn into a contract by accepting. That's not what usually happens, however.

What usually happens in the building trade is that a property owner asks a builder or contractor for a bid. Sometimes, a public body actually

What Can You Do if You Don't Have a Written Contract?

Suppose you should have had a written contract and didn't. Do you have any hope of getting paid?

You might.

Sometimes, even in those states or those situations which require a contract be in writing, it's possible for a contractor without a written contract to collect for his work. The answer often depends on what state you're in, and what kind of work you did. If the job was a commercial site, many consumer protection laws about written requirements may not apply. In that case, not having a contract won't be a big legal problem. But even if it was a residential job, it still might be possible to get paid. Some states allow a contractor, who can't enforce the actual contract because it wasn't in writing, to get paid for the work he or she has already done on *an unjust enrichment* or *quantum meruit* legal theory.

The idea behind an unjust enrichment lawsuit is that you actually did the work, while the property owner just stood by watching. If the owner didn't say "No, stop, you don't have an enforceable contract," it would be unjust to allow that property owner to benefit from your work without some reimbursement to you.

However, even if you win an unjust enrichment or *quantum meruit* lawsuit, you probably won't get the profit you would have made on the job. These aren't breach of contract lawsuits. The damages that you could win in one of these suits aren't necessarily the same as what you could win in a breach of contract suit. Unjust enrichment damages are based on the value of the work to the property owner, which might be more than you expected in profit, or it could be a whole lot *less*!

If you're in a situation where you hope to use a *quantum meruit* or unjust enrichment lawsuit, you'll definitely need the assistance of an attorney.

issues a formal invitation to bid on public projects. Although that invitation is very detailed, it's still not an offer, simply because it's not intended to be an offer. It's the *intent*, not the *details*, that makes the difference.

Suppose Harry the homeowner says to Cal the carpenter, "I want you to fix my floor." That's not an offer, because it's obvious that Harry doesn't intend Cal to be able to turn it into a contract by simply saying, "Sure, I'll do it."

What Harry wants is for Cal to *bid* on fixing the floor. Harry wants to hear Cal say something like: "I'll fix your floor for $500." That would be Cal's offer. When Harry says something like "Okay" — that's Harry's acceptance. His acceptance creates a contract between them.

If, instead, Harry had said to Cal, "I'll give you $500 if you fix my floor," that's an offer, because it's specific enough that it's clearly intended to be an offer. When Cal says "Sure, I'll do it," Cal has accepted Harry's offer.

That creates a contract between them. You can see what they intended by looking at the language they used and the circumstances of their relationship.

Is an Estimate an Offer?

No, it's not. An estimate isn't an offer — it's just a guess. It needs to be put into the language of an offer before it can create a binding contract.

Some estimates come with language at the bottom of the estimate that turns the estimate into an offer that can be accepted with the client's signature. That creates a contract, because the language at the bottom of the estimate turns that estimate into an offer. That language would look something like this: "If acceptable, please sign and return." Language like that is clearly intended to be an offer that, if accepted, would create a contract.

Is a Bid the Same Thing as an Offer?

Yes, a bid is an offer that the recipient can turn into a contract by accepting. I've also heard bids called *quotes.* That's okay. You can call a bid anything you want as long as it's clear that you intend to make an offer.

Can an Offer or Bid Be Withdrawn?

Yes, most of the time. As a general rule, a bidder can withdraw a bid any time up to the moment it's accepted. We'll discuss the exceptions to this rule in the following sections.

For example, suppose Cal gave Harry a bid that said it was good for ten days. Then, for some reason, Cal decided to withdraw that bid the very next day — before Harry had a chance to accept it. Cal can do that if he wants to. All the ten-day term does is set an expiration date for the offer. Except for the exceptions we'll look at later, Harry can't treat the ten-day expiration date as a promise to keep the bid open for ten days. That would make the ten-day term a contract term. There are no contract terms between Cal and Harry, because there's no contract. There can't be a contract until the bid is accepted.

Are There Any Situations Where a Bid Can't Be Withdrawn?

Here's the situation that's usually the problem: Many contractors base their bid to a property owner on the bids they get from the subcontractors that they'll use to do the work. But the contractors don't actually accept the subcontractors' bids until after they hear back from the property owner, in case they don't get the job.

For example, suppose Able Concrete gives Bigger Builders a bid for pouring a foundation. Able Concrete knows Bigger Builders intends to use Able's foundation bid as part of Bigger's own bid on a new strip mall. Meanwhile, Able puts out some other bids, which are accepted. So now Able wants to withdraw its foundation bid on the Bigger's job, because Able just doesn't have the time or the crew to perform. Can Able do that? Or can Bigger Builders treat Able's bid as a contract, even though Bigger specifically *did not accept* Able's bid. After all, Bigger Builders didn't want to be bound to a contract with Able if Bigger Builders' bid on the mall was not accepted.

In Some States a Subcontractor Can't Withdraw a Bid if ...

Some states don't allow a subcontractor to withdraw a bid until a "reasonable time" has passed. How many days amount to a reasonable time depends upon what's customary between the parties, and also on what's customary in the local industry. That's why a well-advised subcontractor would put an expiration date, like ten days, on his bid. Then everyone knows what the reasonable time is. It's ten days.

About half of the states take a different approach. When a contractor gets a bid from a subcontractor, *and* reasonably relies on that bid, *and* if the sub who made the bid knew the contractor would rely on the bid, then that subcontractor can't withdraw the bid. This is called *reliance* or *promissory estoppel.* Clear as mud, right? I'll explain some more.

The idea is that the subcontractor knew the contractor intended to use that bid in the contractor's quote, so it isn't fair to let the subcontractor pull the rug out from under him. However, what if the contractor had said something like "Give me a ballpark figure," or "What's your best guess?" That's not an offer that the subcontractor can't withdraw, because the subcontractor wouldn't have necessarily known the contractor was going to use it in his bid.

What Happens if the Subcontractor Can't Perform on Its Bid?

Suppose Bigger Builders' bid on the strip mall is accepted, but then Able Concrete can't do the work for some reason. What happens? In the "reasonable time" and "reliance" states, Able has a problem. In those states, if Able doesn't perform on its bid to Bigger Builders, Bigger can sue Able and possibly collect damages (or sometimes two kinds of damages); breach of contract damages and consequential damages.

Breach of contract damages mean that if Bigger Builders has to pay another concrete company more money to do the work than Able Concrete's price, Able will have to pay Bigger the difference between its bid and the actual price. Of course, if the actual price is less than Able's bid, there won't be any breach of contract damages.

Consequential damages means that if Bigger Builders loses money in other ways that were caused by Able's breach of contract, Able will probably have to reimburse Bigger Builders for that money. An example of consequential damages would be if Bigger had to pay damages to the property owner because of the delay while Bigger was finding a different concrete company.

Are There Any Exceptions to These Exceptions?

Of course there are. That's what makes the practice of law so much fun! One exception to the "reasonable time" and "reliance" rules is when the subcontractor's bid was clearly a mistake. In that case the contractor can't bind the subcontractor to that mistake by rushing out and accepting that bid, or by using it.

For example, if Able Concrete had left out the material costs and only figured labor costs into its bid, it should be clear to Bigger Builders that there's something wrong with that bid. It would only be about half of what it should have been. Bigger Builders can't hold Able to that bid, because Bigger obviously realized, or should have realized, that there was a mistake.

Does an Expiration Date on the Bid Protect the Subcontractor?

Sometimes a subcontractor will put out bids on more work than he can actually handle, on the theory that they won't all be accepted. What can he do to protect himself in case he gets more acceptances than he expects? He should put an expiration date on his bid. It doesn't matter how much reliance there might be, or how many cases there are in that state about "reasonable time." A bid with an expiration date *ends* on the expiration date if it's not accepted before that date. The expiration date won't protect the subcontractor if a problem comes up before the expiration date, but it does make this kind of problem less likely to happen.

Are There Bids That Must Be Accepted?

Most of the time, the property owner doesn't have to accept a bid. But there are two exceptions to that general rule.

Bids Made to Public Agencies

Some public works contracts are located in states where the public body is required by law to accept the lowest bid unless the public body can demonstrate good reason why it should not. For example, if the low bidder has a history of not completing work or has a history of fraud, the agency can refuse the bid.

Bids Obtained by Fraud

There are a few instances where a private owner must accept the bid. For example, if the owner puts out an invitation to bid that says the lowest bid will be accepted, some courts have considered that the lowest offer is automatically the accepted bid. It becomes a binding contract the moment that low bid is received.

These cases recognize that contractors use a lot of time, money and resources to create bids. Since the property owner persuaded the contractor to make a bid with the understanding that it would be accepted if it were the lowest bid, it wouldn't be fair to allow the owner to refuse it. This kind of legal theory is called estoppel. Because of his own actions, the property owner is now estopped from not accepting the bid.

A Contract Must Benefit Both Parties

Consideration is what the law calls a benefit in a contract. Enforceable contracts must involve benefits for both parties. This is also called "mutual promises." In other words, there must be something in the deal for the parties on both sides.

For example, if I promise to give you my car for your birthday, that's not an enforceable contract, because there's nothing in it for me. There might be something else that may be enforceable, but it's not a contract. However, if I promise to sell you my car for $500, that's an enforceable contract. The deal is that you get my car, and I get your money. We'll both benefit from the contract.

Change Orders Must Also Have Some Consideration

To be enforceable, a change to the contract that involves extra work must have some sort of benefit to the contractor, usually either more

Get Those Change Orders in Writing

The phrase "change order" is self-explanatory. If the parties agree to do something different from the original job specifications or payment terms, that's a change to the contract. Just as it's best to always get your original contract in writing, you should also get in writing any change orders to that contract. In fact, some states won't enforce a change order that's not in writing.

Don't let the writing requirement make you nervous. What should make you nervous is the casual:

"Can we change this to that?"

"Sure. No problem."

Remember, we're not talking about John D. Rockefeller's will. It's enough to add a sentence across the bottom of the original contract that says what's different, or what has been added onto the contract, and what it will cost. Or write a simple note — a Post-It note will do in a pinch — that's initialed by both the contractor and the customer.

But get it in writing.

money or an abandonment of another piece of work that the contractor was supposed to complete. The contractor is entitled to be paid for the work when it's finished. If no specific promise of payment has been made, then the contractor is entitled to a "reasonable" amount of compensation. The law assumes the contractor didn't intend to work for free, and if the homeowner didn't realize that, he should have.

For example, suppose the contractor and homeowner sign a contract with plans attached for a new kitchen. Then the homeowner decides to change those plans so that the new kitchen includes a counter and bookshelves for a built-in office. To make this change an enforceable part of the contract, the homeowner needs to do one of two things:

1. Pay extra for the built-in office (it is, after all, *extra*);

2. Make a trade-off that has the effect of reducing the contractor's costs on the original contract.

The homeowner might decide that he could do without the stained glass inserts on the cabinet doors, which were part of the original contract. Giving up those inserts would reduce the contractor's cost, so that's a benefit to the contractor. It doesn't have to be a dollar for dollar benefit, but there does have to be *something* of benefit to the contractor.

An Offer Has to Be Accepted Before There's a Contract

Usually it's easy to recognize acceptance: The other party signs the contract. If there's no written contract, acceptance could be saying "Yes," or starting work, or paying money. Any words or actions that make it clear that the parties are agreeing to a contract will do, unless the state law requires that acceptance be in writing. Some states do require that. Then actions or words alone probably won't be enough, except as detailed in the following section on *unjust enrichment*.

What Constitutes Acceptance?

If there's a written document involved, it's generally not enough to just sign it. The signed contract also has to be delivered to the other parties. The contract can be *delivered* by mailing it or by simply handing it to the other party. Signing the contract and keeping it on your desk is *not* acceptance.

But there are a surprising number of lawsuits involving situations where the property owner told the contractor that he had signed the contract and put it in the mail, when he hadn't. When the contractor went ahead and started the work without the contract in hand, the court usually ruled that the owner was estopped from denying that there was a binding contract. Although most of the contractors won these cases, they obviously could have avoided an enormous amount of expense and hassle by either waiting until the contract arrived before starting work, or by dropping by the owner's house and picking it up. That way, even if the owner breached the contract, the contractor's lawsuit would have been quicker and less expensive. While the contractor's lawyer would still have to prove breach of contract, the lawyer wouldn't have to also prove that there was a binding contract in existence.

What About Faxes?

Faxes of a written contract are a modern problem. Traditional law held that a copy of a signature wasn't good enough. But modern building practices often involve faxing a signed copy of the contract so the contractor can start work on the project immediately. The most recent court cases have held that a contractor *can* rely on a faxed copy.

Is a Counteroffer an Acceptance?

Suppose Harry the homeowner had said, "Fix my floor and I'll pay you $500," and Cal the carpenter responded, "Okay, I'll fix it, but I want $700 to do it." That isn't an acceptance, because Cal hasn't agreed to the terms of Harry's offer. Harry didn't offer to pay him $700. Cal has made what's called a counteroffer. If Harry agrees to Cal's request for $700, that's an acceptance. At that point, they have a contract.

Consumer Protection Notices That May Be Required

Some construction contracts must have certain consumer protection notices written into them. Some of the clauses may be required by the state you live in, and some are required by federal law. Federal laws require that the contractor include notice of the *Right of Cancellation*, the *Right of Rescission*, and the *Magnuson-Moss Warranty Act* in some of their contracts.

The Right of Cancellation

When the contract is signed in the customer's home in the presence of the contractor or his agent, many state laws require that the contract include a notice of the customer's right to cancel the contract and notice of when the right expires. For more information, see Chapter 14.

The Right of Rescission

The Truth In Lending Act gives construction customers a right of rescission (cancellation) if the contract involves a security interest or a lien on the customer's home. They have 72 hours after it's signed to rescind the contract, or 72 hours after the homeowner is given notice of the right of rescission, whichever comes later. Rescission (or to rescind a contract) means to put the parties to the contract back in the position they were before there was a contract. In other words, cancel it. For more information, see Chapter 14.

What About Contract Warranties?

The federal Magnuson-Moss Act regulates how consumer product warranties — or the disclaimer of those warranties — should be phrased. Many contractors don't think they fall under this act, but remember that residential construction jobs often involve products like stoves, bathtubs, or furnaces, which are all consumer products.

When the contractor buys the product himself, adds a markup, and then installs it, that contractor is selling that product, whether he realizes it or not. If the customer is a homeowner, he or she falls into the "consumer" category and Magnuson-Moss covers that contract. For more information about Magnuson-Moss, see Chapter 14.

What About State Consumer Protection Laws?

There are a number of consumer protection laws at the state level that require specific language in the contract. Some states, such as Michigan, require "cooling off" periods for consumers, which give the customer a certain number of days to change their mind about the contract. Some states require notice of the possibility of a lien or mortgage. You should always check your state requirements, because the penalties for violating these requirements can be very harsh. It's easy to find out what those requirements are; just call your state licensing agency and ask. If they can't tell you themselves, they can tell you who you should be calling. If there's a Consumer Protection office in your state, you should call them, too.

For a more complete discussion of consumer protection laws, see Chapter 14.

What If the Contract Doesn't Have Everything in It?

The contract between Harry the homeowner and Cal the carpenter may be a little vague in places. Maybe it doesn't say *exactly* when Cal will start work on Harry's floor, or *exactly* what kind of flooring Cal will install in Harry's new kitchen. Those kinds of problems don't necessarily mean that Harry and Cal don't have an enforceable contract.

If it's clear the parties intended to make a contract, and it's possible to figure out in broad terms what each party was promising, the law will "imply" some of those missing details. But that's only true if these really are just details, and don't actually go to the heart of whether or not the parties intended to have a contract. And these details can't be implied if there's a state or federal law that required those details to be there.

In other words, if it's possible to see what Harry and Cal intended to agree to, and if it's possible to imply these missing details in a way that's consistent with what they agreed on, the contract is still good. And there's one more *if.* It also has to be consistent with the consumer protection laws.

But if the missing details are critical to the contract, then the contract may be too vague to be enforced. In that case, Harry's remarks would have only amounted to an invitation to Cal to bid. They need to negotiate some more before they actually have a contract.

For example, suppose Harry and Cal agreed to install a bumpout on the rear second floor of Harry's Cape Cod so Harry will have a new bedroom. They've signed a contract complete with architectural drawings and specifications. However, the contract fails to use the term "paint-ready" in the specifications, so Harry thinks that he's supposed to get a new bedroom that's fully painted.

When Harry's new bedroom isn't painted, he withholds his last payment. As a practical matter, Cal ought to see if he can negotiate a way out of this. But what if he can't, and he winds up suing Harry for that last payment? The court will probably reason that the contract implies that Harry and Cal agreed to what's standard in the industry with regard to details not specifically detailed in the contract. If contractors in that area don't typically hand over fully-painted additions, Cal will win. Of course, if Harry can bring experts who testify that local contractors always expect to have to paint the interior of new additions, then Cal better break out the brushes.

As another example, let's look at something a court wouldn't be likely to imply was a part of the contract. Suppose Harry contracts with Cal to build an apartment building on Harry's property. After the contract is signed, Harry then decides to use the building as a senior citizen residence, which means another $100,000 in additional building costs to met the licensing standards. Harry says Cal will just have to eat that extra $100,000 because he has already agreed to build the building for a specific amount of money.

But Cal *didn't* agree to build a senior citizen residence that required special facilities. This couldn't be implied in the contract by reading the other terms of the contract and finding that it's consistent with them. At the time of signing the contract, Cal didn't know that Harry intended a special use for the building. Cal's obligation is to build an apartment building that could be rented out to the general population. There's no industry expectation that this would be a building appropriate for a particular population with special needs (beyond those required by the ADA).

The important thing to remember is this: If the parties intended to make a contract, the law is weighed toward enforcing that contract even if it does mean filling in a few blanks.

In the next chapter, we'll take a closer look at some of those blanks that need to be filled in on your construction contracts.

4

Contract Terms: Filling in the Blanks

In the last chapter we looked at what makes contracts enforceable. This chapter is about filling in the blanks on your enforceable contract. That can be difficult. In construction, you're often dealing with projects that are as complicated to put together as the Battle of the Bulge — and with unknown factors lurking beneath the surface like land mines.

For example, on many projects, Cal the carpenter doesn't know how much to charge until he tears out a floor to see if the joists have moisture damage. He doesn't know exactly how long it will take to frame an addition if the weather's bad. He doesn't know if the price on the lumber he needs will go up between the time he bids the contract and the time he actually buys the lumber.

So how does Cal write an enforceable contract that's missing some important details — like exactly what the specifications are, how long the job will take, or how much it will cost?

Blank Copy on CD-ROM

There's a blank copy of Figure 4-1 included on the disk in the back of the book.

He can do this by filling in the contract terms — what I'm calling the blanks on your contract — with language that recognizes the pitfalls ahead, and plans for them. Figure 4-1 is a sample remodeling contract that shows how you can prevent many common contract problems.

Who Are the Parties?

The first section in a contract is usually the one that identifies the people who have obligations in that contract. For example, if Harry the homeowner and Cal the carpenter agree that Cal should build an addition onto Harry's house, Cal and Harry should both be named in the contract. They are the *parties*, because they're the people who have made promises to each other in this contract. Harry promised to pay for the work, and Cal promised to do the work.

Bigger Builders Inc.
22 Commerce Drive • Lansing, MI 55555
Phone (555)555-1234 • Fax (555)555-6789
Website: www.biggerbuildersinc.com

REMODELING CONTRACT

(This document is intended as a guide. Although language for different options is included in some of the contract clauses, this is not a universal document. You may find your situation requires language or legal assistance that isn't included here, or you may find that a combination of some of the options used here to be the most useful.)

I. Parties

(Opening statement identifying the parties is always first in a contract. Put the names of all of the parties, their addresses, and the date of the contract here. If the address of the place where the work is to be done is not the same address as the customer's, then that address should also be included here. Choose one of the options available and delete the others.)

(Option one: Contract between married homeowners and a contractor who is a sole proprietor.)

This contract is made and entered into on <u>July 17, 2000</u> *(month, day, year)* and specifies the terms of the agreement between <u>John & Carla Customer</u> *(name of both husband and wife)*, homeowners, and <u>Calvin Smith</u>, remodeling contractor, whose address is <u>21 Commerce Drive, Lansing, MI</u>, to <u>remodel</u> *(construct, build, remodel)* <u>the kitchen according to the attached plan</u>, *(identify the kind of structure to be built and/or remodeled)* on the property located at <u>21 West Street, Lansing, MI</u>. *(The mailing address goes here. In larger jobs, the legal description should also be included here, or in the specifications.)*

(Option two: Contract between an incorporated contractor and married homeowners.)

<u>Bigger Builders Inc.</u> *(name of construction company)*, whose business address is <u>22 Commerce Drive, Lansing, MI</u>, hereby enters into this contract with <u>John and Carla Customer</u> *(name of both husband and wife)*, whose address is <u>21 West Street, Lansing, MI</u>, and who own the property at <u>21 West St. Lansing</u> *(if property is other than the clients' home, add that address and legal description to the contract)* on this day of <u>July 17, 2000</u> *(month, day, year)* as follows:

- 1 -

Figure 4-1 *Sample remodeling contract*

(Option three: Contract between an unincorporated sole proprietor contractor and an incorporated business.)

This contract is hereby made and entered into on <u>July 17, 2000</u> between <u>Calvin Smith</u>, remodeling contractor, whose address is <u>21 Commerce Drive, Lansing MI</u>, and <u>Bigger Builders</u> *(name of incorporated business)*, who is doing business at <u>22 Commerce Drive, Lansing MI</u>. This contract is to <u>frame the addition</u> *(describe the job)* on the property located at <u>21 West Street, Lansing, MI</u>.

II. The Contract Documents

(This clause is to identify those things, which are part of the contract, but which are on separate documents, such as architectural drawings, permits, lists of allowances, limited warranties, specifications sheet drawings, and so forth.)

(Option one:)

The remodeling contractor will perform all the work that is required by this agreement and all the work that is required by the documents incorporated by reference into this agreement. *(All separate documents that relate to the job should be named here. The ones named in this example are examples only. If you have more or different documents, name those.)* The contract documents are:

<u>Architect's drawings, dated 1/1/00</u>   *Alvin A. Archer, AIA*

<u>Specification sheet, dated 7/1/00</u>   *Calvin Smith, Contractor*

<u>Notice of Customer's Right to Rescind</u>

(Option two:)

The contract documents include the terms of this contract and, by reference, the documents listed below:

(Don't forget to fully identify the documents by including their name, who signed them and the date when signed.)

1. <u>Architect's plan by Al Archer dated 1-1-00</u>

2. <u>Specification sheet dated 7-1-00 & signed by Calvin Smith, Contractor</u>

3. <u>A printed notice of the customer's right to rescind</u>

Figure 4-1 *Sample remodeling contract (continued)*

III. The Scope of the Work

(This clause describes what the project is.)

(Option one: General language, which assumes separate specifications and/or architectural drawings.)

The remodeling contractor will furnish all the labor, materials, and equipment necessary to complete the alterations and improvements described in the contract documents. The work does not include <u>finish painting, window replacements or exterior improvements</u>. *(This is where to put those things that are not included in the contract such as painting, electrical, hazardous material abatement, etc.)*

(Option two: This example assumes the job is a simple kitchen renovation without a separate specifications sheet. When the project is not detailed in another document, it should be described here in as much detail as possible.)

The remodeling contractor will furnish the labor and materials necessary to do the following:

<u>1. Tear out and remove existing cabinetry and countertops.</u>

<u>2. Haul debris to landfill and pay dump fees.</u>

<u>3. Install new cabinets of the customer's choice from the attached list of allowances.</u>

<u>4. Install new countertop of the customer's choice from the attached list of allowances.</u>

<u>5. Repair existing drywall where necessary and install new drywall where necessary to a paint-ready condition.</u>

<u>6. This agreement does not include labor or materials for electrical work, paint, windows or appliances.</u>

IV. Change Orders

(Anything that is different from the original contract should be documented. Otherwise, the contractor may have difficulty getting paid for it, or even demonstrating the change was what the customer wanted.)

All change orders must be in writing and signed by all the parties. The owners agree that changes resulting in the furnishing of additional labor or materials will be paid for prior to the commencement of the extra work. The owners agree that either of them may sign a change order, and that signature will be binding on both.

- 3 -

Figure 4-1 *Sample remodeling contract (continued)*

V. Permits, Licenses, and Approvals

The remodeling contractor will obtain and pay for local building and construction permits, and will obtain and pay the fees for the governmental inspections that are necessary for the construction and occupancy of the finished structure, except as otherwise provided in this contract. The owners will secure and pay for any easements, variances, zoning changes, necessary modifications of restrictive covenants, or other actions. The owners will indicate the property lines to the remodeling contractor and will provide boundary stakes by a licensed land surveyor if the owners are in doubt about the property boundaries.

VI. Insurance and Risk of Loss

(This is sample language only. This clause describes who is supposed to get what insurance. The contractor and the customer may reach a different arrangement about insurance. The important thing is that somebody should get casualty, property damage, theft, liability and workers' compensation insurance on the project.)

The owners agree to maintain insurance covering the replacement cost of the improvement under contract in the event of loss through fire, casualty, storm or other disasters, and theft of materials from the site. Before work begins, the property owner will furnish a certificate of that insurance to the remodeling contractor. The remodeling contractor agrees to maintain workers' compensation insurance and liability insurance to protect the owners from liability claims for damages because of bodily injury, including death, and from liability for damages to property. Before beginning the work, the remodeling contractor will furnish a certificate of that insurance to the property owner.

VII. Access

The property owner will allow free access to work areas for workers and vehicles and will allow areas for the storage of materials and debris. Driveways will be kept clear for the movement of vehicles during work hours. The remodeling contractor will make reasonable efforts to protect driveways, lawns, shrubs, and other vegetation.

VIII. Site Conditions

(Problems which were not discoverable at the time of the original contract can change the schedule, materials and money that the project will cost.)

The property owners acknowledge that this contract is based upon the remodeling contractor's observation of conditions. Conditions which could not be known by a reasonable inspection, such as termite damage, hidden water damage, hidden code violations, or other concealed conditions, may require extra labor or materials, which are not part

- 4 -

Figure 4-1 *Sample remodeling contract (continued)*

of this contract. If such hidden conditions are discovered, the remodeling contractor will notify the property owner and will attempt to reach an agreement for a change order to this contract that addresses those problems.

IX. Payment

(Option one: Time and materials.)

The customer will pay an hourly fee for labor in the amount of $30.00 for all time spent on the job plus the cost of all materials.

(Option two: Cost plus a fixed amount for overhead and profit.)

The property owner will pay the cost of all materials used in construction plus delivery and handling costs, the wages of all carpenters and other workers, and the cost of all subcontractors. The owner will also pay a fixed fee of $ 10,000 to the contractor for overhead and profit.

(Option three: Cost plus a percentage for overhead and profit.)

The owner will pay the cost of all materials used in construction plus delivery and handling costs, the wages of all carpenters and other workers for the actual time spent on the job, and the cost of all subcontractors. The owner will also pay 30 percent of those costs to the contractor for the contractor's overhead and profit.

(Option four: Cost plus a percentage for overhead and profit up to a maximum amount.)

The owner will pay the cost of all materials used in construction plus delivery and handling costs, the wages of all carpenters and other workers for the actual time spent on the job, and the cost of all subcontractors. The owner will also pay 30 percent of those costs to the contractor for the contractor's overhead and profit. The contractor guarantees that the total cost of the work will not exceed the amount of $ 60,000, excluding the cost of change orders.

X. Payment Schedule

(Some states restrict the amount of deposit a contractor can collect, so check with your state's consumer affairs office. When you set up your payment schedule, aim for as small a final payment as possible to avoid collection problems.)

- 5 -

Figure 4-1 *Sample remodeling contract (continued)*

(Option one: Payments due upon specific dates.)

Payments for the work will be due as follows:

A deposit in the amount of <u>25</u> percent *(this could be a dollar amount instead of a percentage)* of the contract price will be due upon contract signing.

$ <u>15,000</u> is due on the date of <u>8-1-00</u>.

$ <u>15,000</u> is due on the date of <u>9-1-00</u>.

$ <u>10,000</u> is due on the date of <u>10-1-00</u>.

(The payments could be a percentage amount instead of a dollar amount. Also, instead of a specific date, a certain of number of days or weeks after the work has started may be used as the schedule.)

The final payment of $ <u>5,000</u> is due upon substantial completion. Before final payment, the remodeling contractor will deliver a lien release to the customer. *(Consider using a punch list to trigger the final payment. See the punch list language in Clause XI.)*

If payments due to the remodeling contractor are not paid in accordance with the payment schedule in this contract, the remodeling contractor may suspend work until the scheduled payment is made.

(Option two: Payments due upon the completion of parts of the work.)

Payments for the work are due as follows:

A deposit in the amount of <u>25</u> percent of the contract price is due upon contract signing. Additional payments will be due as the following items of work listed below are completed. *(You could use work starts as the payment triggers).*

When each payment is due, the remodeling contractor will prepare a statement of money due in writing and submit it to the owners. All payments are due from the property owner no later than ten days after receipt of the statement. The remodeling contractor will furnish lien releases for work completed through each request, upon receipt of payment.

Figure 4-1 *Sample remodeling contract (continued)*

20% of the remaining contract price is due when <u>the tearout is complete and the debris removed</u>. *(Describe a particular task to be completed before each payment is due.)*

20% of the remaining contract price is due when <u>the appliances are installed</u>.

20% of the remaining contract price is due when <u>the new countertop and cabinets are installed</u>.

20% of the remaining contract price is due when <u>the electrical and plumbing work is completed</u>.

The remaining contract price is due upon substantial completion of the work. Upon final payment the remodeling contractor will deliver a release of all liens.

If payments due to the remodeling contractor are not paid within ten days of the written demand, the remodeling contractor may suspend work until payment is made.

XI. Final Inspections and Liens

(This clause is optional, depending upon the agreement between the parties, and is a punch list procedure.)

very important

Upon notification by the remodeling contractor of substantial completion of the work, the owners and the remodeling contractor will inspect the work performed, and at that time the owners will prepare a punch list that identifies any incomplete work or deficiencies in workmanship or materials. The owners may retain the value of the punch list work from the final payment until the punch list items are complete. Completion of the punch list items must be made within <u>10</u> days from the date of the punch list preparation. When the punch list items are completed, the owners will pay the remodeling contractor the balance of the contract price within <u>10</u> days of the demand. At that time, the remodeling contractor will deliver to the property owners a release of all liens.

XII. Warranties

The remodeling contractor guarantees the work will meet trade standards of good workmanship. The remodeling contractor will make every effort to blend existing textures, colors, and planes, but exact duplication is not guaranteed. The remodeling contractor warrants that materials of good quality will be selected. The contractor will maintain all manufacturers' warranties. The customer is limited to the manufacturers' warranties for defects in the manufacture of materials. All contractors' warranties are limited to a period of no more than <u>one year</u>. *(The period can be whatever the parties agree to.)* The remodeling contractor's warranties are limited to the cost of labor and materials only, and exclude ordinary wear and tear or abuse by others.

- 7 -

Figure 4-1 *Sample remodeling contract (continued)*

XIII. Dispute Resolution

All the parties will cooperate with each other to resolve conflicts informally. In the event that is not possible, conflicts between the parties will be resolved by <u>arbitration</u> *(mediation or arbitration)* provided by <u>American Arbitration Association</u> *(a professional group such as the American Arbitration Association)*. The conflict will be decided according to the Construction Industry Rules of the American Arbitration Association, and the laws of the state where the project is located. The arbitrator will award reasonable costs and expenses, including attorney fees, to the prevailing party.

XIV. Signatures

We, the undersigned, have read and understood this entire contract, including documents attached by reference. We acknowledge that this document constitutes the entire agreement between the parties. This contract is not binding upon the remodeling contractor or the property owners until it is signed by all parties.

Dated __July 17. 2000__   Signed __Calvin Smith__
(month, day, year)   *(The remodeling contractor signs here)*

(If the company is incorporated, the contract must be signed by an officer of the corporation who is authorized to sign contracts, and who is identified by his or her position with the corporation.)

Dated __July 17, 2000__   Signed __John D. Customer__
(month, day, year)   *(The property owner signs here)*

Dated __July 17, 2000__   Signed __Carla Customer__
(month, day, year)   *(The owner's spouse signs here)*

Contract documents:

(List all the relevant construction documents here if those documents are not identified in a contract documents clause.)

_____

_____

_____

_____

(Ask the property owner to sign this page and initial all the other contract pages.)

- 8 -

Figure 4-1 *Sample remodeling contract (continued)*

There could be other people who should also be named here because they're also involved in the project, even if they're not supposed to sign the contract. For example, suppose Harry had hired an architect to design his deck before he accepted a bid from Cal. That architect ought to be identified in the contract, too, because if the design has stairs up to the deck that turn out to be 6 inches too short, everyone ought to know who to blame.

The location of the project can also be identified in this section, although sometimes the address of the job site is put into the *Scope of the Work* clause, or even in its own clause. It doesn't really matter where in the contract the address is, so long as the job site location is always clearly and fully identified some place.

Sometimes the legal description of the property is included in the contract along with the property address, or even instead of it. If the property is unplatted, it's essential to include the legal description. In some states the legal description must be included if there will be subcontractors on the job who haven't waived their lien rights.

Scope of the Work Clauses

Suppose Harry wants a deck built onto his house. The contract language about building that deck is often called the "Scope of the Work" clause, but it doesn't have to be called that. The AIA sample contract calls it the "Work To Be Done" clause. Other contracts use terms like "The Work" or the "Specifications" clause.

 **Key Terms**

Scope of the Work clauses are written by either describing *what* work is to be done, or by describing the work in terms that say *how* the work is to be done.

Whatever it's called, it's the clause that identifies and describes the work that's the basis for the contract. The clause can identify that work by describing it, or by referring to other documents (like architectural plans or drawings or lists of specifications). The clause names those documents and then incorporates them into the contract by reference. "By reference" means that those named documents are part of the contract even though they're separate documents. For example, the contract may say:

> Architectural plans for Harry Homeowner's deck, prepared by Thomas Drafter and dated January 5th, 2001, are hereby incorporated by reference into this contract.

Contractors often run into problems when they're doing the work. When they do, how these clauses are written makes a difference in whether the contractor can use his own judgment to fix the problem, or if he has to go back and consult with the property owner or the architect.

Scope of the Work clauses are written by either describing *what* work is to be done, or by describing the work in terms that say *how* the work is to be done.

When There's a Mistake in the Contract

The basic rule is that if the bid has been accepted and there's a contract in place, that contract is enforceable, mistakes and all. For example, if a contractor made a bid based on trim work at $1 a foot and the real price was $1.10, once that $1 a foot bid is accepted, the contractor is stuck.

However, there are exceptions to this rule. The mistake must be mutual (both parties must be mistaken). If one of the parties realized — or should have realized — that there was a mistake, then the contract may not be enforceable.

For example, suppose that instead of a few cents per foot mistake, the contractor made a bid that was several dollars a foot short of the real price. The property owner should have realized this bid was a mistake, because the price was so dramatically out of line with other bids or with current lumber prices. In that case, the owner can't take advantage of the contractor's mistake to create a binding contract at a mistaken price. The rule is that if the other party knew or should have known that there was a mistake in the bid, the other party can't take advantage of the mistake.

The other situation in which a mistake may make the contract unenforceable is if, because of the mistake, performance is impossible. What if the contractor promised to build new interior walls made of Peruvian Enameled Tile, and it turns out Peruvian Enameled Tile hasn't been available for years? If it can't be done, it may release the contract — or at least that particular term in the contract.

Clause Describing What the Job Is

When the job is described in terms of performance — what work is to be done — then the contractor can use his own best judgment about how to do that job.

For example, a Scope of the Work clause written in performance language would read something like this:

Install 10 x 14 redwood deck at the rear of the house.

The contractor has an obligation to build a 10 x 14 deck, and he has to build it out of redwood because that's a detail described in the contract. Otherwise he can use his professional judgment about how to do the work.

He can use his own judgment because that language concentrates on *what* the contractor is supposed to do, not *how*. It doesn't tell the contractor exactly where to place the footings or how many steps to build or what the width between the posts in the railing should be. It just says build it. How to build it is up to the contractor.

Clause Describing How the Job Is Built

There's another way of writing Scope of the Work clauses. The clauses can be written in descriptive language that describes *how* the contractor is to do the work.

For example, a descriptive language clause in the contract would read something like this:

> Tear off existing steps from the rear entrance on the south wall of the house. Dig and pour six piers 42 inches deep, install 4 x 4 posts on the piers with post anchors, put two 2 x 12s on top of the posts to join the six piers, then lay 12 S.P.F. joists. Cover deck with 2 x 6 x 10 redwood.

Or the clause could read like this:

> Construct the deck in accordance with the architectural plans prepared by Arnold the Architect dated October 8th.

This means the deck must be constructed exactly according to those plans.

When the specifications are described in terms of what the contractor has to do to complete the work, the contractor *must* take those steps exactly the way the contract says — even if the contractor knows a better way. If the contractor sees a flaw in the plans or specs, he needs to get a change order or a contract modification before he can do the work differently.

And because of the contractor's implied warranties, there's a big potential problem.

The Contractor's Implied Warranties

Key Terms

Implied Warranty
guarantees that construction will be fit for its intended purpose.

By law, the contractor gives the property owner an implied warranty of fitness of purpose and an implied warranty of good workmanship. Those implied warranties mean the contractor is promising that the building will be built up to the standards of the trade and that the building will be fit for its intended purpose. But what if it won't be because of problems with the plans or specifications?

For example, suppose that Harry the homeowner hired Cal the carpenter to build his deck and, in the contract, required Cal to use Arnold the architect's plans. Suppose that Arnold's plans made the deck protrude into the rear lot setback.

What if the deck can't get a final occupancy permit after it's built, because it sticks out into the rear lot line setback? There have been cases where property owners have been required to tear off decks or other building additions because of setback violations.

What if the homeowner says to Cal, "I can't use that deck because I can't get an occupancy permit. That means it's not fit for its purpose, so I'm suing you for breach of warranty."

The Customer's Implied Warranty

When the property owner supplies architectural plans or detailed specifications, the law says that the owner is, whether he realizes it or not, giving the contractor an implied warranty that those plans will work for the job. It's possible that they won't, but if the contractor follows those plans, he will have the protection of the property owner's implied warranty of fitness of those plans. The property owner can't claim that the contractor has breached his warranty if the contractor was working from plans the property owner gave him.

So in theory, if Harry the homeowner winds up with a deck he can't use because of a design flaw in his architect's plans, Harry has to sue his architect, not his contractor.

But there are two situations where the customer's implied warranty may not protect the contractor. One is an error or oversight in the achitect's or owner's plans; the other is if there's a violation of ADA requirements.

The contractor's duty to warn — Even though the owner's plans and specifications come with the owner's implied warranty that those plans are fit for their purpose, the contractor still has a duty to warn the owner about errors that he or she actually sees — or should have seen.

If, in the example, Cal the carpenter realized, or should have realized, that the deck was probably going to be too close to the rear lot line setback, he has a responsibility to warn the property owner and the architect, if there is an architect involved, about this potential problem.

So, what do we mean by "should have realized?"

We mean that if a reasonable person in Cal's situation would have realized it, then Cal should have realized it. For example, suppose Cal had built other additions onto lots like Harry's. Based on that experience, it's reasonable to assume that Cal has heard of setbacks and knows what those local setbacks are. So Cal should have realized that deck looks like it's going to be a little close to the lot line. This is particularly true when there is no architect involved, just the homeowner, who has probably never even heard of a setback.

If Cal does warn the property owner, and/or the architect, and they chose not to believe him or to ignore the problem, he needs to protect himself by warning them in writing. Even better, he should try to get them to initial a copy of his warning letter that he can keep in his files. Now he has the best evidence possible that he did warn them.

The ADA laws may be a problem — In some circumstances, the property owner's implied warranty that the plans are fit for their purpose may not protect the contractor because of the provisions of the Americans With Disabilities Act or the Fair Housing Laws. Those laws give handicapped persons certain legal rights when the buildings are not constructed in a way that allows the access required by law. Based on the current language in those acts and the decisions in some lawsuits, it appears that handicapped persons can sue the property owner for damages. And they can also sue anybody who worked on those buildings, including the contractor — even though that contractor followed the architect's plan exactly after warning the property owner and the architect of the problem.

These cases put an extra burden on the contractor. I would suggest reviewing any plans for commercial establishments or multiple housing to make sure they comply with handicapped accessibility laws. If there's any question in your mind about compliance, consult with your attorney, who may be able to structure a bond, or some other legal device, that will create some additional protection for you.

The Payment Amount

The one clause in the contract that you can count on everybody reading carefully is the clause which says how much the job will cost. The property owner wants to know how much he has to pay and when he has to pay it. The contractor wants to know what he has to do to get paid.

But it can be tricky to figure out in advance exactly what a job will cost. Until you tear open that wall, you may not realize the foundation is full of carpenter ants. Until you start digging, you won't know that the largest fieldstone in North America is right where you have to dig out a basement.

A contractor who wants to protect himself from unforeseen or hidden conditions should put language in the contract that says something like this:

> Hidden conditions, which could not have been ascertained in advance, and which are not in keeping with what would have reasonably been expected, will be an additional charge to the extent that those hidden conditions cause extra expense.

This language is fair to both parties. It puts some burden on the contractor to do some educated guesswork about what he can expect to find when he tears open that wall, and, at the same time, it allows him to charge for those things that he simply couldn't have reasonably expected to find. It will take care, for example, of uncovering a thousand-year-old Indian burial mound.

But even with conditions that can be, and are, expected, there's no way to know exactly what most construction jobs will cost until that job is finished. That's why, over the years, a variety of formulas have been developed that try to reconcile the need of the property owner to know what the job will cost, with the need of the contractor to recover his costs plus his overhead and some profit.

Lump Sum Contracts

Some construction contracts are for a specific dollar amount. Cal the contractor says, "I'll fix your floor for $500." Harry the homeowner says, "Fine. Start tomorrow."

It sounds really simple and it is — from the customer's point of view. With a payment term like this, the customer knows exactly how much he's going to pay for the job. The problem is that the contractor doesn't know exactly how much money he'll make. His profit will depend on how complicated the job is and what hidden problems come up.

If the job matches the estimate and the stars are right, Cal can make the money he expected to make when he calculated the job's cost. But what if Cal finds a lot of moisture damage in the subfloor when he pulls up the old floor? Cal might not make anything on this job. He could even wind up losing money.

In fact, there are two ways Cal could lose money on this job. First, he could lose money because the materials and the other job costs (like labor) exceeded the amounts he had estimated when he bid the job. Second, this job may use time he could have used to make more money on another job.

Time and Materials Payment Clauses

In an effort to structure a payment that better reflects the contractor's actual costs, some contractors write time and materials clauses that say that the property owner will pay a flat hourly rate for labor, plus the cost of all materials.

The problem is that time and material contracts don't include money for overhead items like new tools, advertising, truck expenses, office expenses, or estimating costs. The contractor can try to fix that by calculating money for overhead into his hourly price. For example, the contractor could add $20 an hour for overhead costs onto his $40 an hour labor costs.

But there's a problem with that, too. What overhead costs run per hour depends on how many hours you actually work during a year. If you're busy and have a lot of working hours, your average per hour overhead cost is less. If you don't have many working hours, your average per hour overhead cost will be more. And you won't know how many working hours you actually had until the end of the year.

For example, if you have $100,000 annual overhead, and you expect to work 2,000 hours, then you could add $50 per hour to your hourly rate. But if you don't have a good year and only work 1,800 hours, $50 per hour won't recover all your overhead. On the other hand, if you're very busy and work a lot of overtime, you could make more money for your overhead than you actually spent — which isn't all bad.

Cost Plus Contracts

 Key Terms

The **plus** in Cost Plus may be a fixed amount or a percentage.

Here's how a number of popular pricing formulas recover overhead costs: They charge for the actual labor and material costs of the job. Then they add onto those charges either a fixed fee or a percentage of those charges to cover overhead and profit. There are a variety of formulas for this.

Cost Plus a Fixed Fee for Overhead and Profit

In these contracts, the contractor tries to estimate a lump sum — the fixed fee — that represents that job's share of overhead and profit.

The problem with a fixed fee for overhead and profit is the same as in a lump sum contract: The costs fluctuate based on how much or how little business you actually have over the entire year.

Cost Plus a Percentage for Overhead and Profit

Because overhead isn't fixed, and tends to fluctuate with the total number of jobs, some contractors simply use a percentage of their actual costs to recover their overhead, plus some money for profit.

Cost Plus a Percentage up to a Guaranteed Maximum Cost

Property owners like to know in advance what the job will cost them. Some contractors try to ease property owners' fears by writing a payment clause that asks for a percentage of the costs for overhead and profit, but only up to a maximum dollar amount.

The Payment Terms

How much the job will actually cost, and how those costs will be calculated, is only part of the payment equation. Since contractors are builders, not banks, they don't want to finance the job. But that's what they're doing

---

Can a Contractor Stop Work When Progress Payments Aren't Made?

In a word, yes. Contractors aren't required to work when they're not being paid. Lincoln did free the slaves, after all. If the property owner doesn't pay, the contractor can stop work and sue for breach of contract.

Of course, there are some variables here. If the property owner stopped making payments because the contractor wasn't performing properly, that's not a breach of contract by the owner. The owner can withhold payment for work that's defective or doesn't meet the contract specifications. However, if the defect is cured, the owner has to pay.

For example, suppose the property owner observed his roofing contractor installing the chimney flashing upside down, so the property owner refused to make his payment for the roof. Once the contractor goes back and corrects the flashing, the owner then has an obligation to pay for it. What the owner doesn't have an obligation to pay for is the time and materials it took the contractor to correct his own mistakes.

But if the property owner was wrong, and the flashing was correctly installed from the beginning, the property owner has breached the contract by withholding payment.

---

if they pay for materials and labor, and then wait to be reimbursed by the customer. Most construction contracts try to structure the money so that at least enough money comes in advance to pay for materials.

There can be a problem with local laws, though. Some states limit the amount of the down payment or money in advance that a contractor can collect. Those laws are designed to protect the consumer from contractors who accept money and then don't perform. You should check with your state Consumer Protection Office, or with the agency that licensed you, to find out what the rule is in your state.

Progress Payments

A progress payments clause in the contract is a way that you, as a contractor, can solve two problems: How to keep your material and labor costs from getting too far ahead of the money coming in, and how to keep that last payment down to a manageable amount.

Some contracts set up a straight payment schedule for their progress payments. For example, 20 percent of the contract price is payable in advance, and then 10 percent of the remaining balance is due every Monday.

Other contracts use a percentage of work completed to trigger each payment obligation. Still others use a milestone sort of trigger for payment obligations. Or the contract can use a combination of both. For example,

20 percent of the contract price is payable upon contract signing, $_____ is due when the foundation is poured, $____ is due when the framing is complete, and so forth.

My personal experience has been that straight payment amounts due at specific dates usually work best for the contractor, but customers (especially those who have been raised on a diet of crooked contractor horror stories) seem to prefer milestone type contracts.

Allowance Clauses

Key Terms

An **allowance** is a specific dollar range given to the customer by the contractor for the selection of items that a customer hasn't decided on at the time the contract is signed.

Some construction contracts allow the customer to make certain decisions after the building process has already begun. These decisions can impact the final price, so the contractor often sets a dollar range for choosing those items.

Let's suppose that Cal the contractor agreed to build a bathroom for Harry the homeowner for $9,000. But at the time of the contract signing, Harry still hadn't picked out a tub. Cal could write into the contract that Harry could select a tub without an additional contract cost, provided that the tub costs no more than $1,000. Or, Cal could write into the contract that the cost of the tub would be an additional material cost to the stated contract price.

Final Payments

The last payment is often critical in a construction contract, because it's the one the customers will withhold if they're not satisfied. When writing a contract, it's a good idea for the contractor to be very specific about exactly what triggers that last payment.

Substantial performance or *substantial completion* are the phrases that are usually used to describe what triggers the final payment. The word *substantial* is used because that's a way to deal with that handful of customers who will never consider a job completed, because they can always find a nail off-center.

It's always a good idea to define a phrase like *substantial completion* or *substantial performance* in the contract, more as a way of educating the customer than because it needs a legal definition. The courts already know what they mean, but some customers are afraid it means "not entirely finished." You can define it with language like this: Substantial completion means the work has been completed to the point the owner can occupy or utilize the work for its intended purpose.

Sometimes, the problem isn't with the property owner. Occasionally, a dispute crops up between the general contractor and a subcontractor when the final payment is being withheld to get leverage on other jobs.

Substantial Performance

Sometimes the contractor's performance is somewhat less than perfect, but it's still practically everything called for in the contract. In that situation, the contractor can use the doctrine of substantial performance as a defense if the property owner sues for breach of contract.

Also, if the property owner won't pay, the contractor can sue for payment, as long as the contractor has substantially performed his or her contract obligations. The property owner might have a counterclaim against the contractor for the decreased value of the product, but the property owner wouldn't be entitled to simply not pay.

For example, suppose the contractor failed to install the Andersen windows called for in the contract, but used other windows of a comparable quality. The property owner can't reject the work, refuse to pay the contractor, and hire someone else to do it over. (He could hire someone to do it over, but not using the money he owes the first contractor.)

If, however, those windows had been of a lesser quality, the property owner could deduct the decreased value from the contract payments. In other words, the property owner has to pay for the contractor's work, but, depending on the circumstances, the property owner may not have to pay the original contract price.

For example, Bigger Builders might say to Conroy's Concrete: "We don't like the quote you gave us for pouring the concrete on The Eastend Office Building. We're not going to pay you for the work you did on the Northside Strip Mall until we negotiate a quote from you for Eastend that we like better."

Is this legal? In a word, no. The courts don't support this, so the subcontractor can go to court to get paid for the Northside job. However, he could have avoided some of this grief, aggravation and expense by using the substantial completion or performance language. Then his lawyer doesn't have to spend a lot of time arguing about the perfection of the concrete — all he or she has to demonstrate is that the client can use it.

The subcontractor should also put a clause into the contract with the general contractor that says if the subcontractor has to take the general contractor to court, and if he wins, the general contractor has to pay both the judgment *and* the subcontractor's legal fees. Bringing to the attention of Bigger Builders that they'll have to pay *everybody's* legal bill will discourage this kind of blackmail. Even one side's legal bill may well exceed the amount being argued over. Two certainly will!

Retention Clauses

Some contracts allow the customer to withhold a percentage of the payment until the customer has completed an inspection — usually called a *punch list* — and the complaints that the customer identifies in that

Key Terms

A **punch list** is a list of items of work to be completed or corrected by the contractor. The list is prepared during an inspection by the owner or architect.

inspection have been dealt with to the customer's satisfaction. Sometimes during this process, you reach the point where you feel that the customer is being unreasonable and simply can't be pleased. If you get to that point, you can get out the contract and read the part about substantial completion to the customer.

Some contractors don't like to use punch lists. Why, they say, give the customer the opportunity to make trouble? Personally, I think that if the customer isn't satisfied, he or she will make trouble anyway. If you give them the opportunity for a formal inspection, you can deal with any complaint right then, and look like a hero. Also, if there's not a complaint about a particular item during that inspection, but one comes up later, it gives your lawyer a great argument. "This wasn't a problem for the customer at the time of final inspection," which suggests that it's a problem that either has been waived, or never existed.

Satisfaction Requirements

The contracts offered by some property owners and the AIA sample contract include phrases that say the work must be completed to the satisfaction of the owner (or the architect, or an engineer — or all of them) before the final payment is due. But what does "satisfaction" mean? Does it mean the owner is happy with the work? Does it mean that the work is completed according to the contract? *Exactly* according to the contract? Exactly according to whose ideas?

Most courts say *satisfaction* means what a reasonable person would consider satisfaction, but who wants to go to court to win this argument? You should insist that the contract define *satisfaction*. That can be done by inserting a sentence like this into the contract:

> Satisfaction means that the work meets the standards of the trade.

Or here's an alternative:

> Satisfaction means that the work can be used or occupied for its intended purpose.

This doesn't mean that you might not be forced into court, but if you are, at least when you're there, the other party has already agreed on the definition of *satisfaction*. That helps keep those legal bills from skyrocketing while the lawyers drone on and on about what the parties really meant by the word satisfaction in the contract.

Work Schedules

Many contracts set up a schedule for the completion of the work, and also state that change orders or contract modifications will extend that time. Contracts also usually provide that acts of God, fire, labor or supplier strikes and so forth, automatically act to extend the time for performance. However, even if the contract doesn't say that, case law in most states will allow a reasonable extension of time where it's impossible for the contractor to finish on time. However, that doesn't mean you won't have to pay a penalty for the delay.

Time Is of the Essence

Some contracts include clauses that state that *timely performance is the essence of the contract.* That phrase means that time is so important that the failure to complete the work by the stated date amounts to such a breach of contract by the contractor, it excuses the property owner from payment.

Fortunately for contractors, these clauses aren't enforced in most states unless time really *is* of the essence.

For example, suppose a contractor agreed to build a display stand at a local fair by August 15, the day before the fair opened. If the contractor doesn't complete the project on time, he might as well not bother doing the work. They don't need the display stand after the fair. So, in this example, time really is of the essence and the contractor will have substantially breached the contract by not performing in a timely way. Under these circumstances the party who contracted for the display stand ought not to have to pay, because the work, if completed after the due date, is worthless to him.

However, if the completion date is in the contract simply for the convenience of the property owner, but won't destroy the value of the work altogether, most states won't enforce such a harsh and essentially unfair outcome as excusing all payment for the contractor's work.

A better way of writing the contract (and one that the courts will usually enforce) is a properly-calculated liquidated damages clause.

Liquidated Damages for Contractor-Caused Delay

 **Key Terms**

Liquidated damages are a specific amount of money that the parties to a contract agree would be adequate compensation for problems that occur during construction.

This kind of clause imposes a fixed dollar amount that the contractor will be required to pay for each day of delay. The dollar amount can't be arbitrary or simply a penalty. Before agreeing to pay liquidated damages in the event of delay, you ought to give some thought to how tight your profit margin is, and just exactly how much in your control the target completion date really is. You're actually increasing your risk in this contract, and may want to negotiate a higher contract amount to reflect that increased risk.

Although the courts won't usually enforce a liquidated damages contract against a contractor if the property owner's actions actually caused the delay, you should still insert the phrase "contractor-caused delay" into the liquidated damages clause. That makes it clear that the only risk you're accepting is responsibility for delay that you caused.

Some states won't enforce liquidated damages clauses at all. They say that it's the job of the court to determine damages. The customer can still sue the contractor for the actual damages that the contractor's delay caused the customer.

When the Owner Causes the Delay

Many property owners like to put a clause into the contract that they won't be responsible if they cause a delay and that delay costs the contractor money. This is called a *No Damages for Delay* clause. Usually the courts won't enforce this kind of clause unless it was included because of the possibility of a particular type of delay, which both parties knew might occur when they were negotiating the contract.

For example, the property owner might not have his financing package completely in place. But if you have to hold yourself and your crews ready to start work, that will probably cost you money that you could, in most states, recover in a lawsuit against the property owner.

However, if both the contractor and the property owner realized this financing problem existed at the time of the contract negotiations, and the contractor still agreed to a No Damages for Delay clause, the contractor will simply have to eat that extra cost.

Change Orders

Blank Copy on CD-ROM

There's a blank copy of Figure 4-2 included on the disk in the back of the book.

It's not required by law in most states that change orders be in writing, but it makes everyone's life easier when they are. It certainly makes life easier for the contractor who has to deal with clients who don't remember requesting that change, or who didn't realize that the change would be so expensive. Figure 4-2 shows a simple Change Order form. A change order can be as simple or as complex as you want to make it. It's important that it include a description of the change, the date the change was requested, the cost (or savings) to make the change, and the signature of the owner or owner's representative and the signature of the contractor or contractor's representative.

And you can just imagine how much easier written change orders make life for the contractor's lawyer when that lawyer is in court. With written change orders to put into evidence, the lawyer wouldn't have to spend all that time (at $200 an hour — and trial lawyers cost more) sorting out who said what to whom.

Bigger Builders Inc.
22 Commerce Drive • Lansing, MI 55555
Phone (555)555-1234 • Phone (555)555-6789
Website: www.biggerbuildersinc.com

CONTRACT CHANGE ORDER

(This is a sample. A change order does not have to be in this form to be enforceable.)

Project: <u>Kitchen Remodel at 1227 Woodville, Lansing, MI</u> *(Put the name of the project and its address here.)*

To: <u>John D. Customer</u> *(Put the owner's name here.)*

Date: <u>August 21, 2000</u>

Contract change: <u>Delete formica brand countertop and self-rimming sink and replace with solid surface countertop of client's choice not to exceed $5000 and undermounted sink of client's choice not to exceed $1000.</u>

Material cost adjustments: <u>Subtract $3000 from material costs in the contract and add additional material costs as noted above.</u>

Contractor fee adjustments: <u>There will be additional labor costs for this contract change, not to exceed an extra $2000.</u>

Work schedule adjustments: <u>No schedule adjustment is necessary.</u>

This change order may increase the contract cost or may extend the contract schedule.

_____
(Contractor signs here)

_____
(Contractor address)

_____
(Property owner signs here)

_____
(Property owner address)

Figure 4-2 *Sample change order*

Waiving the Requirement for Written Change Orders

It's helpful when the contract has language in it that makes it clear to the property owner that only a certain person on the contractor's staff, or the contractor himself, has the authority to authorize change orders — and that all change orders must be in writing. But that language won't mean a thing if the actual practice is different. When the lead carpenter, for example, is allowed to regularly agree to change orders and to immediately implement those orders, that practice effectively waives the change order requirements in the contract.

Most construction contracts do include a provision that change orders must be in writing and signed by an authorized person to be enforceable. The problem is that too often, either the property owner or the contractor asks for, or allows, change orders without requiring specific written authorization. The courts usually hold that when that happens, the requirement that change orders be in writing is waived. The contractor can't object to a change order later on the grounds that it violates the contract, because he's already waived that term in the contract.

For example, suppose Bigger Builders agreed to a contract on a new home that said all change orders must be in writing. Then let's say that during the actual building, the homeowner and the site superintendent regularly made verbal decisions about small changes to the plans on the job site. By small, I mean the "Now that I see it, I realize that the kitchen counter is too short. Can you add on another 6 inches?" sort of changes.

Bigger Builders might be tempted to let this go on without an objection. "What's 6 inches of countertop? If I give a little now, he'll give a little later if I need it." But when the site superintendent and the homeowner verbally agree to add another bay to the garage and that another thousand dollars would be enough to cover it, Bigger can't later object. Bigger has already given up the protection it had in its contract against this kind of problem. Bigger has waived the contract requirement that change orders have to be in writing and approved by Mr. Bigger himself.

Indemnity Clauses

 Key Terms

Indemnification is the right to be reimbursed for losses caused by someone else's errors, omissions or negligent acts.

Some property owners, architects, and sometimes general contractors dealing with subcontractors, will demand an indemnification clause in their contract. You usually see indemnification clauses in contracts where the party who's asking for indemnification has significantly greater bargaining power than the other party.

The idea is that if, for example, the property owner is successfully sued for damages because of injuries that occurred on the job site, then the contractor has to reimburse the property owner for whatever the courts ordered the property owner to pay. So what's the problem with that? Why

---

Breach of Contract

When a person breaches a contract, that means they're failing to meet their obligations under the contract in a serious and substantial way. There are several things the other party can do, but the first thing they should do is consult with an attorney. That's because you could breach the contract yourself by taking action based on the belief that the other party has breached it, when they actually haven't.

Here's an example. Suppose that Harry the property owner has contracted with Bigger Builders for a small office building. Harry believes that Bigger Builders has breached the contract with him, and so he responds by withholding payment. If it turns out that Harry was wrong and that Bigger Builders didn't breach their contract with him, then Harry has breached his contractual obligation to pay them. In other words, if Harry doesn't have the breach-of-contract excuse for not paying, he'll be liable for contract damages. The reverse is also true.

If the contractor has actually breached the contract, the property owner can:

1. Allow the contractor to continue, but withhold from the progress payments an amount of money sufficient to compensate the property owner for the damage he suffered because of the contractor's failure to perform properly. But the property owner should always check with his attorney first.

2. Terminate the contractor and bring in someone else to do the work, then sue the contractor for the difference in cost.

3. Rescind the contract.

When the owner has actually breached the contract, the contractor can:

1. Stop work, but remain ready for a reasonable period of time to continue performance after the property owner has cured his or her breach. What this usually amounts to is that the property owner cures the breach by making payments that he has withheld.

2. Stop work and sue for the contract value of the work already completed.

3. Rescind the contract and sue for the reasonable value of the work already completed.

---

are so many contractors and subcontractors wary of indemnification clauses?

In some states, indemnification agreements are interpreted as meaning that if the property owner or architect is sued, the contractor has a duty to get into court and defend them. Even if the defense is successful, we're still talking big legal fees.

An even bigger problem with indemnification clauses is that sometimes they're an attempt to require the contractor (or whoever's doing the promising) to reimburse the property owner or architect for every claim — including those that occurred because of the property owner's or the architect's own negligence. Many courts say that's what the contractor agreed to do when he signed the contract with the indemnification clause in it.

But not everyone who agrees to an indemnification clause understands that's what the clause means. For example, suppose the clause reads, as it often does, that John the subcontractor agrees to indemnify Cal the contractor "for claims and damages rising out of the work performance for which the contractor may be liable." One of the things for which the contractor would be liable is the contractor's own negligence. But did John the subcontractor understand that when he signed the contract?

Some states won't enforce an indemnification clause that attempts to pass off the damages for one's own negligence onto someone else, but some states will. Some other states make a distinction between what they call "active" negligence and "passive" negligence. They'll stick the party agreeing to an indemnification clause with the damages only for "passive" negligence.

Suppose the indemnification clause is between the property owner and the contractor. Here's an example of passive negligence: Say the property owner shows up on the job site with a guest. Then the property owner takes a nail gun out of an unlocked — and obviously unsupervised tool crib — to demonstrate how neat nail guns are. Oops! The guest winds up with a nail through his foot. The guest sues the property owner and collects. The property owner then waves his indemnification clause at the contractor and says, "Sure, I shouldn't have taken the nail gun out, but you're the dummy who left the tool crib unlocked so you have to reimburse me for the money my guest collected from me." The property owner is saying his negligence isn't the same as the contractor's negligence, and therefore doesn't count.

I'd like to take a minute to point out that this is only one of the many reasons I recommend that visitors to the job site, including the property owner, *never* be allowed to wander about unsupervised. Write this into your contract:

> There will be no visits to the job site except in the company of the contractor or his designated employee.

If you're ever asked to sign an indemnification agreement and feel you have no choice, at least make sure that clause only requires you to pay for damages caused by your own negligence. Language like this would be okay:

> The contractor shall indemnify Harry Homeowner for claims, damages, or losses rising out of, or resulting from the performance of the work, but only to the extent caused by the negligent acts or omissions of the contractor.

Settling Disputes

Many contractors prefer to use a contract that requires dissatisfied customers to use arbitration or mediation if there's a dispute in an effort to reduce some of the time- and money-eating aspects of litigation. Going into court is such a time-consuming and expensive process that almost anything, including being burned at the stake, appears to be a better deal.

 Key Terms

Arbitration is a means of settling disputes without going into court.

It's true that in many circumstances, using arbitration to settle a problem does work better than going to court. The arbitrator is usually a person with some background or expertise in the construction area, and the process is quicker and less formal. It's possible to go to court to appeal an arbitrator's decision, but the courts almost never overturn an arbitrator's decision unless serious fraud can be proven.

Arbitration isn't the answer to every problem. Arbitration used to be a way to save money on legal expenses, but these days, almost every party in arbitration is represented by lawyers. If the problem is that the customer won't pay, the contractor might be better off going straight into court. Also, an arbitration award, unlike a judgment in a lawsuit, doesn't allow the winner to immediately move to attach or to garnish the property of the loser.

For a contractor, the best way to use arbitration is to put it into the contract, but make it optional at your choice. You can use language like this:

> Disputes may be resolved by arbitration, if the contractor demands arbitration, by giving written notice of intent to arbitrate to the property owner no less than 60 days after the dispute arises.

Remember that giving notice of intent to arbitrate does not mean you now *must* go ahead to arbitration. It just preserves the right to arbitrate if the dispute can't be settled between the parties themselves.

Warranty Clauses

There are both implied warranties and express warranties in construction. Contractors warrant their work as fit for its intended purpose and up to industry standards of good workmanship, whether they realize it or not. These are *implied* warranties. *Express warranties* are spoken or written. They add additional warranties on top of the implied warranties, or can define and limit all the contractor's warranty obligations whether those warranties are implied or express.

For more information about warranties, see Chapter 13.

Consumer Clauses

Both state and federal laws impose many special consumer protection requirements on contracts with homeowners. Those clauses can include:

▌ Restrictions on the amount of down payments

▌ Written explanations of the mechanic's lien laws for the consumer

▌ Options giving the consumer a certain number of days to cancel the contract

▌ Written warnings about arbitration clauses, explaining that the consumer may be giving up his right to go to court

▌ Notice that the contractor is required by law to be licensed

▌ Notices about certain protective state agencies

For more information about consumer protection laws, see Chapter 14.

Signing the Contract

Sometimes contractors aren't sure who should sign the contract, because there may be subcontractors and/or architects named in the contract as well as the property owners. Or it might be a rental situation where the tenant is having the work done.

The parties who should sign are the ones who are making the promises. You have to sign because you're promising to perform some construction work. The person who's promising to pay for the work should also sign.

If the person promising to pay is the property owner, and if that person is married, both husband and wife should sign the contract. Otherwise you or the subcontractors may have a problem enforcing construction lien rights. If only one spouse is the property owner, and the other spouse doesn't want to sign, consult with your attorney about local property laws relating to married persons. In some states, married persons have certain legal rights that can affect title to property even if they aren't named in the title.

If the person ordering the work is only a tenant, then it's a good idea to ask the landlord to acknowledge in some way — such as signing or initialing the contract — that the work is being done with his consent.

Sometimes contracts are signed in the presence of all of the parties who are bound to the contract, then each party simply takes a signed copy home with them. (If a husband and wife are involved, give *each one* of them a copy.)

If it's more convenient to leave the contract with the customer for them to look it over, it's okay if you simply sign all the copies and leave them with the customer. Ask the customer to sign and return one of the copies.

But, if you do leave a signed copy with a customer for them to sign and return, *put an expiration date on that contract.* You don't want to have this contract turn up six months down the road when you're busy with other contracts that were accepted in a timely fashion.

Part Three:
Legal Guidelines for
Running a Business

Chapter 5

What If You Hire Someone?

Chapter 6

What Do You Have to Do for the IRS?

Chapter 7

How Do You Collect What's Owed You?

5

What If You Hire Someone?

Hiring people is a big step for any small construction company. There's a lot more to think about than whether or not a potential worker has good construction skills. If you hire someone, you'll have several IRS reporting and withholding requirements imposed on you. Also, you'll have to deal with employee workers' compensation rights and unemployment rights. There are also antidiscrimination laws, immigration laws, and laws regarding hiring the disabled that may affect you as an employer.

Of course, you can sidestep these complications by deciding not to be an employer. Some construction companies never hire employees at all. Instead they work entirely with independent contractors. But sometimes the difference between an employee and an independent contractor is not very clear. You may think you're dealing with independent contractors, but in the eyes of the law, they may be employees. Believe me, it pays to be sure, because making a mistake in this area can be very expensive.

This mistake is most often made unintentionally. A small company needs help, but can't afford, or doesn't need, a permanent employee. So they get help for brief periods of time from an independent contractor who has the particular expertise that they need. Then, as the company grows, it needs this person more and more. At some point that person becomes so enmeshed with the company, that he or she has become an employee, and no longer an independent contractor.

Sometimes, calling a worker an independent contractor instead of an employee isn't a mistake so much as wishful thinking. The company *hopes* this person can be classified as an independent contractor, because using independent contractors takes less paperwork and is almost always less expensive than hiring employees. But just because someone is part-time, or supplies his own tools, or only works seasonally, doesn't necessarily mean that worker is legally an independent contractor rather than an employee. How do you tell the difference?

The "Safe Harbor"

Even if you have misclassified employees as independent contractors, there may be some relief available from the heavy penalties and back taxes you'd normally face.

The Classification Settlement Program sets up a "safe harbor" — a special provision of the law which offers some relief to taxpayers who incorrectly treated a worker as an independent contractor. There are three standards for relief:

1. You must have filed Form 1099 for the worker who you incorrectly identified as an independent contractor, whenever that worker earned more than $600 during the year. If these 1099s were filed, some relief is available, even if you don't meet the next two tests.

2. You were consistent in how you treated other workers like the independent contractor. In other words, if the independent contractor was a painter, every other job site painter in basically the same working conditions must also have been treated as an independent contractor.

3. You had some legitimate reason to believe that worker could be treated as an independent contractor. For example, if you had consulted with an accountant who advised you that you could consider that worker as an independent contractor, that probably would amount to a reasonable belief.

Remember that none of this relief is available if you didn't file Form 1099 for that worker (if the worker earned more than $600).

Is a Worker an Employee or an Independent Contractor?

In deciding if a worker is an employee or a subcontractor, there are two tests you have to consider. The first test is *control*. Who actually controls how the worker does the job? Who supplies the tools? Who sets the hours? Who decides when and how the work will be done? In other words, who has the most control over the worker: the worker himself, or the person he's doing the work for?

The second test is a little more subtle. Does this worker, who is supposed to be an independent businessperson, actually *act* like someone running their own business? Does this worker ever work for other contractors, submit bids for other jobs, use his own tools, keep records, bill by the job? Does he or she have a federal ID number, insurance and a business phone?

The IRS has a publication intended as a guideline for employers who need to decide if a particular worker is an employee or an independent contractor. It's IRS Publication 15-A, *Employer's Supplemental Tax Guide*.

You can, if you want to, ask the IRS to determine whether or not a particular person is an independent contractor or an employee by filling out and sending in IRS form SS-8.

For more in-depth information about the independent contractor vs. employee problem, see Chapter 11.

Employees' Taxes and Social Security Payments

If you've determined that your workers are employees, not independent contractors, you're required to withhold money from their wages for income taxes. You can be severely penalized for not doing it — and even more severely penalized if you withhold the money, but don't turn it into the IRS. Since these are common contractor "oversights," the IRS watches for this. If you don't take my advice on anything else, take my advice here: *Don't play loose and easy with federal withholding.*

In addition to withholding money for federal taxes, you must also withhold half of your employee's social security (FICA) and Medicare payments. Then you've got to contribute the other half of the money for employee's social security and Medicare payments. In other words, the employees pay half and you pay half. In some cases you've also got to pay unemployment taxes.

Find the amount of money to withhold by looking at the tables in *IRS Publication 15, Circular E, Employer's Tax Guide.* The IRS details the entire withholding and reporting process in Circular E. You can get this guide and other IRS forms free of charge by calling 1-800-829-3676, or you can download them over the Internet. Go to the IRS Web site at www.irs.gov and click on Forms & Pubs at the bottom of the page. You'll need Adobe Acrobat to print them. If you don't have it, you can download it free from the IRS Web site.

If you can understand the instructions for your personal taxes, you'll be able to understand these instructions and tables. Just hang in there!

To use the IRS tables, you need to know how many dependants each employee is declaring. Employees declare their dependants by filling out a Form W-4, *Employee's Withholding Allowance Certificate.* You don't have to file this form anywhere, unless the employee declares more than ten dependants or earns more than $200 a week and claims not to be subject to withholding. If the employee falls into one of those exceptions, then you must mail their W-4 to the IRS. Otherwise, you just keep the W-4s as part of the employee's personnel file.

Some people actually *aren't* subject to withholding. They may have another job where sufficient withholding is being deducted, or for some reason they may be filing their own withholding. Of course, the Internal Revenue Service wants to check on that.

The money that is withheld from employees is considered a trust fund. Although it may still be in your hands, it no longer belongs to you. You're just holding it on behalf of the employee. The IRS requires you to deposit the withheld money into an approved account every quarter.

The IRS doesn't fool around with problems concerning employee withholding. They take it very seriously if they feel that money isn't being handled properly, and they'll impose some very nasty penalties on you. In fact, they'll show up and shut your business down in no time at all.

Reporting Requirements

The IRS requires you to report on Form 941 exactly how much money has been withheld at the end of every quarter during the year. Then, during January of the following year, you have to fill out W-2 forms for each employee showing that employee's total wages and the amount of money withheld from those wages. One copy of the form goes to the employee, one copy to the IRS, and a copy to each of the local taxing authorities (states or cities that also have an income tax). Also, see Chapter 6 for more information about the IRS.

FUTA Payments for Employees

Federal unemployment taxes (FUTA) aren't withheld from the employee's wages. The employer pays it all, and must report it on Form 940, *Employer's Annual Federal Unemployment Tax Return.* Employers have to pay a percentage of the employee's salary for every employee who earns more than $7,000 a year. (That's the current requirement; this wage base may change.)

Most employers have to pay both state and federal unemployment taxes. For state tax rates, check with the unemployment office for the base wage and the payment percentage in your state.

Employers Can't Unlawfully Discriminate in Hiring

There are several federal antidiscrimination statutes that protect people with certain problems or ethnic, religious or racial backgrounds from job discrimination. Many states also have state hiring laws that protect people from unlawful discrimination. These laws don't require an employer

Avoid the Appearance of Illegal Discrimination

It's quite possible for people who have no intention of discriminating to do or say things that make it appear they *do* intend to discriminate in their hiring activities. Since it's impossible for employers to lift off the top of their heads and show their good intentions to people, it's worth the effort to avoid the appearance of discrimination.

There are some specific steps you can take to avoid these kinds of problems when you hire. These steps require concentrating on what you want the applicant to *do*, not what you might want the applicant to *be*.

Be careful how you word your job advertisements. When you're describing the job, use language that describes the job, not the age or sex of the applicant you might hire. If the position is answering the phone, filing and typing, say something like Administrative Aide or Office Worker. If the position is for a handyman, say something about General Construction or Construction Repair, or General Repair. If the position is in sales, say Sales or Salesperson, not sales*man*.

When you're interviewing a job applicant, you can ask questions about the applicant's education, work experience, when the applicant can start work, if the applicant can work overtime, or if the applicant has special training. If the job involves driving, you can require the applicant to provide proof of a good driving record. If the position involves going into people's homes, you can even ask the applicant about a criminal record.

But you can't ask applicants about their religion, ethnic background, birthplace, or what languages they speak unless speaking a certain language is necessary in the position. You can't ask for the applicant's photograph before you hire that person.

You can't ask applicants if they're citizens, but you can ask if the applicant is legally entitled to work in the United States. Do not request evidence of legal residency, such as green cards or birth certificates, until after you have announced your intention to hire them if they're legally entitled to work in the United States.

to *hire* a person who falls into a protected group. What the laws say is that an employer can't *refuse to hire* someone just because that person falls into a protected group.

"Unlawfully" discriminate simply means that you can't refuse to hire someone for the wrong reasons. Regardless of what you may have heard on the radio, the antidiscrimination laws don't require an employer to hire people who can't do the job. Those laws do, however, prohibit employers from making the decision to hire or not hire on the basis of such factors as age, gender, race, ethnic origin, or the presence of a handicap.

An employer who makes his or her hiring decisions based on whether the job applicant can do the job is *not* violating the discrimination laws. If the applicant falls into a class of people protected from unlawful discrimination, but that applicant actually can't do the job, the employer can defend the decision not to hire. The employer defends the hiring decision by demonstrating that the applicant did not have the necessary "bona fide occupational qualifications."

For example, if you're hiring foundation people, you might assume that someone more than 40 years old probably wouldn't be able to handle those bags of cement. Handling bags of cement in foundation work is a bona fide occupational qualification — it's something you have to be able to do to accomplish the work. So if someone can't do that, you don't have to hire him. But, if he's over 40, you'd better be sure he can't do it. Ask him to demonstrate. Otherwise, how will you know?

What Is a Bona Fide Occupational Qualification?

Bona fide occupational qualification is the term that means a real requirement of the job position. For example, you could refuse to hire a person as a brick mason because that person couldn't lift 50 pounds. Lifting heavy weights is a part of the job. But you couldn't legitimately refuse to hire an electrician because he or she couldn't lift 50 pounds, because what does lifting 50 pounds have to do with the job?

To meet the test of whether or not that lifting requirement (or any other requirement) is a bona fide occupational qualification, you have to be sure of three things:

  ▌ First, that the job actually requires the employee to lift 50 pounds.

  ▌ Second, that the applicant can't lift 50 pounds. Don't assume that because the applicant is a woman, or of a certain age, that the applicant can't lift that weight. My husband, for example, who is more than 65 years old, can lift significantly more than 50 pounds. He lifts me, and I fit into that "significantly more" category. Offer the applicant the opportunity to try.

  ▌ Third, the person who actually *did* get hired can lift 50 pounds — and you know that for a fact because you asked him or her to show you that they could.

Remember that not every skill is a bona fide qualification for every position. For example, the ability to speak good English could be a "bona fide occupational qualification" in some positions, but not in others. If you refuse to hire someone because they don't speak good English, the ability to speak good English must be a necessary part of that job.

If you were hiring a sales person, certainly that person would need to speak, read and write understandable English. Having an accent would not be enough to disqualify him or her from that position. However, if you were hiring a brick mason, good English isn't likely to have anything to do with the job position as long as the person can understand the requirements of the job.

Skill tests, written tests, and educational background requirements should relate to the job position. Casual labor doesn't need to have the same reading skills that someone who would be working with power tools might need. For example, Joe, who is hired for casual labor, has enough literacy for the job if he can understand the safety posters OSHA puts out — and they're mostly pictures. But if Joe's an electrician who would be working with live wires, his ability to understand and read instructions and safety guides is much more important. However, if the issue isn't reading itself, but the ability to read *English*, remember that most of those manuals are printed in more than one language. Consider that before you refuse to hire Joe, who can read another language, but not English.

The Age Discrimination Employment Act

The Federal Age Discrimination Employment Act protects people who are 40 years and older. It only applies to companies with more than 20 employees. This doesn't mean you can never refuse to hire someone who's more than 40 years old, but it does mean that if you refuse to hire a person over 40, you should be certain you can demonstrate a bona fide occupational qualification that this person doesn't meet.

That may sound like a contradiction to you, but it's not. Antidiscrimination laws are not intended to force you to hire unqualified people. They're intended to give people of other ages, race, gender or religions as much chance at employment with you as a person who isn't from a protected group.

The Civil Rights Act

The federal Civil Rights Act of 1991 bars making hiring decisions on the basis of race, ancestry, ethnicity or gender. You can't reject an otherwise-qualified individual: "I'm not hiring you because you're a woman." Or "because you're Hispanic, or a Muslim."

The Americans With Disabilities Act

The federal American With Disabilities Act applies to employers with 15 or more employees. It prohibits refusing to hire someone because that person is handicapped, if there's some reasonable means by which that person could do the job.

For example, a person in a wheelchair couldn't work as a roofer; there's simply no reasonable way to accommodate a wheelchair for roof work. However that person could keep inventory in the warehouse if the area were arranged so he could move his wheelchair around in it. Arranging the area so the wheelchair can move around in it wouldn't be a big problem in most warehouse settings, so doing it would be a reasonable accommodation.

Mandatory Workplace Posters

Some federal laws require employers who are subject to those laws to put up posters that explain the impact of those laws on their employees. Those posters must to be in a place where their employees can see and read them.

An Occupational Safety and Health Act poster explaining the employee rights under federal safety laws must be posted. These posters are available from OSHA. Failure to post them may subject the employer to a fine of up to $7,000 for each violation, along with possible criminal penalties.

Every employer subject to the Fair Labor Standards Act must put up a federal minimum wage notice. Failure to post it is a federal crime. You can get these posters from the Department of Labor.

A notice that employee polygraph tests are illegal must be posted. Any employer who violates the Polygraph Protection Act may be assessed a penalty of up to $10,000. These posters are available from the Department of Labor.

Employers must also display a poster describing the equal opportunity laws and the ADA laws that affect employment. These posters are available from the Equal Employment Opportunity Commission.

The Family Leave Act applies to employers having 50 or more employees who reside within 75 miles of their place of employment. An employer subject to this law can get the required poster from the U.S. Department of Labor, Employment Standards Division.

Employers Must Conform to the Immigration Laws

As if there wasn't already enough in place to make hiring people difficult, Congress has passed the Immigration Reform and Control Act, which affects every employer regardless of how many or how few employees that employer has.

Anyone who "knowingly" hires an illegal alien can be fined up to $20,000 per hire. What, you ask suspiciously, does "knowingly" mean, especially considering that it's illegal to discriminate on the basis of national origin, and that asking questions about somebody's nationality could be used as evidence of discrimination?

This is a big problem, because the act says that "knowingly" doesn't have to mean that you actually *knew* your employee was an illegal alien. What it means is that the circumstances were such that you *should* have known, or that you *could* have known if you had checked that person's documents, such as driver's license, birth certificate, social security card, or the so-called green card.

Can an employer avoid this problem by simply not hiring anybody who looks like they might be an illegal alien? No. That's not a solution. This act, like the civil rights statutes, prohibits discriminating against possible employees because of their national origin.

The solution is to make your hiring decision first, and then demand that people show you their documents. Waiting to ask for evidence of legal residency, such as green cards or birth certificates, until after you've announced your intention to hire that person is probably the best way — maybe even the only way — to stay out of trouble with this law.

The Forms You Need for This Law

When you hire someone who's a legal alien, you must fill out and keep a form that's available from the Immigration and Naturalization Service, the *Attestation Form I-9*.

In Form I-9 you swear that you know your employee is a legal alien instead of an illegal alien because you took reasonable steps to confirm that. The reasonable steps the act expects you to take include checking immigration papers or birth certificates. You are also supposed to take reasonable steps to determine if those papers are authentic.

"Reasonable steps" would include things like asking the applicant why his name on his driver's license is Joe, while his name on his INS card is Larry. But be sure you're right if you do refuse to hire someone because you believe their documents are invalid. In fact, I'd suggest that if you suspect you're looking at false documents, you seek professional advice or contact the INS for further guidance.

You should make copies of all of the papers you examined and keep them with the Form I-9 in that person's personnel file. You don't have to file these forms anyplace, but you do need to keep them in your office files for at least three years after hiring that person or for one year after terminating that person, whichever comes first.

Your Duty to Protect Others from the Negligence of Your Employees

As an employer, you could be held responsible if one of your employees is negligent in the course of their duties and someone is injured. That injured person could sue you.

For example, suppose you hired someone with a history of drunk driving convictions. Then you gave them a company truck and sent them off to the lumberyard to pick up materials. While they're on the way over to the lumberyard, they stop for a few beers, then run a red light and kill somebody. You're looking at big liability, because you recklessly put that person into a position where they could injure someone. You should have known better.

This is the kind of situation in which that liability insurance policy proves so important. But even with a liability policy, you want to avoid those situations. Insurance policies usually have dollar limits. If you have a $2 million policy and the judgement is for $3 million, guess who gets to pay that million-dollar deficiency. So what can you do to prove you weren't negligent if you're ever sued for it? You can (and should) take these steps:

- If any employee or subcontractor will be driving for you, or driving vehicles that you own, you should check their driving histories. There have been a few problems under the ADA laws with refusing to hire someone because of a drinking problem in the past, but there's no rule or case law that requires you to put that person into a vehicle's driver's seat.

- If the employee will be unsupervised while he or she is in people's homes, you should check for criminal records. If you send a convicted thief to retile someone's bathroom, and some jewelry turns up missing, that's a problem.

- If your employee will fill a position that requires some kind of licensing, for example, an electrician's position, you should check to see if that person actually has a valid license.

What you *can't* do is ask the applicant to take a lie detector test. For practical purposes, the Federal Employee Polygraph Protection Act has outlawed the use of polygraph tests for most industries.

Drug Tests

Many companies are instituting mandatory drug tests for new hires, because so many construction positions involve driving heavy equipment, or running power tools, or working with live electricity. In those situations, drug tests could save everyone a lot of grief.

Basically there are three different kinds of drug laws:

- First, there are laws about new hires and drugs.

- Second, there are laws about random drug tests.

- Third, there are laws about mandatory employee drug tests.

Which drug laws, or combination of drug laws, you're working under depends on what state you're in.

State drug testing laws run the gamut. For example, Michigan, at this time, has no statute at all. In California, the law states that employers can't discriminate against substance abusers provided they have entered or completed a substance abuse program and are not currently using drugs.

In Hawaii, employers can test for substance abuse provided the employer pays for the test and follows certain procedural safeguards. Vermont requires probable cause to test for drugs.

The message here is that if you're considering drug testing, you should first consult with a labor law attorney in your state.

Employee Handbooks

An employee handbook can avoid confusion and labor problems, and also save an employer enormous legal and personnel headaches. In fact, any company that takes on employees ought to have one.

At a minimum, the handbook should include each job description, a clear explanation of the grounds for termination, and the termination procedure. There should be a thorough description of company benefits, such as vacation plans, insurance and retirement plans, and when pay increases may be expected, along with a specific statement reserving the right to change benefit policies.

The handbook should state, clearly and concisely, the company policies on change orders, vehicle use, material pick-ups, safety polices, job site cleanup, and OSHA compliance. There should also be an explanation of what each employee should do if injured.

The handbook is also the place for company conduct rules such as courtesy to the customer, and the use of radios and other entertainment equipment on the job site. If the company has a drug testing policy, a statement about that policy should be included in the handbook.

Every employee should be given his or her own copy of the handbook, and should also be required to sign a statement that they have read and understood that handbook. Don't ask the employees to sign as you hand them the book. Make sure they actually *do* read it.

An Employee Handbook Is Like an Employment Contract

While an employee handbook isn't technically a contract, courts do tend to enforce them in a fashion very much like contracts. This means that when the employer writes the handbook, that handbook should make it clear when and under what circumstances people may be discharged. Certainly a warning system and a system for recording warnings should be in place.

The handbook also needs language that makes it clear that under some circumstances, such as when the employee creates a clear danger to himself or others, that employee could be discharged immediately.

Remember the example where the company driver took a company truck and stopped for a few beers on his way to the lumberyard? That's potential liability no employer can afford to keep on the payroll.

Avoid Language That Guarantees a Job

It's dangerous for an employer to write a handbook that promises employees a job for as long as they perform well or meet the handbook performance standards. The company may have to downsize at some point, or the company may change directions.

For example, suppose a small builder had been doing all sorts of residential remodeling, but then decided not to do roofs anymore. So they tell Ralph the roofer they're going to have to let him go. If Ralph gets a lawyer and sues for wrongful discharge, Small Builders doesn't want the issue to be whether or not Ralph has been doing a good job. Small Builders wants the issue to be whether or not the company needs Ralph.

Discharging Employees

Employees who don't have an employment contract are called "at will" employees. At will means that the employee can be discharged whenever the employer wants to discharge them - in other words, "at will." For protection from possible Wrongful Discharge lawsuits, an employer should explain in the employees' handbook that in his company people are hired "at will." The employees' handbook should also explain what "at will" means.

However, the phrase "at will" sounds like the employer has a lot more power than he really has. For practical purposes, when an employer fires

If You Fire Someone for Cause

Your hiring policy, as stated in your employee handbook, should include a catchall phrase such as this: In the event the action of the employee recklessly places the employee or another person in immediate danger, that employee may be terminated without further notice.

But most firing situations aren't a matter of life and death. In most situations, the employer should use a termination procedure that begins with a written warning system. This is used for two reasons. First, it can have the effect of improving behavior. Even if it doesn't, it does establish grounds for termination so you have a defense to a wrongful discharge lawsuit. Copies of all warnings should be kept in the employee's personnel file. It's very important that your warning and your termination procedure be enforced the same way against every employee. If there's some reason for not doing that, your reasons must be carefully documented.

someone for cause, the employer needs to be in a position to prove that it wasn't done illegally. That's why a well-thought-out termination procedure should be in the company handbook before there's actually a problem with an employee. That termination procedure should include keeping records of every problem with an employee, every warning that has been given to that employee, and every effort to train the employee to do better. It should all be carefully documented and saved for at least three years after the employee is gone.

Restrictions on Outside Employment or Employment with Competitors

If there are company restrictions on moonlighting or outside employment, those restrictions should be stated in the handbook. But be aware that some of those restrictions may not be enforceable.

Construction companies have a chronic problem. It goes like this: Better Builders is adding on a family room for Harry the homeowner. Harry asks Cal the carpenter, who works for Better Builders, if he'd come back later and build some shelves while he's "off the company books." Harry knows that Cal can build those shelves for less than what Better Builders would charge. Better Builders doesn't think this is fair and wants to keep it from happening, but it's very difficult — close to impossible — for a private company to control what employees do on their own time. If Cal is determined to build those shelves, the company can't stop him. What the company can do is make it grounds for termination, especially if that's clearly stated in the company handbook.

Another problem that some construction companies have is when their best workers leave to start their own company, or go to work for the opposition. It's difficult to prevent this, because trying to stop it is, among other things, clearly a restraint of trade. Most states will uphold covenants not to compete, but only within very narrow guidelines. To have any hope of enforcing a policy that their employees can't compete with them, the construction company will need a written contract with each employee they hope to restrain. That contract should be limited to a certain area, such as the county in which the employer is located, and should also be limited in time, such as for one year after employment termination.

If you, as an employer, want to restrict what work your employees can do on their own time, and where they can work after leaving your employment, it would be a good idea first to talk to an attorney who does labor law work in your state.

Affirmative Action Programs

Affirmative action hiring plans and requirements are so often in the headlines that people tend to forget those programs don't impact private construction *unless* those private construction companies are bidding on public works. Any contractor who puts in a bid on a public project should inquire before putting the bid together about any possible requirement of minority ownership or employees.

6

What Do You Have to Do for the IRS?

I wrote this chapter to let you know what the IRS, your favorite business partner, requires from you. I'll warn you about what you might have trouble with, and what you can do if you do have trouble. Contractors seem particularly prone to IRS scrutiny — mostly because so many have the opportunity to deal in cash, in payments from customers and in payments to workers. Some construction companies have even folded because of IRS difficulties. I've seen people so intimidated by the forms and requirements that they simply didn't follow through with them — and that's a straight shoot into trouble.

However, if you can do your own long Form 1040 on April 15th, you can cope with these other forms, too. It may take you a while to figure them out, but you can do it. If you can't, get somebody else to do it. Find a company that specializes in handling taxes for small businesses.

When you're thinking about what the IRS wants from you, remember there are two different things they require. First, of course, they want you to send in the money you're supposed to. Second, that means you have to file the papers that you're supposed to. Pay and/or file. Sometimes one or the other, sometimes both. If you can't do it yourself, hire somebody.

Here's the best advice that I, as a construction attorney, can offer you: Don't mess with the IRS! Follow their rules and pay what they say you should. It just isn't a battle you can win.

The Self-Employed and the IRS

When you're self-employed, you have to do everything for the IRS that an employed person does, and more besides. As a self-employed person, you'll have to file your annual 1040 tax return just like you did when you were an employee — with some extras added in. First, you'll have to file more forms than you did before. Second, and even more painful, you'll now have to pay *all* of your own social security. When you were working for someone else, they had to pay half of it. Third, you have to send in your own withholding.

When you're self-employed, you're supposed to keep good business records of your income and your expenditures. If you don't, and you're audited, the IRS will probably rewrite your tax bill because you can't properly document your deductions. It doesn't mean the IRS will throw them all out, but they *will* probably cut back on your estimates of your deductions. After all, if you don't have the records, all you've got are estimates. And they might have their own estimates that they prefer over yours!

Estimated Quarterly Payments

When you worked for someone else, they withheld your taxes and sent them in for you. Now you get to do that for yourself. That withholding is called your *quarterly estimated tax payments.* The current IRS rule is that if you had to pay more than $1000 in taxes when you did your last tax return, you'll have to pay in quarterly tax payments during the following year. The idea is that the taxpayer is more likely to be able to pay his or her taxes if they send the money in installments during the year than if they wait until there's one backbreaking tax bill at the end of the year.

How do you make estimated payments? You send in your quarterly payment to the IRS along with a payment voucher called a Form 1040-ES. An estimated tax worksheet is included with the instructions that come with the 1040-ES. Call the IRS at 1-800-829-3676 and they'll mail you payment vouchers and instructions, or dial 703-487-4160 to have them faxed to you. Or you can download those or any other IRS forms from the Internet at www.irs.gov.

If you have trouble with the worksheet, or just don't want to do it, you could take your total taxes from last year, divide by four and send in that amount. If you send in 100 percent of that amount and it turns out not to have been enough, there won't be a penalty. But remember that 100 percent includes *all the taxes owed in the previous year including self-employment taxes.* If you made more than $150,000 in adjusted gross income last year, the rules will be different. But, of course, if you made that much, you'll have a tax accountant on board. (If you don't, you should.)

Underpayments

If you don't fit into an exception discussed in the previous paragraph, there will be a penalty for not sending in enough money. If you did underpay, you ought to send in extra money as soon as possible to stop that meter running. You can send in more money using IRS Form 2210, *Underpayment of Estimated Tax by Individuals, Estates, and Trusts.* Or you can wait until the end of the year and send in a check for the rest of money you owe with your income tax return. If you do owe a penalty, you don't have to figure out the amount — which is lucky because it's very hard to figure since it's tied to the current yield in U.S. short-term bonds. Just don't fill in line 65 on your 1040, or line 33 on the Form 2210, and the IRS will figure out your penalty and send you a bill.

Self-Employment Taxes

If you earned more than $400 in the taxable year, you'll need to report your self-employment taxes (I snicker every time I see this term) on your Form 1040, Schedule SE, *Self-Employment Tax.* Self-employment taxes are not income taxes. They're the same as the FICA withholding that you saw on your pay stub when you were an employee. It's the money for your social security. However, when you were an employee, half of your social security payment was withheld from your pay, and your employer paid the other half. When you work for yourself, you pay it all.

If you're an independent contractor, like a subcontractor on a construction site, the people who contract with you are supposed to file a Form 1099 whenever they pay you more than $600 in a calendar year. If the 1099s they file don't match your earnings report, you should expect an audit. The IRS believes that people in your position have the most opportunity to under-report income, and they're ever on the alert for evidence of that.

Other Forms You Have to File If You're Self-Employed

Which forms you need to file and what kind of payments you have to make on behalf of your business depend on your business structure. Are you a corporation, a sole proprietor, or a partnership? If you're a corporation, what kind of corporation are you?

The IRS has some surprisingly readable — and free — publications to help you. You can pick up the IRS Publication 334, *Tax Guide for Small Business*, at your local IRS office, or you can call them and have them send it to you.

If You're a Sole Proprietor

If you're a sole proprietor, you are self-employed. As a self-employed person, you have to file your annual 1040 tax return, along with a 1040 Schedule C, *Profit or Loss From Business,* showing how much money you made — or lost — from your self-employment. And don't forget those quarterly payments with your 1040-ES payment vouchers. You'll probably have to file a Schedule SE, *Self-Employment Tax* for your social security payments if you made more than $400 in the taxable year. There are also other forms you may need to file if you claim certain deductions, such as business depreciation.

If You're a Partner

If you're a partner in a business, the partnership will report its profits and losses to the IRS on a Form 1065, *Partnership Return of Income,* and will also attach a Form 1065 Schedule K-1, *Partner's Share of Income, Credits, Deductions,* for each partner to that 1065 form. Then the partnership gives you a copy of the Schedule K-1. Think of your K-1 as about the same thing as the W-2 you used to get when you were an employee. All of these forms, including the Schedule K-1, come in the partnership package that the company gets from the IRS along with its Taxpayer Identification Number.

It's important to remember that a partner is *not* an employee of the partnership. A partner is a self-employed person who must meet the rules for self-employed people. However, a partner doesn't file a Schedule C. Instead, each partner gets from the partnership a copy of a Schedule K-1 (think of it as a partner's W-2). Then the partners report their partnership income on the back of Schedule E, *Supplemental Income and Losses.* Then each partner takes the total from that form and enters it on line 17, Form 1040.

Partnership earnings, losses, credits, and deductions are taxed during the year they are earned, unless there's a specific provision in the tax code that states otherwise. Unlike a sole proprietorship, it's possible for a partnership to have a fiscal year that's somewhat different from the calendar year. If, for some reason, you wish to do this — for example, the calendar year might not be consistent with when the business started — you should first consult with a tax accountant, because the procedure for declaring a tax year that's different from the calendar year is difficult.

If Your Company Is Incorporated

If your business is a corporation, then you *aren't* self-employed. You're employed by your corporation. If your company is a corporation and you do work for it, you are its employee. Even if you're the only shareholder, the only worker, the only manager and the company president, too, for tax purposes you're the corporation's employee and must be treated like an employee when it comes time to report to the IRS and to pay taxes.

In other words, the corporation withholds income taxes for you, contributes one-half to your social security and Medicare, and gives you a W-2. Of course, there's a big exception to this. (Isn't there always? That's what keeps us lawyers in business.) Corporations that qualify as Subchapter S corporations have different tax rules. There's more information about that in following sections.

If you're incorporated, you may have two different kinds of income from your company. You could receive dividends from that corporation and/or wages from the corporation. How your dividend earnings as a shareholder are taxed depends on what kind of corporation it is, and what you do for that corporation.

A Standard C Corporation

A straight corporation, sometimes called a C corporation, pays corporate taxes on its income, but the company's shareholders only owe taxes on that income when and if the corporation distributes some of that money to its shareholders as dividends.

If the corporation decides to distribute profits to you as a shareholder, that's dividend income. If it exceeds $400, you need to report it by filling out Part II of Schedule B, *Interest and Dividend Income.* That's on the back of Schedule A — *Itemized Deductions.* Then enter that final figure from line 10 onto line 9 of Form 1040.

If you work for a corporation, you are its employee. You may be the only employee that corporation has; you may also be its only shareholder. That's okay, you're still its employee. The money that your corporation pays you for your labor is your salary, and it's treated like any other salary. You get a W-2 from the corporation and you attach it to your 1040 tax return.

There are a number of benefits that are available to corporate owner/employees such as health or life insurance plans that aren't available to sole proprietors or partnerships. A corporate owner who wants to put together a corporate benefit package should consult with an accountant and/or attorney. We'll discuss retirement plans in Chapter 17.

A Subchapter S Corporation

S and C, when talking about corporations, actually refer to parts of the tax code, not a particular kind of corporation. They're simply different ways of taxing corporations. But not every corporation can be taxed as an S corporation. Also, not every corporation that could be taxed as an S corporation chooses to be. It's optional with the corporation itself.

Earnings from a Subchapter S corporation are taxed differently than earnings from a C corporation. If your corporation qualifies as a Subchapter S corporation in the tax code, *and* you've filed a timely Form 2553 asking to be treated as an S corporation, your corporation's income will be taxed like a partnership's income. That means the corporation doesn't have to pay corporate taxes on its earnings.

That money is just passed right through the company straight into the shareholder's tax return as earned income. You don't have to worry about the difference between dividends and wages because in a Subchapter S corporation, there is no difference.

Like a partnership, an S corporation doesn't pay taxes on profits or take deductions for losses. These things are "passed through" straight to the shareholders.

Qualifying As a Subchapter S Corporation

Subchapter S is a section of the tax code which allows a company to keep one of the major benefits of being a corporation: the shareholders don't have to pay corporate debts out of their own money. At the same time, it allows the corporation to treat its earning and losses the way a partnership does.

To qualify for subchapter S treatment by the IRS, the corporation must have no more than 75 stockholders, be a U.S. corporation, and must only have stockholders who are citizens or which are estates or certain kinds of trusts of the U.S. The corporation must also have only one class of stock.

If the corporation does qualify, it must then ask to be treated as a subchapter S corporation by the IRS by filing a Form 2553. The Form 2553 must be filed on or before the fifteenth day of the third month from the beginning of the corporation's taxable year. In other words, if the corporation's fiscal year is the same as its calendar year, the form should be filed by March 15th.

The Subchapter S corporation reports the business's income, losses, deductions and credits to the IRS on Form 1120S. The corporation attaches an 1120S Schedule K-1, *Shareholder's Share of Income, Credits, Deductions,* for each shareholder to the Form 1120S that the corporation files. (All these forms come in the package with the Taxpayer Identification Number — the TIN — from the IRS.) Then the S corporation gives each shareholder a copy of the 1120S Schedule K-1.

The shareholder in a Subchapter S corporation reports his share of the company's earnings on the shareholder's own Form 1040 Schedule E, *Supplemental Income and Loss,* Part II in the year the income (or loss) is earned.

Remember though, that not all states recognize the Subchapter S status for state corporate tax purposes. A corporation that does not have to pay federal corporate taxes because it's an S corporation may still have to pay state corporate taxes. If you're in one of these states, the state will let you know.

Deductions Available to the Self-Employed

There are many deductions available to the self-employed which aren't available to others.

Vehicle Deductions

Vehicles used for business are deductible. Running them, licensing them, insuring them and maintaining them are all business expenses. There are two ways to deduct vehicle costs. You can deduct every single dime on Form 4562, or you could use the standard mileage deduction.

Actual vehicle costs — If you report your vehicle expenses on Form 4562, you must report exact records of mileage, depreciation, repair and everything else that goes on with the vehicle.

The standard mileage deduction

Working out the actual expenses is complicated and time consuming, so unless you enjoy that sort of thing, you might want to use the standard mileage deduction that's reported on the 1040 schedule C. The standard mileage deduction only requires that you keep a record of your mileage. The standard deduction is usually enough to reflect a true vehicle cost and is so much easier to use. In fact, if the price of gas goes down, you might make money using the standard mileage deduction.

When you use the same vehicle for both business and personal use — Many small business persons use the same vehicle for business and for personal use. Not to worry, the IRS has a solution. They want you to keep a record of your mileage on a trip sheet, and then figure out how much of that mileage was for business and how much was for personal use.

Just in case you're audited on this, you should save all your mileage logs, trip sheets, repair receipts, credit card receipts, gas, parking and toll receipts, and any other piece of paper that comes into your hand. It's okay if you just throw these receipts into shoe boxes and write the year across the top of the box — but *keep them*! The IRS won't necessarily accept a canceled check to an oil company as sufficient evidence of business purposes, not when there's overlap between family and business use. There may even be some people who overestimate the proportion of business use, so the IRS can get a little touchy about this.

Tools and Equipment

Items that have a life longer than a year are capital expenditures, not expenses. Expenses are costs that recur every year, and are written off against the income of the year of purchase. Capital expenditures are supposed to be depreciated instead of just written off in the year you purchase them.

Obviously, there are some problems here. You wouldn't buy a hammer that wasn't going to last a few years, but you don't want to divide its $20.00 purchase price by the ten years it will last and then deduct $2.00 each year, which is what you would have to do in straight-line depreciation. Just the bookkeeping on something like that will turn your hair gray.

Section 179, accelerated depreciation — So, the tax code has adopted a system that allows some items to be written off in the year you buy them no matter how long they may last. When you do that, it's called *expensing* the item, instead of *depreciating* the item, because that's what you're doing. You're treating that hammer as an expense even though it will last for years.

Section 179 allows personal property items that don't exceed a certain value to be expensed instead of depreciated — so you can write them all off in the year you buy them. When you're starting a business, this can be a way of offsetting some of those big start-up expenses, so that in addition to the cost of all this new equipment, you don't have a big tax bill.

However, there are some criteria you have to meet before you can use Section 179:

▌ You can't write off property that you won't use in your business more than 50 percent of the time. If you buy a home computer that you use for your business, but mostly your kids and you play a lot of games on it, you probably can't deduct it.

▌ You can't write off more than a certain amount of dollars worth of purchased items each year. That amount is being gradually increased each year. For example, in 1998 you couldn't expense more than $18,500 of personal property items, but by the year 2003, you'll be able to expense up to $25,000. However, this amount is reduced if you purchase more than approximately $200,000 worth of property. If you fall into that situation, and you don't have a tax accountant, it's time to get one.

▌ You can only write off "personal property." What that means is that you can't write off real estate investments or income-producing property like a backhoe you rent out to other contractors.

Other kinds of depreciation — There are other ways of dealing with depreciation. Since I run screaming from the room when people start talking about accelerated, declining balance depreciation and things like that, I can only recommend a tax accountant for those problems. If you can afford to buy equipment that exceeds the Section 179 limitations, you can afford a few hours of an accountant's time.

Home Office Deductions

In past years, people in the construction trade couldn't deduct the use of their home office because it wasn't their "principal place of business." But starting in 1999, a home office is deductible if it's the place where the bulk of your administrative and management work is done. But the space for your home office must be used *only* for business purposes. When you run your business out of your home, you can deduct that business expense by reporting it on Form 8829, *Expenses for the Business Use of Your Home.*

Your Employees and the IRS

If you have employees, you must withhold money from their paychecks to pay income taxes unless your employee claims more than ten dependents or claims not to be liable for withholding because he doesn't pay taxes. For example, it may be that his income is so low, and his number of dependents so high, that in combination with the earned income credit, he doesn't have to pay taxes.

Any employer that doesn't withhold when they are required to will be severely penalized. Also, you have to withhold a percentage of the employees' wages for the FICA (social security) contribution, then match that contribution with company funds.

The money that you withhold from employees is considered to be a trust fund. It no longer belongs to you. You're simply holding it on behalf of the employee. The IRS requires you to report quarterly how much money has been withheld. They also require that the withheld money is deposited into an approved account every quarter. If you want a real quick trip into real hot water, try forgetting that money isn't yours, and using it!

The only exception to these quarterly deposit and reporting rules is if you accumulate less than $1,000 in employee withholding (until 1999, it was $500). Then you're only required to report and deposit annually.

W-4 (Withholding) and W-2 (Reporting) Forms

Every new employee (even one you don't have to withhold money from) has to fill out a Form W-4, *Employee's Withholding Allowance Certificate.* You keep this form as part of the employee's personnel file. It's your justification for reducing the amount of money withheld from the employee's paycheck because of the employee's dependents. Then, during January of the following year, you have to fill out a set of W-2 forms for each employee showing how much that employee earned that year, and the amount of wages you withheld. W-2s come in a set with carbon copies. You must give them to the employee no later than January 31 of the following year.

If an employee hasn't filled out a W-4, you have to withhold the maximum amount of tax from the employee, with no reductions for dependants. If an employee wants to change the number of dependants shown on their W-4, they're entitled to file a new W-4 with their employer at any time.

There are a couple of exceptions to the general rule that the employer doesn't have to file W-4s with the IRS. You'll have to send in the W-4s when any employee who earns more than $200 a week claims not to be liable for withholding, or if any employee claims more than ten dependents.

What If You're Audited?

Self-employed people, especially those in the construction industry, are more likely to be audited than many other people. That's mostly because of the potential for cash transactions. Computerization has made it possible for tax returns to be audited without any face-to-face contact. If the computer decides you've made an error, it will send you a bill for additional taxes, plus penalties. Even on these computer audits, you can appeal the computer's decision to a human being.

There are three types of audits which involve more direct contact between the taxpayer and the tax collector.

The Correspondence Audit

In this type of audit, the IRS sends you a letter asking for specific evidence to support a claim on your tax return. For example, if you deducted medical expenses, they might want to see your medical bills. If you receive one of these letters, make a copy of everything they've requested and send it to them. *Keep your originals!* You can send a written explanation along with the documents if you feel it will help clarify your situation. It's not usually necessary to seek outside help to deal with this unless your return was prepared by someone else.

If you want to, you can request a personal interview with an agent. You can bring your attorney, accountant or anyone else you want with you. Or you can send them to the meeting without you. You don't actually have to be there.

If you object to the agent's decision, you can appeal it. The process and the time limits for appealing will be explained in the Notice of the Deficiency that you'll receive from the IRS if the agent decides against you.

The Office Audit

You may receive a letter from the IRS asking you to come into their field office and bring certain material with you. If the time and place of the audit aren't convenient, you're entitled to ask for a different time and place. If you and the IRS can't agree upon a time and place, then the IRS can determine when and where the audit will take place. Usually, your only option for the location is a different IRS office.

The office audit isn't a fishing expedition. It starts because a tax auditor has a specific question about your return. Read the notice carefully to see what they want. Think about what you need to take with you. Cooperate with the auditor, but don't answer questions you aren't asked. You are entitled to bring someone along to help you. If you don't, and you suddenly decide that was a mistake, you have the right to suspend the interview at any time until you can get someone to help you.

The Field Examination

The field examination can be thought of as an informed fishing expedition. The IRS has serious suspicions about a particular item, so they want to see your books and records for themselves, instead of letting you pick out what you want to show them. You don't have to answer their questions, but you *do* have to let them look at your records. You can insist that you or someone representing you be present when the field agents examine your books.

Financial Status Audits

This is a full court press. This is what happens when, for example, you and your spouse live in a $500,000 house, take fancy vacations, drive luxury cars, and report a joint income of $30,000 a year. In other words, they don't believe a word of it. They also do these to a certain number of randomly selected (and unlucky) taxpayers each year, to check for compliance in the general population. You're entitled to consult with a tax professional — and you probably should.

Appeals

You're entitled to object to a decision by an IRS agent or a tax auditor, but you must do so within a certain number of days after that decision is made. The procedure for doing this will be on the Notice of Deficiency advising you of the original decision. Your appeal will be referred to the Appeals Office in your region. There will then be, depending on the size of the claim, a hearing or a meeting about your issue. If basically factual issues are involved, the appeals officer may try to compromise them or return them to the field officer for reexamination. If your appeal in the Appeals Office is unsuccessful and you aren't offered any acceptable compromise, you can appeal to the Tax Court.

What If You Haven't Filed Your Tax Returns?

Even if you don't have the money, you should file a tax return. Remember, not filing a required tax return is a crime. Not paying your taxes isn't a crime. In this country, people don't go to jail for failing to pay their debts — except for child support payments. The IRS can make your life miserable with their collection efforts, but they can't put you in jail — not if you've filed those tax returns, and they're as honest as you can make them. If it's been so long that you simply don't know any more what your income was, make your best guess. Get those returns in. If necessary, you can amend them later. It's best to get help from a professional tax accountant if you can afford it.

Of course, if you deliberately file a pack of lies, that's called income tax evasion. Then jail is a real possibility.

On that happy note, we'll end this chapter on how the IRS collects from *you*. In the next chapter, we'll take a look at how you can collect what's owed *you* for the work you've done.

How Do You Collect What's Owed You?

This is a tough one, and one that's close to the hearts of all contractors. It shouldn't be a problem, but it's one of the most common. People pay their mortgages, they pay for their groceries, and they pay for their gas. But the contractor who put up their room addition or reroofed their house — his bill, they seem to feel, is optional.

Collecting money is difficult, time-consuming, and not what you wanted to do when you went into business for yourself. I can't give you much advice on collections without going to court, but I can give you some advice on avoiding the problem. Structure your payment schedule so you get paid as you go along. Be careful about clients who talk about all the problems they had with previous contractors. You might want to try to contact those other contractors and find out more about the situation. Be careful of clients who haggle about everything. You don't want to do business with someone who, when he owes you $10,000, offers to settle the debt for $9,000.

I'm a great believer in going with your gut. I've seen too many contractors get into trouble because they wanted a job so much that they ignored the bad feeling they got about a particular client. Deep down, they knew they were going to have trouble — and they did. You can't afford to do business with a client who won't let you make money.

There are a number of ways to collect money for work that's been done, but not paid for. The ways I'll cover in this chapter involve using the legal system. But first, here's some up front advice: Most of the time you'd be better off trying to work out a payment plan or a settlement instead of going to court. There's not much about protecting your legal rights or going to court that's cheap, quick or easy.

It's best to try some non-legal solution first, because you'll often find that after a certain amount of time and aggravation, customers will pay up without you needing to bring out the legal guns. Or maybe you don't want to go to court because the people have had some kind of temporary

Arbitration and Mediation

Arbitration and mediation clauses are most useful when they're used for settling misunderstandings and disputes revolving around the job site or the meaning of contract terms. As a vehicle to work out serious disputes, they're usually quicker, cheaper and less damaging to business relationships and reputations than going to court. That's why they're often included in contracts. The one place they're not particularly helpful is debt collection.

In mediation, a mediator (who is agreed upon by both parties) sits down with the parties and, instead of making a decision, tries to bring them to the point where they can agree on a solution to the problem themselves.

In arbitration, the contract between the homeowner and the contractor, or between the contractor and a subcontractor, identifies a professional arbitration organization. In the event of a dispute that triggers arbitration under the contract terms, that organization appoints a third party to be the arbitrator. The arbitrator listens to both parties, and then makes a decision about the dispute. If one of the parties is dissatisfied with the arbitrator's decision, he or she can appeal that decision to a regular court. However, it's rare for a court to overturn a qualified arbitrator's decision unless the appealing party can prove fraud or gross misconduct on the part of the arbitrator.

problem, a health problem or a job loss. Perhaps these are people you hope to do business with again. I can guarantee you that if you sue someone they won't be doing business with you again.

However, even if you don't want and don't intend to ever go into court, you should still take the steps necessary to protect your lien rights on every job. This doesn't mean you're going to take your customer into court. It just means that if you're forced to at some point, you've put all the legal hammers into place that the law allows you. There are two situations where it's especially important to take these steps:

1. If you're a subcontractor who has never even met the owner.

2. If you're a subcontractor in one of those states where payment to the contractor automatically discharges all subcontractors.

Remember that what you're worried about when you take steps to protect your lien rights is not just that your customer might not pay. Think about all the other things that can go wrong in life. What if your customer drops dead, and you find yourself dealing with his nephew who recognizes that if he pays you off, there won't be much left for him?

Then there are those situations where, if you don't sue, you could wind up with nothing. If you do have to sue for payment, you'll want to use the least expensive, most efficient, method. For most relatively small amounts, that's Small Claims Court.

Small Claims Court

Most states have a special procedure for going to court to collect small amounts of money that's considerably easier, quicker, and cheaper than a regular lawsuit. It's usually called Small Claims Court, and it's intended to be an informal, uncomplicated procedure that you can do yourself, without a lawyer. Some Small Claims Courts even have rules against using a lawyer.

What determines whether or not you can use Small Claims Court is the amount of money that's owed you. Here in Michigan, the debt must be less than $1,750. In California, it's $5,000. Find out the limit in your state, and keep it in mind when you're making a payment schedule. For example, if you're in California and building an addition for $25,000, try to pace the advance and progress payments so the amount owed you for the work you've completed is never more than $5,000. If they suddenly stop paying, you stop working, and you can go to Small Claims for $5,000 or less to collect what is owed you.

Usually you can get a booklet from the Small Claims Court that will tell you exactly what to do. Call your county clerk and find out the location of the Small Claims Court in your area. Then, to start the ball rolling, go there and fill out a form called a *complaint*. The court clerk will take your complaint and assign a hearing date. There will be no attorneys at the hearing and it will be much more informal than a standard trial. On the day of the hearing, you show up, along with your evidence and any witnesses. That evidence should include:

- Your contract with the customer (If you don't have a written contract, you're going to have a tougher time.)
- Material receipts
- Change orders
- Copies of your license
- Photographs of the job site
- A completed punch list if you have one
- Anything else you have that would be helpful in explaining or supporting your argument.

If you don't have every single one of these things, or don't have independent witnesses, don't give up. Remember, you're probably your own best witness.

Completed punch lists are especially helpful, because a customer who hasn't paid often says, "I'm not paying because the contractor didn't do the work right." A punch list can go a long way toward disproving that claim.

For example, suppose Cal the carpenter sues for payment for a deck. Cal can prove he was hired by showing his signed contract, and he can prove that he did the work by showing before and after photographs of the deck. But what if the customer says, "I'm not paying because the deck wobbles when I walk on it." It would help a lot if Cal could whip out a punch list that the customer filled in as part of a walk-through inspection when the work was complete, and that punch list said nothing about the deck "wobbling." Customers are often better at finding defects in your work when the job is complete and they have your bill in their hand. A punch list gets them looking and checking off their approval *before* they get their final bill.

Pretrial Settlements

Often, simply showing up ready to go to trial will motivate the defendant to offer a settlement of the debt. The offer may be less than what you could win by going to trial, but remember that a bird in the hand . . . and so forth. There's always a risk that when you go to trial, you won't get *anything*. You may get a judge who doesn't fully understand your position — or simply doesn't agree with you. Maybe he or she just had a bad experience with a contractor, and subconsciously sides with the customer. Judges are just people, you know. And even if you win (and collect) a judgment, the costs of the lawsuit will reduce your actual award.

If you decide to accept a pretrial offer, insist on being paid on the spot. If you get a check, take it to the defendant's bank immediately.

Winning a Judgment

If you go to trial and win, whether it's Small Claims or some other court, all you actually get is a judgment in your favor. You *don't* get your money. You get a tool you can use to get your money. Once you have a judgment, you can garnish the defendant's wages or attach his assets. You can require the defendant to come into court and tell you under oath what those assets are. With a judgment in hand, you can foreclose on your construction lien and force the sale of the property where you did the work — if you've done the things you need to do to preserve that lien.

The court clerk can tell you what forms you need to fill out to do any of these things.

What Is a Construction Lien?

As a contractor you have some extra legal help in collecting the money that many other creditors don't. You're entitled to a lien on the property.

A construction lien is a kind of mechanic's lien, something that's been in the law since the Middle Ages. The idea behind a mechanic's lien is that if someone hires you to repair or improve their property, then doesn't pay you for your work, you ought to be able to get your money by taking the thing you fixed for that person and selling it.

For example, auto mechanics have a mechanic's lien on a car when they fix it. They don't have to return that car to the owner until they're paid. If they aren't paid, they can sell the car to pay off the debt for repairing it. That's after a certain amount of time and after making the proper notices of lien and foreclosure required by law, of course. When they sell the car, they can take the money that's owed to them out of the proceeds. Then they have to give the rest of the money to anybody else who has a lien on the car. If there's any money left after the liens are satisfied, it goes to the person who originally owned the car. The mechanic doesn't get to keep all the proceeds if that's more money than the debt that's owed to him.

This is easy enough when you're talking about cars, but chopping off a house's new addition and hauling it off to sell doesn't work. And you can't scrape off the paint you put on and return it to the paint store. So, instead of taking actual possession of the property, the builder or contractor takes symbolic possession by putting a lien on the title to the property.

That lien allows the person who did the work to ask a judge to order the sale of the property to pay off the debt. But, of course, the person claiming a lien has to prove to the judge that he is actually owed that debt. The property owner gets what's left over *after* the construction liens and other security interests like mortgages are paid.

Putting a construction lien on a building is a much more elaborate process than what an auto mechanic has to do to establish a lien on a car. The mechanic has the car in his possession and can just keep it. The builder has to establish his construction lien in a way that's very similar to what a mortgage lender would have to do to protect his mortgage.

Who Is Entitled to a Construction Lien?

People who are entitled to a lien are called *lien claimants*. Anyone who works on a building project or supplies materials for that project is entitled to claim a construction lien. Being entitled, however, doesn't mean that anyone automatically *has* a lien they can foreclose on. It's much more complicated than that.

Technically the lien attaches to the property the moment your part of the job is finished. However, to foreclose that lien, to protect it from someone else getting priority over your lien, and to keep it from expiring, you have to file the right papers within a certain number of days from the moment the lien attached to the property. (That's called *recording or perfecting* the lien.)

Contractors

Any contractor or builder who has done construction work on the property has a right to a construction lien if he or she is not paid. To get that lien the contractor must follow precisely the statutory process in his or her state. To find out what that procedure is in your state, contact the office where real estate deeds are recorded.

Subcontractors

Often it's not the contractor who wasn't paid and is trying to collect by putting a lien on the property — it's a subcontractor.

Subcontractors also have lien rights. In fact, lien rights can be critical for subcontractors, who may have never even met the property owner and may have limited rights under the contract between the property owner and the contractor.

In some states, a subcontractor cannot get a lien against a property owner who isn't otherwise aware of his identity. The subcontractor must give the property owner a Notice of Furnishing as soon as his work *begins*. In other states, to preserve his lien rights the subcontractor needs to give notice to the property owner of the work he has performed as soon as his part of the job is *finished* — even if the project itself isn't finished (also usually a Notice of Furnishing). Then, the subcontractor must record a Claim of Lien with the Registrar of Deeds within a certain number of days of completing his work. All subcontractors should make themselves aware of the lien procedures in their state so that they know which requirements apply to them.

The contractor has a duty to protect the property owner from the liens of subcontractors or material suppliers. This means that if the homeowner has to pay off a lien that a subcontractor, laborer, or supplier put on his property, the homeowner has the right to be reimbursed by the contractor. Or the homeowner can withhold some of the money they haven't yet paid to the contractor because the contractor has breached his contractual obligation to pay the subcontractors, or get lien waivers from them.

For more information about subcontractor lien rights, see Chapter 12.

Material Suppliers

Anyone who supplies materials to a job site for building purposes or improvements is entitled to a lien on the building in which those materials are used. Improvements include things like cement for the foundation or asphalt for the driveway. This is true even though the relationship between the homeowner and the supplier may be very remote; the supplier may even have delivered the goods to a subcontractor *of* a subcontractor. That doesn't matter. The key for the right to a construction lien is that the goods were delivered to, and used in, a construction project.

Laborers

Construction laborers have construction lien rights against the property if they haven't been paid. That includes the unpaid employees of a subcontractor who also have lien rights in most states. The key is that they worked on that job site, not who they worked for, and that they have given the notices required by law.

What if the Contractor's Paid, but Not the Subcontractors or the Suppliers?

In some states, unpaid subcontractors and material suppliers are entitled to a lien even if the contractor has been paid in full — but that's not true everywhere. In other states, payment to the contractor discharges all the subs and suppliers who haven't already given notice to the homeowner, or otherwise perfected their lien according to their state law. In those states, the subcontractors and the suppliers are left with only their rights against the contractor.

To protect their lien rights, a subcontractor or supplier should always give notice of completing work to the property owner as soon the work is done. Many states have a specific form they must use, such as a Notice of Furnishing. Then, according to their state law, they record their lien.

How Do You Get a Construction Lien?

Two legal words are used when talking about liens: *attached* and *perfected.*

When a lien is *attached* to the property, that means that the property owner can't deny it, and, in most states, means that payment to a contractor will not discharge an unpaid subcontractor (or whoever else's lien has attached). The problem is what the property owner's other creditors may be entitled to.

When exactly a lien attaches depends on the law in your state. In some states, just completing the work makes the lien attach. In a few states, such as New York, just starting the work will attach the lien. In other states, formal written notice, usually called a Notice of Furnishing or a Completion Notice (see Figure 7-1), must be given to the property owner. In Michigan, the Notice of Furnishing must be accompanied by a Proof of Service, like the one shown in Figure 7-2. In most states, other creditors can get in front of the lien if you haven't yet perfected it. In a few states, a construction lien takes priority over the property owner's other creditors as soon as it attaches.

Bigger Builders Inc.
22 Commerce Drive • Lansing, MI 55555
Phone (555)555-1234 • Fax (555)555-6789
Website: www.biggerbuildersinc.com

NOTICE OF FURNISHING
(This form conforms to the laws of the State of Michigan.)

TO: <u>John and Kathy Jones</u> *(The name and address of the property owner goes here.)*

PLEASE TAKE NOTICE that <u>Harold's Foundations</u> *(put the name of the subcontractor or supplier here)* is furnishing <u>labor in the value of $20,000.00</u> *(describe the goods or labor here)* to <u>Bigger Builders Inc.</u> *(name of the contractor here, or if you are a sub-subcontractor, put the name of the subcontractor here)* in connection with improvements to the real property described as <u>123 East Street, Lansing, MI</u>. *(Put legal description from the Notice of Commencement here.)*

(The legal description comes from the Notice of Commencement, a document that Michigan requires property owners to post on the property and give to contractors, who are then supposed to give it to subcontractors. If this is not done, the time limit on construction liens does not apply and the notice requirements for effective liens are extended. However, the subcontractor claiming the lien must make a written demand to the contractor that he produce a Notice of Commencement. The subcontractor must file the Notice of Furnishing with an attached Proof of Service, plus a Claim of Lien at the Registrar of Deeds. If there's no available Notice of Commencement, get the legal description of the property from the Registrar of Deeds office.)

WARNING TO OWNER: THIS NOTICE IS REQUIRED BY THE MICHIGAN CONSTRUCTION LIEN ACT. IF YOU HAVE QUESTIONS ABOUT YOUR RIGHTS AND DUTIES UNDER THIS ACT, YOU SHOULD CONTACT AN ATTORNEY TO PROTECT YOU FROM THE POSSIBILITY OF PAYING TWICE FOR IMPROVEMENTS TO YOUR PROPERTY.

Date <u>8·15·2000</u>

Signed <u>H. ef Smith doing business as Harolds Foundations</u>

(The lien claimant should sign his or her own name and should include the company name. If the company is incorporated, then he or she should sign as the president or whatever title they hold in the corporation.)

Address <u>22 West Center Road Lansing MI</u> *(Lien claimant's address here.)*

(This notice should be mailed to the property owner, or to the person the property owner has designated as his agent in his Notice of Commencement, by certified mail at the address shown in the Notice of Commencement within 20 days after furnishing the first labor or material. Then attach a Proof of Service to a copy of this Notice of Furnishing, and file both with the Claim of Lien.)

(A property owner who receives a Notice of Furnishing may demand a sworn statement of exactly what labor and materials have been furnished. If the property owner does not receive the sworn statement, the lien claimant risks losing his lien rights.)

State of <u>Michigan</u>

County of <u>Ingham</u>

   Subscribed and sworn to before me this _____ day of _____, 20 _____

   Signature of Notary Public _____

   My commission expires: _____

Figure 7-1 *Sample Notice of Furnishing*

Bigger Builders Inc.
22 Commerce Drive • Lansing, MI 55555
Phone (555)555-1234 • Fax (555)555-6789
Website: www.biggerbuildersinc.com

PROOF OF SERVICE

(This must be attached to a copy of the Notice of Furnishing and filed with the Claim of Lien at the Registrar of Deeds in the appropriate county.)

I, <u>Nancy Smith</u> *(name of person mailing the documents)*, hereby certify that on <u>8-2-00</u> *(date)*, I mailed from <u>22 West Center Road Lansing MI</u> *(give address)*, a copy of the attached Notice of Furnishing and the attached Claim of Lien to <u>John & Kathy Jones</u> *(property owner's name)* at <u>44 Farm Lane Lansing MI</u> *(property owner's address)* by certified mail, return receipt requested with prepaid postage thereon.

Signed *Nancy Smith*

(In some jurisdictions, this signature must be notarized.)

State of <u>Michigan</u>
County of <u>Ingham</u>

Subscribed and sworn to before me this _____ day of _____, 20 _____
Signature of Notary Public _____
My commission expires: _____

Figure 7-2 *Sample Proof of Service*

Bigger Builders Inc.
22 Commerce Drive • Lansing, MI 55555
Phone (555)555-1234 • Fax (555)555-6789
Website: www.biggerbuildersinc.com

CLAIM OF LIEN

(File this document with the office of the Registrar of Deeds)

Notice is hereby given that on the <u>6th</u> day of <u>June</u> , <u>2000</u> , <u>Harold Smith doing business as Harold's Foundations</u> *(name of the lien claimant here)* first provided labor or material for an improvement to <u>123 W. East St., Lansing, MI</u>. *(Give legal description and mailing address of the property where the work was performed.)* The last day of providing the labor or material was the <u>15th</u> day of <u>July</u> , <u>2000</u> .

The lien claimant's contract amount, including extras, is $ <u>30,000.00</u> . The lien claimant has received payment thereon in the total amount of $ <u>10,000.00</u> , and therefore claims a construction lien upon the above-described real property in the amount of $ <u>20,000.00</u> *(Put the unpaid balance here.)*.

<u>Harold's Foundations</u>

(Put the business name of the lien claimant here.)

By: *Harold Smith*

(The lien claimant should sign here.)

<u>22 West Center Road   Lansing MI</u>

(Put the business address of the lien claimant here.)

Dated: <u>8-5-00</u>

State of <u>Michigan</u>

County of <u>Ingham</u>

Subscribed and sworn to before me this <u>5th</u> day of <u>August</u> , <u>2000</u>

Nancy Smith

(Signature of notary public. This document must be notarized.)

My commission expires: <u>Feb. 4, 2004</u>

(Note: In Michigan, this document must be filed with copies of the Notice of Furnishing and a Proof of Service of the Notice of Furnishing attached. It must be filed within 90 days after last furnishing labor or materials to the property. After the Claim of Lien is filed, a lawsuit for the foreclosure and sale of the property must be started within one year.)

Figure 7-3 *Sample Claim of Lien*

A lien is *perfected* by recording it where the state law says to record it. That's usually with the county Registrar of Deeds. Figure 7-3 shows a sample of a Claim of Lien. (Blank copies of these three forms are on the disk in the back of the book.)

When a lien is perfected, that means that the property owner's other creditors can't get in front of it: the legal phrase for that is "take priority over it." Having priority means you get paid first if the property is foreclosed on. For example, in some states where perfection is required for priority, a subfoundation contractor who did the work first does not automatically get paid before the electrical subcontractor, even though his lien may have attached first. Who gets paid first depends on who gets their lien perfected first. If the electrical contractor beat the foundation subcontractor to the Registrar of Deeds, then the electrical subcontractor gets paid fully before the foundation subcontractor.

Don't write me letters complaining that this is unfair to the foundation contractor; fair or not, that's the way it is.

Mortgages also have a place in the priority parade. For example, if you're not in a state where attachment gives a construction lien priority over other creditors, and the property owner takes out a new mortgage on the property, the bank may get their money before you. It depends on whether the bank gets their mortgage recorded at the Registrar of Deeds before anyone else. Then when the property owner goes bust and everything is foreclosed, if the bank has priority, the mortgage will be fully paid before either the foundation contractor or the electrical contractor. This is true even if the foundation or electrical subcontractor brought the foreclosure action. It's possible — and it has happened - that the person going through the expense and aggravation of foreclosing the lien winds up with none of his debt paid. Even in those states where construction liens automatically attach, those liens don't stay attached forever. The contractor must perfect his lien within a certain number of days, or that lien will expire.

The moral here is get those liens perfected even if you don't expect to have to use them. After all, what are you talking about? A quick run to the Registrar of Deeds, or wherever deeds are recorded in your state. Call the tract index and ask if you don't have a Registrar of Deeds. If the bureaucracy is impenetrable, call a real estate broker. They know where deeds are filed.

A lien claimant can *file* a lien even though there's a question about exactly how much money is owed. But lien claimants can't *foreclose* on that lien until after they've proved to the court that they did the work, that they are actually owed money that hasn't been paid, and they are therefore entitled to foreclose. Having a construction lien is something like having a mortgage. If a mortgage isn't paid, then the lender has to go to court to foreclose the mortgage on the property. It's the same thing with a lien.

The Five Steps in the Construction Lien Process

1. A laborer, contractor, subcontractor or supplier provides work, equipment, or materials to a building site.

2. The lien claimant — that's the laborer, contractor, subcontractor or supplier - finishes the work or furnishes material or labor, and gives the property owner or his agent notice that the work has been completed within the required number of days as set out in the state statute. This preliminary notice is usually called a Notice of Furnishing or a Notice of Completion. In some states just starting the work is considered legal notice, but subcontractors especially, who may not have any direct contact with the property owner, shouldn't rely on this.

3. The unpaid lien claimant files a Claim of Lien at the recorder's office, the registrar of deeds or the county clerk (or wherever it is that deeds are filed in that state) within the required number of days after the Notice of Furnishing. Filing the lien is called recording the lien.

4. Once the lien is recorded, the unpaid lien claimant is called a lienholder. The lienholder then enforces his lien by starting a foreclosure lawsuit, and going to trial.

5. If the lienholder wins his lawsuit, the court enters an order to the sheriff or bailiff directing them to sell the property to the highest bidder at an auction. After the sale, the sheriff or bailiff distributes the proceeds of the sale according to the priorities established by the court when it entered its judgment in the foreclosure lawsuit.

You go to court and foreclose on the property. The property owner then has the opportunity to defend against the construction lien by claiming he's already paid, or the work wasn't done.

What this means for a construction company is that if it isn't paid, it can claim a construction lien. But to get that lien, the company must do *exactly* what the lien statute in their state requires it to do.

When I say that to file a lien you must follow the law "exactly," I mean you must follow the procedure exactly. You have to file in the right place within the required number of days and so forth. What I do not mean is that the amount of money owed, or the number of hours worked, or material extended has to be reported exactly. If there is a controversy over those issues, that will be resolved in the foreclosure process. What you must do is give the property owner the right kind of notice, meet the time limits in your state, and file the lien claims in the right place. Usually the right place is the county recorder of deeds or the tract index in the county seat.

You may also have to prepare a statement listing every subcontractor and material supplier that you used on the job, and then either, depending on state law, serve on the property owner or file with the Claim of Lien, or both. Then, after filing your lien, you can sue the customer for nonpayment and foreclosure — but you don't have to. Filing a lien just protects your rights if, at some point, you do have to go to court. If you do get your lien perfected, you still only have a lien; you don't have your money. To get your money, you have to sue for foreclosure.

Lots of trouble, right? Yes — but it still beats not being paid. If you need to foreclose on a construction lien, this would be a good time to talk to your lawyer. I know it costs money to hire a lawyer. However, it's easier and it usually costs less money in advance to get a lawyer for a foreclosure lien because that lawyer knows he or she can be paid out of the foreclosure proceeds. A lawyer will be more willing to work for you if they're sure they are dealing with a lien claimant who didn't let his rights expire.

Most states say that if the lien claimant wants to sue, it must be within a certain number of days after filing the lien. If the lien claimant doesn't sue, the lien just expires.

Is the Lien Claimant Limited by the Owner's Equity?

The lien claimant can never get more than what the property owner who contracted for the work actually owns. That's what equity means: the value of the owner's interest. If there's a recorded mortgage on the property, or someone else already owns part of the property (like a spouse who did not sign the construction contract), the lien claimant can't reach beyond the customer's equity. This is why it's always a good idea for the contractor to get both spouses to sign the construction contract.

Here's an example of the effect of mortgages on construction liens. Suppose that Ralph the roofer puts on a $5,000 roof for Sam. Sam's house is worth $100,000, but it's mortgaged for $120,000. Property values in Sam's neighborhood have decreased since he got his mortgage. Ralph can put a lien on Sam's unit, but it won't get him a cent towards his roofing bill, because Sam doesn't have any equity in his house.

Can Somebody Else Be Paid Before the Lien Claimant?

Someone else may have priority over the lien claimant. If someone else has a mortgage on the property, in most states who gets paid first depends on who got their lien or mortgage perfected first. The legal term for this first-come-first-served idea is *priority*. If the property is sold to satisfy a construction lien claimant, anyone who has priority over that lien claimant can demand that the court pay off their debt first, before the lien claimant's debt.

Priority doesn't depend upon who actually foreclosed first. It depends on whose lien or mortgage gets priority in the state security interest laws. Some states require a lien to be recorded in order to take priority over a mortgage. In those states, if a mortgage was recorded before the construction lien was recorded, then the mortgage will be fully paid before the lien claimant. If the lien was recorded first, then the lien is paid first.

For example, suppose that Cal Contractor has a $20,000 construction lien for remodeling work that he did for Harry Homeowner. Suppose Harry had mortgaged his house for $90,000 after Cal did the work, but before Cal got to the recorder's office to record his lien. The foreclosure sale brings in $100,000. In some states, if the mortgage company recorded its mortgage before Cal did, the mortgage company will get its $90,000 first, leaving only $10,000 for Cal. The mortgage had priority over Cal's lien, because the mortgage was recorded first.

Suppose Harry's mortgage company had their mortgage before Cal did his work, but, for some reason, the mortgage company didn't get down to the county clerk's office to file a record of their mortgage until after Cal did. Then, in most states, if Harry's house is sold for $100,000, first Cal's construction lien of $20,000 is paid, and then the mortgage company gets the $80,000 that's left over after Cal is paid. The mortgage didn't have priority because it wasn't recorded before Cal's construction lien was perfected.

Not every state does it this way. In some states, a lien takes priority over a mortgage if the lien attached before the mortgage is recorded. The idea is that anyone could go to the site and see that construction is going on, so they have notice of a possible lien. They shouldn't be able to defeat it by racing to the tract index or county recorders office with their mortgage.

If you're in a situation (or negotiating a contract) where priority matters, it's very important that you get local legal advice about your state laws on priority. Laws on liens vary widely by state, but the one thing they have in common is that you must follow every step to the letter.

Construction Lien Rights if the Customer Is a Tenant

In most states, your lien rights when work is done for a tenant depends on whether or not the landlord required the tenant to make the improvements to the property as part of the lease. If the landlord required the tenant to do it, then the lien can attach directly to the property itself.

If the landlord didn't require the tenant to make the improvements, then the tenant has no interest beyond the value of his lease to which a lien could attach. It's not that the lien claimant isn't entitled to a lien, it's that he can't use his lien to get a bigger interest in the property than what the tenant who hired him actually had. Most of the time, a lien on lease rights isn't worth much, but that's not always true.

Lien Waivers

Blank Copy on CD-ROM

There are blank copies of Figures 7-4 and 7-5 included on the disk in the back of the book.

A contractor, a subcontractor, or any other person who's entitled to a construction lien, can give up the right to a lien by signing a release that surrenders those lien rights. This kind of release is called a lien waiver. Figures 7-4 and 7-5 are both lien waivers. The lien waiver in Figure 7-4 would be used by individual contractors or subcontractors. The one in

Figure 7-5 would be used by a general contractor. That one is worded the way it is so that the person signing the lien waiver is guaranteeing the non-existence of any other liens that may have risen out of his or her work. If it turns out that there is, for example, a sub-subcontractor who is entitled to a lien, that sub-sub is still entitled to a lien, but the property owner or the contractor, depending on who pays the lien off, is then entitled to go after the person who signed the lien waiver guaranteeing that there were no other lien claimants out there pursuant to the work the lien waiver signatory did.

The key words here are rising out of that work. If there's another lien claimant lurking out there who had nothing to do with the work the person signing this lien waiver did, then this lien waiver has no effect on him and vice versa.

Can a Contractor Waive Everybody's Lien Rights?

Some contractors or property owners put a blanket lien waiver into the construction contract that automatically waives all liens as soon as the contract is signed. Then when the sub performs work, a few states say the subcontractor has no lien rights because all of his rights rise out of the contract — which gave up his lien rights. However, most states don't enforce this kind of blanket lien waiver.

Conditional Lien Waivers

Lien waivers can be unconditional or they can be conditioned upon payment. When a lien waiver is conditioned upon a certain event, like payment, and the event doesn't happen, then the lien waiver isn't enforceable.

For example, suppose before getting his money, Sam the subcontractor signs a lien waiver that says that he waives his lien rights upon payment by Harry Homeowner. Then Harry doesn't pay him. Sam can still get a lien because the lien waiver that he signed was conditional, and the condition didn't happen. This example is assuming that the time limits in the state law for Sam to get a lien haven't expired.

In some states the tender of payment by cash or by check will satisfy the condition. But suppose Harry's check bounces? In most states, this means that the condition has not been met. However, I'd recommend that you protect yourself if you sign a waiver. Instead of language about "payment," you should require language like this: "This lien wavier is conditioned upon full satisfaction of the debt." With that language, there's no question about it - the check has to clear the bank. A bad check does not satisfy the debt.

Bigger Builders Inc.
22 Commerce Drive • Lansing, MI 55555
Phone (555)555-1234 • Fax (555)555-6789
Website: www.biggerbuildersinc.com

LIEN WAIVER

State of _____

County of _____

My/our contract with <u>John and Kathy Jones</u> *(Name the property owner, or, if you are a subcontractor, name the contractor.)* to provide <u>framing</u>_____ *(Describe services)* to the property located at <u>18 Apple Lane, Lansing, MI</u> *(Give address and legal description of the property where work was done.)* having been fully paid, I/we hereby waive my/our construction lien in the amount of $ for labor or materials.

Signature _____
(The contractor or subcontractor signs here.)

Title: _____
(The title of the person signing above.)

Company Name: _____

Company Address: _____

Date: <u>8-15-2000</u>

Figure 7-4 *Sample Full Unconditional Lien Waiver*

Bigger Builders Inc.
22 Commerce Drive • Lansing, MI 55555
Phone (555)555-1234 • Fax (555)555-6789
Website: www.biggerbuildersinc.com

LIEN WAIVER

State of _____

County of _____

The undersigned <u>Sam Smith</u> *(Name the company or person entitled to a lien.)* hereby releases, waives, and quitclaims rights to a construction lien in the amount of $ <u>5,000.00</u> for improvements to, or materials furnished to, the property described as <u>18 Apple Lane, Lansing, MI</u> *(Insert mailing address and legal description.)* through the date of <u>8-15-2000</u>.

The undersigned warrants that all laborers and subcontractors employed by it, and all suppliers from which it has acquired materials, have been paid their respective portion of prior claims, and that none of such laborers, subcontractors, or suppliers have any claim of lien against the project through <u>8-15-2000</u> *(date)*.

This waiver is conditioned upon full satisfaction of the amount shown above.

Signed on <u>8-15-2000</u> *(date)*

Signature: _____
(Signature of Lien Claimant)

Address: _____
(Address of Lien Claimant)

Figure 7-5 *Sample Full Conditional Lien Waiver*

What Is a Stop Notice?

By law, no one can put a construction lien on a public building. A contractor, subcontractor, or a supplier who would ordinarily be entitled to a construction lien, is not entitled to that lien when the construction is for a publicly-owned building — even if he or she is unpaid. So, instead of a construction lien, a Stop Notice is used in public works projects such as libraries, schools, roads or other kinds of buildings owned by the government — any government, whether it be federal, state or local.

It would be bad public policy to not provide a way for small material suppliers, laborers or subcontractors to collect for unpaid work, especially if the contractor is collecting money from public agencies but isn't using it to pay off the subcontractors or suppliers. That's why the law allows the use of Stop Notices.

A Stop Notice procedure isn't a construction lien. It's a way for subcontractors and suppliers to get at the contractor when the contractor is being paid by the public agency, but isn't paying the subcontractors and suppliers. Stop Notices can't be used to recover funds already distributed to the contractor, but they can be used to intercept payments not yet made by the public agency to the contractor.

Stop Notices aren't available in every state. But in the states that do allow them, the subcontractor or material supplier can use a Stop Notice to order that public agency or lending institution to hold money back from the prime contractor. That makes funds available to pay a subcontractor or material supplier.

In effect, a Stop Notice escrows the funds until the claimant (the subcontractor or supplier) can prove in court that they're entitled to the money because they worked on the project or delivered goods to that project, but weren't paid by the general contractor.

If you need to use a Stop Notice, you must be quite careful to follow the state law about the procedure. Usually this is what's required:

▌ The Stop Notice must be delivered by certified mail to the lending institution (we'll call it the bank, although it might be a mortgage company or a federal finance institution) where the public funds to pay for the program are on deposit. In other words, mail your Stop Notice to whoever has custody of the money. You should already know what bank this is, because whenever you get involved in a public works project, the first thing you should find out, before even making your bid, is who's holding the money. But if you don't know, don't forget the value of those Freedom of Information Act laws.

▌ The Stop Notice must have a bond mailed with it. That means before you can mail your Stop Notice, you have to make arrangements for a bond with a bonding company that promises to protect the bank. You need a bond to protect the bank just in case it turns out that the general contractor really has been paying you properly.

This may seem like a difficult procedure, but if you're having a problem getting paid, don't give up on using a Stop Notice. It's an extremely useful device. Hire a lawyer who specializes in this kind of work. You'll probably find that hiring lawyers isn't as expensive when they know where the pot of money is that's going to pay their fee. And that's what a Stop Notice does. It puts a pot of money into the freezer.

Most of the states that have this procedure restrict it to public projects, but a few allow it on private projects as well.

Payment and Performance Bonds

A construction payment bond or a performance bond guarantees payment or performance if the principal contractor defaults and doesn't finish the project, or doesn't pay the subcontractors or suppliers. Exactly what is guaranteed depends on what kind of bond it is. Most states and all federal projects require payment and performance bonds on public works. Some private projects also require payment or performance bonds.

The company or person that gives the bond is called a *surety*. That surety is promising to make good, if someone else doesn't. If the surety has to pay off on the bond, the surety always has the right to sue the contractor for any money the surety had to pay out to fulfill the contractor's obligations.

What Is a Payment Bond?

A payment bond is a guarantee that the subcontractors and suppliers will be paid if the contractor doesn't pay them. It's intended to protect the property owner from construction liens.

The bond is purchased from an insurance company or a professional surety company, usually by the contractor, for the benefit of the property owner. The payment bond doesn't directly pay the subcontractors' or suppliers' bills. What it does do is reimburse the owner when the owner has to pay off a lien because the contractor didn't pay a subcontractor or supplier. Then the bonding company sues the contractor for reimbursement.

Most payment bonds only pay off liens. So even if there's a bond in place, the unpaid subcontractor or supplier won't be paid unless everything has been done that the law requires to get a lien perfected on the property.

Sometimes, on larger jobs, the contractors will require their subcontractors or suppliers to obtain payment bonds. That way if the contractor has to reimburse a property owner because a subcontractor's failure to properly pay off his suppliers or sub-subcontractors ended in a lien being put on the property, the prime contractor can go to that bond for reimbursement.

What Is a Performance Bond?

A performance bond guarantees the work itself. The surety promises to protect the owner from damages caused by an unfinished job. Often that involves making some alternative arrangement to get the job finished. Sometimes, instead of requiring the contractor to get a performance bond before the work is started, the project owner simply reserves the right to require a bond in the event of a dispute. The problem with having that term in the contract is that it's difficult to get a performance bond for a project that's already in trouble.

When it appears that the project won't be completed, the surety can intervene. Or someone else (the lender, the property owner or the contractor, depending on the situation and the terms of the bond) calls for the surety to intervene. There are several things that the surety can do.

1. The surety can lend money to the contractor to complete the project.

2. The surety can undertake to complete the contract itself, through its own agents. The surety can ask the lender for a "set-aside letter" in which the lender agrees to set aside a portion of the project loan, and advance that money to the surety for project completion. If the surety undertakes the construction itself, or through an agent, the surety or its agent must be properly licensed.

3. The surety can pay damages up to the penal amount in the bond. Many people don't realize that the standard performance bond form *doesn't actually guarantee that the project will be finished*. It only guarantees that some named person, usually the project owner, will be protected if the project isn't finished. One way of protecting that person is to simply pay them the money that not finishing the project will cost them. If the property owner had advanced $200,000 to the contractor, and the contractor went south with the money, the surety could either finish the project, or, instead, just return the $200,000 to the property owner.

4. The surety can deny liability. The surety could claim that for some reason, the terms of the bond have not been met and the surety is not obligated to intervene

How Do Change Orders Affect the Performance Bond?

Significant change orders in the construction project may have the effect of losing a performance bond's protection. The bond surety accepted the specifications on the original contract, not on change orders.

Part Four: Legal Problems on the Jobsite

Chapter 8

What Laws Affect the Building Site?

Chapter 9

How Is Safety Regulated on the Job Site?

Chapter 10

What If Someone Is Injured on the Job Site?

Chapter 11

What If You Use Subcontractors Instead of Employees?

Chapter 12

What Contract Problems Do Subcontractors Have?

What Laws Affect the Building Site?

Anyone who builds or remodels has to consider the requirements of both the building code (which issues building and occupancy permits) and the zoning code (which regulates land use and building site issues).

The difference between a building code and a zoning law is their primary focus. The building code aims to protect the safety of the public, while the zoning laws aim to protect property values.

It's important to find out about the rules that impact your building plans before you start the work, because zoning and building inspectors have a great deal of power. They can shut a project down. They can even (and have in some instances) order a project that has been started, or even completed, to be torn down.

The example I like to use to show this power involves a resort community in Michigan that required a builder to remove the fourth floor of his waterfront apartment building before he could get an occupancy permit. Did I feel sorry for him? Not especially. The three-story height-restriction was in the local ordinances, which he could (and should) have read. Those ordinances weren't hidden away where the public couldn't find them, and he surely must have known that building height is regulated in many communities. The only part that bothered me even a little bit was that he actually had received a building permit for the four floors. I thought the local authority should have realized there was a problem when he first brought his plans in for a permit. However, a building permit is only permission to go ahead. It's not a guarantee that the plan meets all the local laws.

Building Codes

Most communities have building codes. Unlike zoning laws, which are usually aimed at aesthetics and maintaining surrounding property values, building codes are intended to make buildings safe for human use. That includes the people who presently use the building and the people who may buy it or enter it at some time in the future.

Model Building Codes

Instead of writing their own building codes, most communities adopt one of the major model building codes such as BOCA or the Uniform Building Code. All of these codes are put together with industry input.

These codes aren't identical. There are even different versions of the same code. You may be familiar with the code in one community, but don't assume the rules are necessarily the same in another one, even if it uses the same code. Always check with the building inspector while you're still in the design stage, because sometimes different communities use different editions of the same code. For example, here in Michigan, where I live, our community uses the 1987 BOCA code, while one nearby community uses the 1994 edition of the BOCA code, and another uses the 1997 edition.

Building Permits

The building codes require a building permit before starting work. You start the process of getting a building permit by paying a fee and showing the building inspector your plans. Depending on how complicated and extensive your project is, you may also have to show the inspector your architectural drawings, engineering calculations, soil reports, and whatever other plans and specifications the inspector needs to decide if your plan meets the code requirements.

Remember, however, that getting a building permit issued that allows you to start work is not a guarantee that your building will meet the code.

Who's Responsible for Getting the Building Permit?

The general rule is that the owner must provide access rights, easements, rights of way, and *all the permits* necessary for the start of construction, unless the parties agree otherwise. However, this rule is of very little benefit to a contractor who's gone ahead and started the work without a building permit. The contractor is required to do the work in a way that conforms to the local laws — and local laws say you need a building permit in hand before you can start work.

Contractors who start work without a building permit in hand could have all kinds of legal trouble. They might have trouble getting paid, because it's hard to enforce an illegal contract. They could be delayed until a permit is obtained — and we all know that in the construction industry, time is money. In some communities, the contractor could be facing legal penalties that may include a fine and/or time in jail. Now I don't expect a contractor to go to jail for starting work without a building permit even in those communities with an ordinance that talks about jail. That's just not what typically happens. Judges are usually reluctant to send someone to jail who's just trying to earn a living. Judges are not, however, reluctant to fine them.

Usually, a homeowner has to get a permit even for do-it-yourself work if the value of the project is above a certain dollar amount, or if the work is of a specific kind (like electrical work). The dollar limit varies by area, so check your local code. A permit is usually needed even if the project just includes interior work, if it meets that dollar limit.

Do You Need Plans and Specs Prepared by an Engineer or Architect?

That depends on the licensing laws in your state, and on what your building official feels is needed to adequately review the project. As a general rule, *unless the state laws require an engineer or a licensed designer,* the plans can be prepared by anybody. However, under most building codes, the building official has the authority to insist that your plans and specs be reviewed by an engineer or architect, even if the state law doesn't require it.

Do You Need a Permit to Demolish a Building?

Yes, you do. Even if you're required by the local authorities to tear the building down because it's unsafe, you still must get a demolition permit first.

Inspections

Regular inspections are usually required during the building process. Those inspections can include a foundation inspection, a concrete or underfloor inspection, a frame inspection, a gypsum board inspection, and others. The kinds of inspections and the number of inspections that are required depend on what's in the plan.

Although the building inspector has a lot of power in the inspection process, violating the building code isn't a crime, and a building inspector isn't a police officer. That's both good and bad. Inspectors can't arrest you, but they can do things a police officer can't — like enter a building if they have reasonable grounds to believe that an unsafe condition exists inside the building, or that the building code is being violated. Of course, there are a few things inspectors are obligated to do before entering the building. They must present credentials and request entry if the building is occupied, or contact the holder of the building permit if it's not occupied. They must always make a reasonable effort to obtain formal permission before entering.

The Final Inspection

The last inspection is made when the work is done. The report of the completed inspection is called an occupancy permit. It certifies the building or the remodeling as ready for use. The project can't lawfully be used until that time without some sort of special permission. For example, the builder may want to display the house he has built as part of a home show. In most communities, he couldn't do that if the building hasn't had a final inspection unless he gets a home show permit, which gives him a limited right to allow the public into the building.

Who's Responsible if the Building Doesn't Meet the Code?

The builder, as part of his implied warranties, guarantees the fitness of purpose of the building to the property owner. *Fitness of purpose* means the property owner can use the building in the way he had expected to use it. If the property doesn't pass its final inspection and the owner can't get an occupancy permit, the builder hasn't met his warranty of fitness of purpose. That builder could be liable to the property owner for whatever it costs to do the work needed to qualify the project for an occupancy permit. After all, the property owner didn't bargain for a building he couldn't use.

If the problem with meeting the code is because the builder or his subcontractors haven't done their job correctly, then it's up to the builder to get the problem fixed or pay for having it fixed. However, if the problem is in the plans that were supplied to the builder, that could be a different situation.

If there's an architect involved, or if the builder is using owner-supplied plans, and the failure to get a building permit is because of a flaw in the plans, that may give the builder a defense to a charge that he has violated his warranty of fitness of purpose. That's because those plans came with their own warranty. The builder has a right to rely on the plans, because there's an implied warranty that those plans are fit for their purpose.

For example, suppose when Cal the carpenter looks at the stair plans for the new addition he thinks that those stairs probably won't conform to the new BOCA standards. He mentions that to the architect, who says, "I'm the architect, not you. Just shut up and build them." To protect himself, Cal should probably write a note to the architect with a copy to the property owner. At that point, Cal has discharged his duty to warn. It's not his problem if the architect won't listen. Anyway, who knows? Maybe the architect's right.

But suppose there's no architect involved, just a homeowner who's using plans he bought from a magazine. In that kind of situation, Cal probably can't satisfy his duty by simply warning the homeowner with "Hey, I don't think these stairs will meet code." If the homeowner won't listen to him, Cal needs to make a big issue out of his fears. *Cal* is the expert, not the homeowner. In fact, unless the homeowner has some special expertise or is relying on the advice of some other professional in the construction field, Cal should find out for sure if those stairs meet code. If they don't, Cal should be reluctant to build them. Usually it won't go that far, because a few words from the building inspector can make a believer out of the homeowner.

COPYRIGHTED BUILDING PLANS

Federal copyright laws cover building plans and constructed buildings. In 1990 the laws were tightened up to guarantee the person who designed a plan the right to be paid for the use of that plan. Now, a plan is protected by copyright even if it's not stamped with a copyright insignia. A sample copyright notice is show in Figure 8-1.

When a builder or a remodeler uses someone else's plans, they can only do so with permission from the copyright's owner. That kind of permission is called a "license" to use the plan.

▌ If you use a copyrighted plan without the permission of the copyright's owner, you may be sued.

▌ If you use blueprints created since 1990 with no copyright mark on them, but with no permission from the copyright owner to use those plans, you may be sued.

▌ If you use a plan from a plan book or magazine dated after 1990 without permission from the owner of the copyright, you may be sued.

▌ If your customer brings you a copy of a plan — even one the customer ripped out of a magazine or from a book that the customer bought — and you use it without permission from the copyright owner, you and your customer may be sued.

▌ If you use somebody else's plan as a starting place, but make significant changes to it without permission from the copyright owner to make those changes, you may be sued.

▌ If you have permission from the copyright's owner to build one building, and you build two buildings from the same plan, you may be sued.

So how does a copyright owner give permission that's good enough to protect someone who uses the plans from being sued for copyright infringement? The copyright owner can sign an agreement granting permission for a one-time use of the plans (see Figure 8-2), or they can contract to sell the right to use their copyrighted material using an agreement like the one shown in Figure 8-3. There are blank copies of these forms on the disk in the back of the book. You can obtain U.S. Copyright forms online at www.loc.gov/copyright/ or by contacting the Library of Congress at 202-707-9100.

The Zoning Laws

The idea behind zoning is that a house next to a factory won't be worth as much as the identical house that's *not* next to a factory. So zoning laws typically group uses and put them together: all the stores in a commercial area, all the industries in an industrial area, all the rural activities in an agricultural zone, and all the houses in residential areas. The power to zone is based in the health and welfare clause of the constitution, which has allowed zoning to be expanded into all sorts of building and site regulations, such as building height or materials.

COPYRIGHT NOTICE

Figure 8-1 *Sample Copyright Notice*

What Do Zoning Laws Include?

Zoning is a catchall term for the laws that regulate what land uses are allowed in a certain region. Zoning laws can also regulate such things as:

▌ How buildings have to be placed on the site.

▌ What kind of building material can be used.

▌ How buildings can be decorated.

▌ How much parking must be available for that building.

▌ What size sign can identify the building.

▌ How much green space must be preserved on the site.

Not every community has the same zoning laws, because zoning is always a matter of local regulation. Some communities choose not to have a zoning system at all.

In communities that do have zoning laws, there's lots of variation. It depends on each community's local needs and, of course, on local politics. Some communities have minimal zoning ordinances that may only have commercial, residential and agricultural zones, or perhaps not even that. Other communities may have zoning ordinances that tell the property owner how tall their building can be, how many windows it will have, whether it will be built of brick or wood, and what the landscaping will look like.

To get an idea of the impact and power of zoning, think about this example: Suppose Harry the homeowner decides that he wants his home to be built right on the very front property line of his lot, because then he'd have a very nice-sized back yard. "Why," he thinks, "waste all that land on a front yard when I really only intend to use the back?"

AGREEMENT FOR A ONE-TIME USE OF COPYRIGHTED ARCHITECTURAL PLANS

(Architectural plans are automatically copyrighted as soon as they are completed, but putting a copyright notice on the plan, which you can do even if the plans have not been registered with the copyright office, means no one can claim that they believed the plans were in the public domain. It's an easy way to establish ownership. It's also useful to register copyright plans, because registering the copyright means that the copyright owner does not have to prove that the copyright infringement cost him or her actual cash damages. For copyright applications, call the U.S. Copyright Office at 202-707-9100.)

On 8-21-2001 *(date),* Build And Design, Inc. *(Insert copyright owner's name.)* of 22 West Street, Lansing, MI *(Insert copyright owner's address.)* hereby agrees with John and Nancy Jones *(Insert licensee's name. Licensee means the person — builder or property owner — who is going to use the plans.)* of 18 South Street, Lansing, MI *(Insert licensee's address.)* as follows:

This agreement is to allow the licensee to build one building using building plans owned by Build And Design, Inc. *(Insert copyright owner's name.)* and dated 12-1-00 and identified hereafter as The Plans.

All other rights are reserved by Build And Design, Inc. *(Insert the copyright owner's name.)* The Plans may not be copied, reproduced in any form, modified or reused except by explicit permission or in connection with the actual construction of the building referred to in this agreement. Every reproduction for use during the construction process shall be clearly marked as copyrighted by Build And Design, Inc. *(Insert the copyright owner's name.)*

Build And Design, Inc. *(Insert copyright owner's name.)* shall be paid $5000.00 dollars by John and Nancy Jones *(Insert the licensee's name.)* for the use of The Plans immediately upon execution of this document.

Build And Design, Inc. *(Insert copyright owner's name.)* warrants The Plans are its original creation, and that it is the sole owner of all of the rights in the plans that are conferred by the copyright.

This agreement expresses the entire understanding of the parties relating to the use of the copyright, and both parties hereby expressly waive any other or further representations or warranties.

Both parties further agree that if either party files an action in relation to this agreement, or to the right to use The Plans; the unsuccessful party shall pay to the other party, in addition to all other sums that he may be required to pay, a reasonable sum for the successful party's attorney fees.

Signed *Don Design* for Build And Design, Inc. 22 West Street, Lansing, MI
     (Copyright holder)   *(Company)*   *(Address)*

Signed *Bill Bigger* for Bigger Builders, Inc. 44 Commercial Drive, Lansing, MI
     (Licensee)   *(Company)*   *(Address)*

Figure 8-2 *Sample of agreement for one-time use of copyrighted plans*

AGREEMENT TO SELL THE ENTIRE COPYRIGHT

On <u>10-1-2001</u> *(date)*, <u>Build And Design, Inc.</u> *(Insert copyright owner's name.)* of <u>22 West Street, Lansing,MI</u> *(Insert copyright owner's address.)* hereby agrees with<u>Bigger Builders, Inc.</u> *(Insert the licensee's name. Licensee means the person - builder or property owner - who is going to use the plans.)* of <u>44 Commercial Drive, Lansing,MI</u> *(Insert the licensee's address.)* as follows:

This agreement transfers all rights in the building plans dated <u>8-21-2001</u> *(date)* and owned by <u>Build And Design, Inc.</u> *(Insert the copyright owner's name.)*, and attached hereto. These building plans described hereinafter as The Plans.

<u>Build And Design, Inc.</u> *(Insert copyright owner's name.)* warrants The Plans are his original creation, and that he is the sole owner of all of the rights in The Plans that are conferred by the copyright.

(Option 1: If the sale is for a specific amount of money, use the following language)

<u>Build And Design, Inc</u> *(Insert copyright owner's name.)* shall be paid $<u>25,000</u> dollars by <u>Bigger Builders, Inc.</u> *(Insert the licensee's name.)* for the use of these copyrighted plans immediately upon execution of this document.

(Option 2: If the sale involves a royalty fee, use this language)

<u>Build And Design, Inc.</u> *(Insert copyright owner's name.)* shall be paid a royalty fee of $<u>5000.00</u> dollars which shall be immediately due upon each use of The Plans.

This agreement expresses the entire understanding of the parties relating to the use of the copyright, and both parties hereby expressly waive any other or further representations or warranties.

Both parties further agree that if either party files an action in relation to this agreement, or to the right to use The Plans; the unsuccessful party shall pay to the other party, in addition to all other sums that he may be required to pay, a reasonable sum for the successful party's attorney fees.

Signed *Don Design* for <u>Build And Design, Inc.</u> <u>22 West Street, Lansing, MI</u>
(Copyright holder) *(Company)* *(Address)*
Signed *Bill Bigger* for <u>Bigger Builders, Inc.</u> <u>44 Commercial Drive, Lansing, MI</u>
(Licensee) *(Company)* *(Address)*

Figure 8-3 *Sample of agreement to sell entire copyright*

Very likely the local zoning laws won't let Harry dispense with his front lawn. Most suburban communities require houses to be "set back" so many feet from the front property line. That setback is for the purpose of creating a front lawn. There's no real public health or safety benefit to having front lawns, but the community has agreed that it's good for the economic well-being of the community if all the single homes have lawns. So the community has passed a zoning regulation intended to create front lawns.

Historically, those laws intended to create lawns only required that the buildings be so many feet from the front property line. They relied on an unexpressed expectation that, of course, the property owner would put grass in that space. In the sixties, when some people began to find alternatives to grass, there were a number of "grass lawsuits" between neighbors. That's when people discovered that the local laws generally did not prohibit a nice expanse of goldenrod in the front. Fortunately, this isn't the builder's problem.

Appealing Zoning Laws

Most communities have a procedure for asking for a waiver from zoning laws. That kind of waiver is called a *variance*. Someone asking for a variance from a zoning law is literally asking that the law not be applied to them. Some communities grant variances quite freely while others do so only rarely.

As a general rule, to get a variance, the applicant has to convince the Zoning Board of Appeals of two things: First, that his situation is unique, and second, that enforcing that zoning law would create a hardship for him. For example, a paraplegic in a wheelchair might have a problem with a side yard setback that left him without room to install a ramp up to a side entrance door. His situation is unique, because most other residents who are regulated by the side yard setback zoning law aren't in wheelchairs. He can also demonstrate a hardship because he can't get into his house without a ramp. The zoning laws create a hardship *on him* that's unique *to him.*

The zoning board could grant his variance, or it could decide that the paraplegic could use a ramp at the front entrance, so the side yard setback isn't that big a hardship.

As another example, suppose Harry decides to renovate an existing storefront for a deli. But because he intends to serve food on the premises, the zoning laws require Harry to provide 35 new parking spaces. Harry's problem is that his older building was built back when individual businesses didn't have to provide parking, because people parked on the street. Harry's older building covers the entire lot. There's no place on his lot to put any parking without tearing down part of the building.

Harry could argue to the Zoning Board of Appeals that the parking law created a unique hardship on him, because when that law was passed, it was aimed at new buildings that would have a place to put parking. Unlike these new buildings, Harry *doesn't* have a place to put new parking.

Of course, this argument wouldn't necessarily work. The Zoning Board could say that every commercial building has to provide parking because the community needs more parking in its commercial areas. If Harry can't provide that parking, then they'll wait for a business that can, or one that doesn't generate so much traffic. Or the Zoning Board could grant the variance because they feel the community needs to encourage people to renovate existing buildings.

Who Has to Comply with the Zoning Laws?

The real question we're asking here is who gets to fix the problems that are caused when a building doesn't conform to the zoning laws? If the question comes up before the building's built, it's a contract question. And the answer is that a contract to do something that doesn't conform to the law is unenforceable. So for the rest of the discussion, assume we're talking about a completed building that turns out to be in violation of the zoning laws.

When the building is up (or partially up), there are a variety of consequences to a zoning problem. It may be that someone will have to pay a filing fee and ask for a variance. Or the builder may have to spend money and time to fix the problem, by tearing off a wall and starting over, for example. Whether or not the builder can get reimbursed for this depends on who is responsible. If the zoning problem is something that can't be fixed, the responsible person may have to reimburse the owner for the diminished value of his building.

Is It the Owner's Responsibility?

Technically, it's the owner's responsibility to conform to the zoning laws. I think it's more accurate, however, to think of the responsibility as a rubber ball that can do a lot of bouncing before it comes to rest.

Why am I using the rubber ball analogy? The responsibility can "bounce" because most property owners, unless they're developers or builders themselves, are working with architects and builders who have much more expertise than they do. The people with that expertise had a duty to warn the property owner if they saw, or if they should have seen, that there was a problem with the plans.

Is It the Architect's Responsibility?

Some contracts between the property owner and the architect place all the responsibility for furnishing surveys and information about legal limitations directly on the property owner. Is this something that will protect the architect if he violates a zoning law? Probably not.

When the architect gives the plans to the property owner, he also gives the owner an implied warranty that those plans will be fit for their purpose. It's possible for the architect to draw up a contract that would effectively exclude all implied warranties of fitness of purpose, but that architect might have trouble persuading people to hire him. However, most of the plans that people buy from books and other such sources come with disclaimers of warranties, and these disclaimers are enforceable.

A lot depends on the circumstances and on the property owner. Is he simply a homeowner, or a developer with years of experience? The property owner's background is an issue because the architect has a duty to protect his client. Since the architect is the one with the training and experience, then very likely the architect will be liable for damage suffered by the property owner because of a violation of zoning law. That's especially true if the zoning law involved an architectural feature such as building height or parking lot requirements.

Is It the Builder's Responsibility?

Technically, it's not a builder's responsibility if the builder is working from plans that were supplied by the owner unless the contract places that responsibility directly on the builder. But, like the architect, the builder has a duty to warn. If the problem is one that the builder should have noticed, then the builder's failure to do that can be negligence in the eyes of the law, especially when the builder is the "expert" dealing with an inexpert homeowner. So the answer to that question may be yes. Sometimes it's the builder's responsibility.

Is Zoning Constitutional?

It's amazing how many people believe zoning restrictions are unconstitutional. "It's private property," they say. "I own it and I can do what I want to with it." That's usually wishful thinking by people who believe they could make more money if they *could* do anything they wanted.

However, that battle was lost decades ago. Yes, zoning laws are constitutional, even in those situations where they reduce the profit the property owner can make on that land. The constitution requires that the zoning allow the owner a *reasonable* use of the property, but it doesn't require that the zoning give the property owner the *most profitable* use of the property.

But while zoning itself is unquestionably constitutional, that doesn't mean every single zoning decision in the country is constitutional. When zoning is unconstitutional, it's not because the community can't zone. It's because the community didn't zone in a constitutional way.

Zoning That Leaves the Property Owner Unable to Use the Property

Zoning that makes it impossible for the property owner to find a reasonable use for his property is unconstitutional. Take this example: A small community in Michigan zoned a parcel of property next to a trailer park into a single-family luxury home residential category. The property owner argued that the luxury home zoning made it impossible to use the property at all. He wasn't allowed to build anything but luxury houses on the property — but he couldn't sell expensive luxury homes next to a 300-unit trailer park.

The court agreed that the effect of the zoning was to deny the property owner the use of his property, and ordered the community to rezone the property into something that he could use. That doesn't mean the community had to rezone the parcel as a trailer park, but it did have to be a zoning that the property owner could actually use.

Arbitrary and Capricious Zoning

Zoning that's arbitrary and capricious is always unconstitutional. *Arbitrary and capricious* means that there's no public benefit to the law, and it's so constructed that it impacts some people differently than others, but not in a consistent way. Got that? It's a difficult concept, because obviously zoning laws affect different people in different ways. For example, if you own commercially-zoned property, of course the zoning laws in your community won't have the same impact on you as on your brother-in-law, who owns residential property.

So let's take a closer look. The zoning laws are constitutional (not arbitrary and capricious) if it's just the location and use of the property that makes the difference in the way they impact you and your brother-in-law. But what if your brother-in-law's property is zoned the way it is because he belongs to some peculiar religious sect, and the local authorities want to keep him from building a church in their community? That's unconstitutional, because that zoning law is aimed at *him*, not his property.

Zoning isn't lawful when it's used to exclude people or to exclude certain activities. It's possible, for example, to restrict the location of bars by prohibiting them in residential areas, or near churches or schools. But the community can't use zoning to exclude them altogether. The zoning laws can limit where people do certain things, but if the activities are legal, they have to allow people the right to do them somewhere.

The Accessibility Laws

Making buildings accessible to the handicapped is probably the biggest legislatively-imposed change on the construction industry during the last decade. There are many problems associated with it that haven't been fully resolved. There are cases still moving through the courts.

Anyone building or remodeling has to consider the possible impact on the site of the Americans With Disabilities Act (ADA) and the Fair Housing Act. The ADA regulates making commercial buildings accessible to the handicapped, and also involves hiring issues which are discussed in Chapter 5. The Fair Housing Act regulates what modifications have to be made to the design of multiple-housing units to accommodate people with disabilities.

For example, suppose you construct a new building with a ramp and doors wide enough for wheelchairs, but the building entrance has an airlock (entry doors, then an unheated space, and then a second set of entry doors). Suppose that after it's built, a person in a wheelchair discovers that, while he can get his wheelchair past the first set of doors, he can't get any further because there isn't enough room in the airlock for him to swing open the second set of doors. If this building is a commercial building like a restaurant or a store, the building design is a violation of the ADA. If the building is a multiple dwelling building like an apartment building, the design is a violation of the Fair Housing Act.

Because this is a new building and isn't entitled to the benefit of any of the grandfathering provisions of the various acts, the person in the wheelchair who can't get into the building is entitled to sue to require that the building be redesigned and rebuilt to accommodate him. If he's successful, the defendant will also have to pay his legal fees. It would be, of course, far cheaper and faster to just tear out the doors and change them.

The question that comes up is who is supposed to pay for all this? The builder? The property owner? Someone else? Good question. The current state of the law doesn't offer a clear answer.

The Americans With Disabilities Act

The ADA only applies to buildings with commercial uses or to public accommodations such as a restaurant, a store or a hotel. All new commercial buildings must comply with the ADA standards for accessibility. There's also an impact on existing buildings, but only when those buildings are renovated or upgraded.

ADA Requirements for Existing Buildings

The ADA considers remodeling or building alterations as an opportunity to bring that building closer to compliance with the ADA standards. Of course, not every nail that's driven into a wall triggers the ADA. It takes a change in the building footprint or a change in the primary use to trigger the ADA requirements — but those requirements are significantly less severe than for new buildings. The ADA administration tries to restrict ADA-required modifications to a building that's already in use by a business to those things that are possible without excessive difficulty or expense. The goal of ADA is *not* to put existing enterprises out of business.

As a rough rule of thumb, the ADA enforcing agency limits their requirements to 20 percent of the total project cost. That doesn't mean that if bringing the building up to standard would cost more than an additional 20 percent, the builder can just forget about it. It means that it's possible to choose to do some of the more important work now and the less important work later when there's more remodeling.

To help builders and remodelers make a decision about what needs to be done now, and what they can put off, ADA supplies a priority list about what work is the most important:

▌ The first priority is building access from the sidewalk or parking lot. Makes sense, right? If the handicapped person can't get into the building, it makes no difference how accessible it is inside. If it's too expensive or too difficult to make the main entrance accessible, then it's okay to look around for an alternative entrance that could be made accessible to the handicapped.

▌ The second priority is ease of movement inside. For example, if the building is a restaurant, someone in a wheelchair needs to have enough space to maneuver around the tables and chairs.

▌ Bathroom facilities are also a high priority, for obvious reasons.

The Fair Housing Act

The Fair Housing Act sets accessibility standards for new multiple housing units such as apartment buildings, senior citizen homes, dormitories, or buildings that are converted to those uses.

What Problems Are Likely with Accessibility Laws?

Here's one of the most common problems: Just how far down does the responsibility for accessible design go? Both the Americans With Disabilities Act and the Fair Housing Act use language that appears to put the responsibility for "designing or constructing" in accordance with the acts on just about everybody in the process. These acts give disabled persons the right to sue the people who violated these laws. That right to sue apparently includes suing the property owner, the architect, the contractor — maybe even the subcontractors.

This has the potential to be a serious burden on contractors and subcontractors who, in reality, often have very little actual design control. At this time I can't give solid, complete answers to the question of who is financially responsible for a building that violates these accessibility laws because the issue is still being litigated. But until you know for sure that there's no way it could ever be your neck, you'd better assume that it could be.

There are a couple of ways you, as a builder, can protect yourself from this vagueness. Insurance companies will insure you against anything if you pay a large enough premium. You should also get an indemnification agreement from the property owner and/or the architect (although usually architects want you to promise to indemnify them!). An indemnification agreement is a promise by someone, such as the property owner, to reimburse you for money you have to pay out in legal fees or judgments because of legal difficulties you get into on their project. Drawing up indemnification agreements can be tricky, so I'd suggest bringing your attorney into the process.

Are There Other Kinds of Permits You Must Get?

That depends on your community's local ordinances. Some communities require that the health department and the fire department certify certain kinds of uses as well as the building department. I'm familiar with one community where the fire chief is also the building inspector.

Some subdivisions have local design review boards and covenants and conditions in their plats that must be followed. While the local community government may not enforce these subdivision rules, the other landowners in that subdivision can go to court and enforce them.

There may also be environmental permits such as wetland permits, drainage permits, and watershed certifications. Depending on the project, there will be Department of Health requirements such as soil tests that will be needed before work can start.

So now you've checked all the regulations, got all your permits and you're ready to begin construction. But there's one more issue you've got to consider: job site safety. We'll look at that in the next chapter.

9

How Is Safety Regulated on the Job Site?

When you think about safety regulations that affect the job site, don't forget that they come from several sources: local, state and federal. However, the OSHA rules and regulations have the biggest impact on construction sites. OSHA covers an estimated six million companies in the United States. Because it's federal law, there are some small companies that slip under the jurisdictional net, but that doesn't mean those OHSA regulations won't affect those employers in some indirect way. OSHA regulations can affect the smaller company's insurance rates, and set the standard for just what is careful enough to not be liable to third parties such as injured owners, deliverymen or even trespassers.

Some smaller employers are picked up when their state adopts OSHA rules. Here in Michigan, for example, instead of OSHA, we have Miosha, because Michigan has taken over the OSHA functions and enforcement, and in some instances, has set higher standards. No state can lower OSHA safety standards, but it can set higher standards.

In a lawsuit involving someone who's injured on the job site, a court will typically use the OSHA job site safety rules to decide if the employer had a safe job site. That can be true even if the injured person isn't actually an employee, or if the company is too small to be regulated by OSHA. Although there's never a guarantee in a negligence trial, as a rule of thumb an employer who followed the OSHA regulations isn't negligent. If there *were* OSHA violations on your site, even if they had nothing to do with the accident and your company isn't covered by OSHA, your time in the defendant's chair is going to be a lot less than pleasant.

OSHA Job Site Safety Requirements

OHSA's Statement of Purpose is quite clear. OSHA requires that employers provide a place of employment that's "free of recognized hazards" that may cause death or serious physical harm. OSHA also requires both employers and employees to follow the OSHA rules and standards for their industry.

Free of recognized hazards does not mean you have to provide a place where there's no possibility of anyone ever getting hurt. What it does mean is that you must make your place of business as safe as it's reasonably possible to make it.

Employers' Obligations Under OSHA

The basic rule is that employers must provide a safe place to work. There are two ways that OSHA requires employers to provide that safe place:

1. Employers must follow the OSHA rules that apply to their industry.
2. Employers must provide a place of employment that is "free of recognized hazards" that may cause death or serious physical harm.

Even if OSHA has no specific rule about a condition or situation in the workplace, OSHA requires your company to make sure that condition or situation is free of recognized hazards. If there are safety precautions available that would result in a safer job site, it's a violation of the OSHA laws not to use them — *even if there's no specific OSHA rule about using that particular safety precaution.*

What If the Work Is Inherently Unsafe?

There are certain kinds of work, such as demolition work, that won't be safe, no matter what. That doesn't mean those jobs have to disappear. But, it also doesn't mean that you can simply say: "Well, it's dangerous work and that's just the way it is." Your obligation as an employer is to do everything that would make that unsafe job as safe as it's reasonably possible to make it.

For example, digging trenches is one of the most dangerous jobs on a job site, but there are things you can do to make it not quite as dangerous, including:

▌ Shoring up the trench walls

▌ Training the crew on the safest way to do the work

▌ Having a rescue plan that's ready to go in the event of an accident

▌ Keeping the area at the top of the trench clear of objects that could slide in on top of workers

The OSHA regulations already require these things when digging trenches, but even if they didn't, you'd have to do them anyway. They're all well-known safety precautions that can make the job site safer. If there's anything that's known to make the job safer, you have an obligation to do it, whether OSHA has a specific regulation about it or not.

Keep Your Job Sites Safe

Don't underestimate the disruption and trauma a serious injury can cause to your whole project. The pain and medical problems of the injured worker are just the beginning.

You also have to cope with a disrupted job schedule as you try to replace the injured worker. And there's bound to be lost time as fellow workers stand around and watch the ambulance. The reality is that a serious injury shuts down the job site for a significant period.

There's also the real emotional toll that an injury takes on the other employees — and you, as the employer. Suddenly that job site seems like a dangerous place to work. Employees don't feel as safe there. Also, most employers suffer feelings of guilt and regret about injuries. They didn't go into business to hurt people.

Then there's all the regulatory attention a serious injury attracts. Once you're on their list, it's hard to get back off. It isn't just government agencies that will be giving you a hard time, either. Insurance companies hate injuries, and we all know that insurance companies have ways of getting even if you put them in the position of paying claims instead of collecting premiums.

You can avoid a tremendous amount of hassle simply by making your job site safer. It isn't hard. There are lots of easy things you can do to avoid injuries.

1. Train employees in safety techniques and in the manufacturers' recommendations for handling power tools and toxic substances. Show those techniques to your employees; don't assume that your employees already know them because they could pick up the instruction sheet, or read the safety poster. You might be surprised at how many either can't read or don't bother to.

2. Require employees to use personal protective equipment (PPE) like safety glasses, hard hats, steel-toed boots, dust filters, and safety harnesses. Some of these PPEs aren't comfortable or easy to use, but don't look the other way when the safety harnesses are left on the ground. Make it clear that the failure to use safety devices is grounds for termination. Require your subcontractors to follow safety procedures, too.

3. Pick up and dispose of job site debris. Nobody ever fell and injured themselves on the nail sticking up from the 2 x 4 that wasn't there. Dispose of toxic waste containers immediately.

Finally, remember this: There is no down side to keeping a job site safe.

Employers Must Train Their Employees in Safety Procedures

OSHA requires that employers train employees to do their job safely. Setting up a system that guarantees as safe a workplace as possible takes the cooperation and help of everybody on the job site. You have to train your employees to understand and follow both the OSHA rules and your safety rules as they apply to them. After all, your employees are more likely to work safely if they know how. They should also be trained to recognize and report safety hazards in the workplace.

Not having a safety-training program in place is, all by itself, a violation of the OSHA rules. But not every company has to have the same safety-training program, because not every company faces the same hazards. In construction, for example, a company that does only finish carpentry won't have the same safety problems — or safety programs — as a roofing company.

The safety training that's required by OSHA includes information on safety issues, appropriate safety procedures, the use of personal protective equipment (PPEs), safety meetings, and educational materials such as "how to" posters.

Employers Must Keep Safety Records

OSHA requires that all employers file a report within 48 hours if there's a workplace death or the hospitalization of five or more employees. There's some overlap here with the notice requirements of the workers' compensation laws. Just think how much paperwork you could avoid with a safe job site.

OSHA requires that an employer with more than 10 employees keep an ongoing record of all illnesses and injuries on the OSHA 200 log form. Employees have the right to look at the 200 log forms.

Keeping the OSHA 200 Log

1. The log must show all employee deaths — that's every single death — no matter what the cause. It doesn't matter if the employee died at home of pneumonia. It might have been a pneumonia that resulted from an exposure to toxic material.

2. The log must show one or more lost workdays. About the only thing that doesn't have to be recorded here are vacation days and instances of getting to work late.

3. The log must record every loss of consciousness. Many head injuries aren't readily apparent at the time of the injury.

4. The log must show every instance where an employee is transferred to another job. Since employees have the right to refuse a task that's unnecessarily dangerous, this is one way of tracking those situations.

5. The log must show every time an employee has received medical treatment for a job-related injury.

Employees' Rights Under OSHA

OSHA guarantees certain rights to employees. These guarantees are necessary because using safety equipment and following the rules increases overhead costs and slows the work down. There are some employers who would cut corners on their employees' safety to improve that bottom line without these guarantees. The theory is that those employers are more likely to follow the OSHA rules if they know their employees can enforce those safety rules. It sometimes takes actual employee action before some of those employers will follow the rules.

The Right to OSHA Information

Employees have the right to have copies of:

▌ The OSHA standards and regulations for their industry

▌ OSHA-required safety programs, such as their employer's emergency response program

▌ The OSHA 200 log

▌ The results of employer-paid medical examinations and tests

As an employer, you can't just wait for your employees to ask for this information. You're required to let them know that information exists and that it's available to them. Displaying required safety posters is a simple way of informing the employees of their rights.

The Right to Know About Hazardous Materials

Employees have the right to know about chemical and other hazardous substances used in their workplace. They have the right to the results of monitoring and test programs of chemicals used in their industry. When an employer is using hazardous materials, the employer must, in addition to the usual safety posters, also put up posters with specific instructions about handling and about emergency responses for that hazardous material.

The idea is that if employees are taking certain risks by working in a particular environment, they are, at a minimum, entitled to *know* they're taking those risks. Besides, if they don't know about the hazardous materials, they won't know to take the necessary safety precautions. They're also entitled to know if everything possible to reduce the risk to them is being done. If they don't know about the hazardous materials risk, they won't know to look for the information about the employer's risk reduction.

The Right to Access Certain Records

Employees have the right to review the OSHA 200 log, the results of OSHA inspections, and they have the right to information about their employer's violations of OSHA regulations.

Employees are also entitled to copies of any health or medical examination that they take. That includes the ones that their employer requested — even the ones the employer paid for. Although the employer technically owns those records, the employee is entitled to know the results.

The Right to Complain About Safety Violations

Employees have a protected right to report violations to OSHA. OSHA also allows any employee to participate in company or union safety and health committees. Any employee can request an OSHA investigation of possible safety or health rule violations, and they have the right to accompany and consult with OSHA inspectors. They can also ask for training or information on avoiding potential hazards.

Retaliating against an employee for doing these things is a violation of federal law. If you fire an employee for these reasons, they can bring a wrongful discharge lawsuit against you, and file an OSHA complaint about the firing. Several states also offer relief to employees who are fired for exercising their lawful rights to complain.

The Right to Refuse to Be Exposed to Hazards

If an employee's objection is that the job itself is so dangerous he simply doesn't want to do it, his solution is to find another job. An employee can't refuse an assignment simply because there's a chance of injury — not when it's part of the job. For example, consider trenching, easily the most dangerous activity on a construction site. If the employee simply refuses to get into a trench and dig because it's too dangerous, then he should look for other work.

However, that employee could refuse if that trench is more dangerous than it needs to be. Suppose the supporting structure installed to keep the trench walls from collapsing was not properly maintained. That's an unnecessary risk an employee can't be required to take, and he can't be lawfully discharged for refusing to take that risk. That's true even in a construction company that's so small it's not covered by OSHA. That discharged employee would still have a potential lawsuit against his employer for an unlawful discharge.

Here's another example of an extra risk that would *not* be an inherent part of the job. Suppose the employer simply assigned an employee to rip out asbestos without any training in handling or any personal protective equipment. Both the lack of adequate training and the lack of protective equipment are risks that could be reduced. Because those risks could be reduced, employees don't have to face them. Those are risks that should not be part of the job.

Any employee has the right to notify OSHA within 30 days if they've refused to expose themselves to a hazard and believe they're being punished for those actions.

Employees' Obligations Under OSHA

The OSHA rules may sound like employers have all the obligations and employees have all the rights, but employees have some obligations as well. They must follow OSHA and company safety and health polices, which includes using the assigned personal protective equipment. They must participate in safety training. They must report hazardous conditions to their supervisor, as well as report any job-related injuries or health problems. And the employees must get medical attention and follow through on their medical treatment.

I've never actually seen a lawsuit involving an employee who, when the employer sent him to a clinic, didn't bother to go, perhaps because he preferred to go to his own doctor, or perhaps he didn't believe in medical treatment. However, I'm confident that, while an employer can't fire an employee for being injured on the job, an employer could terminate an employee who fails to get recommended medical treatment for a work-related injury.

The employees must also cooperate with OSHA inspectors. If they don't follow the company safety rules and policies, the employer can discharge them for violating their employee obligations.

For example, some roofers don't like using safety harnesses, because the harnesses are awkward, take a long time to set up, and slow the work down. As the employer, you don't have much choice about how to respond to this. If you don't enforce the safety harness requirement as part of your safety program, you're violating the law. An employee who doesn't use the harness should be warned in writing. Any employee who continues to refuse to use the protective equipment should be discharged. They're not only exposing themselves to harm, they're exposing their employer to serious legal problems.

OSHA Inspections

How does OSHA select companies for inspection? Because of the huge volume of cases it has to deal with, OSHA uses a priority system to decide where to hold inspections. A work-related death bumps a company to the top of the list. Of course, a death doesn't mean an automatic finding of an OSHA violation, because some jobs are just plain dangerous. But it's serious evidence that there *may be* a violation.

Then OSHA puts the next priority on those situations in high-risk industries where there's reason to suspect the existence of a hazard that places the employees at risk of immediate death or serious harm if not promptly corrected.

Finally, OSHA goes to those places where there are employee complaints about unhealthy conditions or rule violations. Sometimes these complaints really reflect labor disputes, but the OSHA rules protect employees who make complaints, whether those complaints are justified or not. As annoying as it is when employees make a complaint just to harass their employer, there must be absolute protection for whistle-blowers, whether they're right or wrong. If they weren't absolutely protected, no one would have the nerve to blow that whistle.

OSHA also puts priority on certain specific high-hazard industries (like the construction industry) and on occupations that involve hazardous substances.

What Happens in an OSHA Inspection?

An OSHA inspector, after arriving on the job site, contacts the highest-ranking person on the site. Then the inspector makes a company tour. The inspector may review records, take notes, take measurements, and do whatever else is necessary to fully investigate the problem. The employer or a representative is entitled to accompany the inspector. So is any employee or union representative. However, the inspector may speak privately with employees about job conditions.

If there's a citation issued, it must be posted for employees to see. Employers or employees may appeal the citations (or the lack of them) all the way to the U.S. Court of Appeals.

The purpose of all these safety rules is to protect employees from injury. But all the rules in the world can only *reduce*, not eliminate, injuries on the job site. In the next chapter we'll cover what to do if an injury does occur.

10

What If Someone Is Injured on the Job Site?

Construction is a high-risk activity that accounts for 7 percent of the economic activity in this country, and 18 percent of the industrial injuries. All sorts of people can get hurt on a construction job site: the employees, property owners, subcontractors, visitors — even trespassers.

When Your Employee Is Injured

Employers are required to compensate employees who are injured on the job for their medical costs and some of their lost wages. It doesn't matter whose fault the accident was. It doesn't even matter if the worker caused his own injury. Workers' compensation covers every on-the-job injury.

You could discover you had Larry, Moe and Curly working on your job site. Doesn't matter. If they hurt each other on the job site, even if it's their own fault, their stupidity isn't a defense to your workers' compensation obligations. If they get into a brawl over a personal argument and one of them is injured — if that brawl takes place on the job site on company time — you'll still have to pay them workers' comp.

Workers' compensation insurance is available to help employers with these obligations. In fact, carrying workers' compensation insurance is mandatory for many employers, although different states have different triggers for when an employer must carry insurance. In some states, it depends on how long the employer has had an employee. Other states do it by the number of employees. Some states allow self-insurance pools.

What's important to remember is that the obligation to help injured workers is always mandatory. It's only the obligation to carry insurance that's sometimes not mandatory.

The Exclusive Remedy Doctrine

Because injured workers are automatically entitled to benefits when they're injured, they're not entitled to sue their employers for anything other than workers' compensation benefits.

For example, suppose Moe is hurt on the job site because Curly, the site superintendent, made dumb decisions. Moe might think he's got a great lawsuit for negligence against the dummies who hired and promoted Curly. No, Moe doesn't. He doesn't even have a negligence lawsuit against Curly himself.

Moe automatically gets his workers' compensation benefits regardless of whose fault the accident was, but that's all he gets: part of his lost wages and help with his medical bills. Workers' compensation laws don't include damages for pain and suffering or those punitive damages that can run negligence lawsuit awards up into the stratosphere.

This is good news for the employers, and actually good for the employees, too. How can this limitation be of benefit to the employees? Prior to workers' compensation laws, injured employees had to sue for, and prove, negligence to get compensation. But lots of accidents just happen without any negligence being involved. That's why they're called *accidents*! Before workers' comp, if there wasn't any negligence, the injured employee wasn't entitled to any assistance at all.

The workers' compensation laws are good for employers because sometimes accidents are caused by negligence. In those cases, the injured employee could recover potentially huge amounts of money. Unlike workers' compensation claims, negligence damages aren't limited to lost wages and medical costs.

The Gross Negligence Exception

The workers' compensation laws were designed to protect all employees, but, at the same time, they limited the amount an injured employee could recover to less than the injured employee might win if he could prove negligence. However, like a lot of other laws, the workers' compensation laws have had some erosion over time. Various court decisions have carved out some limited exceptions.

If the injury was caused by gross negligence, the courts will often allow the injured employee to sue for negligence and collect negligence damages, which will usually amount to more than the regular workers' compensation damages. So what's considered gross negligence? Here's how most courts would define it:

▮ The employer knowingly and deliberately puts an employee into a dangerous situation.

▮ The employer knowingly and deliberately didn't take available safety precautions to keep that employee from being injured.

Unfortunately, there's no one single answer to the question of exactly what behavior amounts to gross negligence. But it usually involves situations where the employer knew of a serious risk, and specifically decided not to take steps to control that risk.

Suppose, for example, that Better Builders ordered its trenching crew to forget the bracing, because "There isn't time for that stuff."

Trenching is one of the most dangerous activities on a construction site. If that trench collapses because Better Builders wouldn't take the time to reinforce the trench walls, that action would make trenching even more dangerous than it usually is. In that case, Better Builders would be facing a gross negligence lawsuit.

Reporting Requirements When an Employee Is Injured

When an employee is injured, of course there are some reporting requirements. The injuries have to be reported to your workers' compensation insurer. In some states, the contractor has to keep an in-house record of all accidents. Most states require a supervisor, or the person who's named in the employee handbook, to accept accident reports and keep a record of them.

All deaths at the workplace and all hospitalization of five or more employees must be reported to OSHA (or the state agency, like Miosha in Michigan, that regulates job site safety) within 48 hours.

OSHA also requires employers with more than 10 employees to keep an ongoing record of all illnesses and injuries on the OSHA 200 log form. That log must show every time an employee misses one or more workdays. The log must also record every loss of consciousness. See Chapter 9 for more details.

What Is the Role of the Workers' Compensation Insurance Company?

An insured employer must keep a record of all injuries. I know of no insurance company in the construction field that doesn't require this. The insurance company may also require injured employees to use certain hospitals, doctors or clinics. Once an injured worker makes a claim, the insurance company handles everything. The insurance company's lawyers deal with any questions about whether the injury actually occurred on the job or somewhere else, whether the employee is only injured or actually disabled, and whether or not the injured worker is an employee or a subcontractor. The insurance company's lawyers will decide whether to litigate or settle the claim.

The insured employer's role, once the claim has been made, is to cooperate with the insurance company's lawyers.

When a Subcontractor or Subcontractor's Employee Is Injured

The general rule is that a contractor is not responsible for injuries to subcontractors or to the employees of subcontractors unless the contractor was negligent. However, the reality is that even when the contractor was not negligent, the courts don't like to see workers who were injured on the job site left without any help. Also, being part of the real world, most judges know that some workers are called subcontractors simply because the contractor doesn't want to pay compensation when those workers are injured. So some very significant exceptions to the general rule have been carved out.

For example, suppose Ralph the roofer works for Valley Roofs, a subcontractor for Better Builders. If Ralph is hurt on the job, and Valley Roofs turns out to not carry any workers' compensation insurance, guess what Ralph is going to do? He'll be looking around to see if there's somebody more collectible that he could get some compensation from — somebody like Better Builders or the property owner.

The Injured Worker May Be Reclassified as an Employee

Ralph could argue that Valley Roofs isn't a subcontractor at all, but is really just part of Better Builders' crew. That would make Ralph one of Better Builders' employees. Ralph could then make a claim for workers' compensation against Better Builders' insurance company. There are several criteria that define the difference between employee and subcontractor, and they're discussed in Chapter Five.

General Contractor and Property Owner Must Provide a Safe Place to Work

Instead of claiming for worker's compensation, Ralph — as the employee of a sub — might be able to sue the property owner or the contractor for negligence because they have a duty to provide everyone on the job site, including subcontractors and their employees, with a safe place to work. If Better Builders hasn't maintained a safe place to work, they could be liable for negligence.

For example, let's say that in order to save a few bucks, the contractor didn't clean up a toxic spill, and a subcontractor fell ill because of exposure to that spill. In that situation, the contractor had a duty not to leave that toxic spill in place. The contractor violated that duty, and because of that violation of duty, someone who was not the contractor's employee was hurt. That someone could sue the contractor for negligence.

What Does Reasonable Care Mean?

A contractor has a duty to exercise reasonable care to avoid injury to visitors on the job site. So what should you do, as a contractor, to be considered reasonably careful?

▮ Don't let visitors, including the property owner, wander about the job site alone. Post a sign at the entrance telling them where to go to check in with the site superintendent.

▮ Keep hard hats on hand and make sure every visitor to the job site, including the property owner, wears one. Post a big sign reminding people about hard hats and telling them where to get one.

▮ Clearly indicate hazardous spots with signs and/or yellow caution tape.

▮ Put tools away promptly and lock them up at the end of the day. Debris, especially material with nails and protruding points, should be cleaned up regularly. Empty used containers and store them so they can't collect rainwater.

▮ Protect all walkways and elevated areas with scaffolding and safety barriers.

There's no such thing as a guarantee against possible liability, but with these procedures in place, you can get close.

Contractor's Duty to Require Subcontractors to Be Insured

There's another way contractors have sometimes been held liable for negligence. Some cases have ruled that contractors are negligent if they don't check to see if their subcontractors carry liability insurance. Those cases say that contractors have a duty to check for insurance certificates. The kind of insurance that would help a contractor who's found guilty of negligence is liability insurance, *not* his workers' compensation insurance.

When a Property Owner or Visitor Is Injured

The property owner or visitors to the job site can sue a contractor for negligence if they're hurt because of the contractor's negligence or, in some situations, the negligence of the contractor's employees. The term "visitor" includes the property owner, the property owner's guests and family, deliverymen, inspectors — even, in some instances, trespassers.

Although as a rule, the subcontractor, not the contractor, is liable for the subcontractor's negligence, the contractor does have a duty to supervise and a duty to keep the job site safe. So sometimes the contractor will be liable for the sub's negligence. The law says that a general contractor has a duty to take reasonable care to avoid foreseeable accidents. It also says "Reasonable care is the care that a reasonably prudent man in that position would have taken to avoid foreseeable accidents." (In this context, that means a reasonably prudent contractor.)

Foreseeable doesn't mean that you only have a duty to avoid accidents that you actually expect to happen. It means you must avoid those accidents that you *would have foreseen* if you had sat down and thought about it, or had spent some time studying safety issues.

For example, suppose you left a large open container with water and other debris in it overnight on a job site that was an occupied house. You know the customer has small children, the neighbors have small children, and the property isn't fenced.

The fact that you didn't actually foresee that a small child would get into the container and then, because of the slippery debris at the bottom, fall into the water and drown, doesn't mean that you weren't negligent. You were negligent, because if you'd thought about the situation in terms of safety, you would have washed out the container and then upended it. What could your negligence cost you? Millions!

When a Subcontractor Negligently Causes an Injury

As a general rule, a contractor or a property owner isn't responsible for the wrongdoing of an independent contractor, like a subcontractor, or for the wrongdoing of that subcontractor's employees. The subcontractor is liable for his own wrongdoing; the people who contract with him are not.

The subcontractor is liable if he through negligence causes an injury to someone. That someone could be the property owner, guests of the property owner, passersby, deliverymen, inspectors — really anybody except the subcontractor's own employees who can only sue him for workers' compensation. In theory, if the contractor wasn't negligent, he doesn't have to worry.

However, I'm sure you won't be surprised to hear that there are some exceptions to this. There have been some successful lawsuits against contractors for the negligence of their subcontractors. Most of those successful lawsuits are based on situations where the contractor brought in Larry, Moe and Curly as subcontractors. The idea is that if you bring a subcontractor onto the job site that you know is incompetent and likely to cause an injury — that's negligence.

There's another exception too. It's called the *peculiar risk* doctrine.

The Peculiar Risk Doctrine

The peculiar risk doctrine says that when a contractor brings in a subcontractor to perform risky activities (that is, activities that have more than the ordinary risk that all construction activities have, such as trenching or roofing on steep slopes), the contractor has a *special duty* to provide a safe place to work. That special duty — beyond his ordinary duty — means that the contractor has to take reasonable steps to ensure these tasks can be performed as safely as it's possible to perform them. So, depending on the facts in one of these extra-risky situations, if a subcontractor negligently injured a passerby, the contractor or property owner might also be sued for negligence, in addition to the subcontractor.

If a Trespasser Is Injured

It drives contractors crazy to think that they could be liable if a trespasser on the job site is injured. Maybe remembering that some of those trespassers could be children or lost hikers would make it less aggravating. Children seem to be drawn to places they're not supposed to be. You might be held responsible if the place they're drawn to is your job site, and they're injured there because you left conditions on your job site that were dangerous.

However, in spite of the problem that trespassers may cause you, there's a limit to what you can do about it. If you take action against trespassers (beyond a No Trespassing sign or a fence), that action has to be consistent with the danger the trespasser actually represents to you or your job site. If you (or your crew) aren't in physical danger from the trespasser, you can't use physical force against the trespasser. The most physical force you could use would be to restrain that person from damaging your property. When there's a problem with trespassers, call the police. Don't take the matter into your own hands.

If the Contractor Is Sued for Negligence

When someone is injured (or claims to be injured), both the property owner and the contractor should seek legal help. Remember that terms like reasonable and foreseeable are open to interpretation, and the outcome of lawsuits, especially a lawsuit argued before a jury, can be very unpredictable.

A liability policy is designed for these situations. Notify your insurance company immediately. Their attorneys will represent you. In fact, if you read the insurance policy carefully, you'll probably find that it gives the insurance company the absolute right to represent you. You can't refuse

Children on the Job Site

Children are a particular problem on a construction site. As soon as the job site is shut down for the night, every kid in the neighborhood is climbing all over it, especially the homeowner's kids. The contractor has to expect that and prepare for it.

No one wants to see a child hurt. There's an emotional cost to everyone when a child is injured on the job site, and—I'm not being cynical here, just realistic—the potential of millions of dollars worth of liability. An injured child could require medical and other care for the rest of his or her life. Think about how much that could cost you, if you're responsible for the accident.

So *keep the job site clean*. Pick up the debris at the end of the day. You don't want kids tripping over a board and falling on a nail that's sticking straight up.

Dispose of containers that held hazardous material that's caustic or toxic. If there's some liquid material left in the containers or if those containers fill with rain, children could put their hands into them or drink from them. Every poison control center will tell you that there's absolutely nothing that's so nasty that some kid won't drink it.

Be careful with containers that a child could pry open, especially containers with hazardous materials in them.

Keep tools locked away.

Be extremely careful about small spaces and excavations. Children love to get inside things. As an adult, it's easy to forget what a tiny space a small child can fit into. Remember there have been cases of toddlers drowning in the rainwater that collects at the bottom of those five-gallon pails that you find all over a job site. Cover all trenches and holes. Lock up dumpsters, portable toilets, lockboxes and tool cribs. And upend those five-gallon buckets.

their help. Nor can you, in most instances, refuse if the insurance company lawyer decides to settle the case. No one wants to see their insurance company pay out on what you know perfectly well is a bogus claim, but you have no say. It's the insurance company's money. They'll make the decisions about how to use it.

Let me give you some advice here. There's a lot of fear in this country about negligence lawsuits. People lie awake nights worrying about being sued for millions of dollars and forced into bankruptcy. But, honestly, the truth is that it doesn't really happen very often. In the construction industry, your legal problems — if you have them — are much more likely to involve unsatisfied clients, workers' compensation claims, or suppliers who deliver unsatisfactory materials and then try to stick you with the consequences. And, unlike some of those problems, you can get inexpensive liability insurance coverage for negligence. So that's what you should do: make your job site safe, buy your insurance, and quit worrying about it.

What If You Use Subcontractors Instead of Employees?

Construction companies use subcontractors to provide skills that the company needs sometimes, but not often enough to justify keeping those workers on the payroll.

Using subcontractors offers a number of advantages. A general contractor doesn't have to withhold income tax or contribute to FICA earnings for a worker on the job site who's a subcontractor instead of an employee. The general contractor isn't responsible for job site injuries to subcontractors or the employees of subcontractors, either. Using subcontractors is so advantageous that there are many major construction companies with only four or five regular employees.

What Is a Subcontract?

A subcontract is structured like this: an independent businessman (that's the subcontractor) agrees with the general contractor to do work that the general contractor has already agreed to do for the property owner.

Let's assume Sam is a plumber with his own business. Better Builders is a general contractor that has contracted with Paul the property owner to build a structure on Paul's property. Better Builders has already promised Paul that Better Builders will provide a building with plumbing in it, but Better Builders doesn't have a plumber on the payroll. So, Better Builders contracts with Sam to do the plumbing. If, for some reason, Sam doesn't do the plumbing or doesn't do a good job, Paul can sue Better Builders because that's who Paul's contract is with.

By agreeing to be a subcontractor for Better Builders, Sam the Plumber has actually entered two contractual relationships. The first is that he has a contractual relationship with Better Builders. Sam has promised to put plumbing into the building they're putting up. Better Builders has promised to pay Sam for his work. That's an enforceable contract between Sam and Better Builders.

Sam also has derivative contract rights against Paul the property owner that rise out of the contract between Paul and Better Builders. Sam has those rights, even though Sam and Paul have had no direct dealings with each other, and, in fact, have probably never even met. About the only time those rights become important is if Sam doesn't get paid. (There are also some warranty implications here, but we'll worry about those later.)

Just as Better Builders is not an employee of Paul the property owner, Sam is not Better Builders' (or Paul's) employee. That's because Sam has his own business, not because Sam's a plumber. It's not the skill that makes a particular person a subcontractor instead of an employee. It's the structure of the relationship. The guy who runs the supermarket where you buy your groceries is not your employee, even though he's performing a service for you. The same is true of any person who's running his own business instead of working for someone else. But in construction work there are so many advantages for a general contractor in working with subs instead of employees, that a lot of wishful thinking that goes on. Many workers on construction sites are called subcontractors — may even believe they're subcontractors — but they're legally employees.

Is this important? You bet your bippy it is.

Why is it so important to know if someone is a subcontractor or an employee? Taxes are one reason. The rules and the responsibilities for withholding and reporting taxes are completely different. Your role in a subcontractor's tax liabilities is nothing compared to your responsibilities if he's an employee. Workers' compensation, unemployment payments, etc. are also solely the sub's burden. And if the subcontractor injures

Checklist for Subcontracting Arrangements

▌ What is the schedule for the work? Are there start and finish dates? What happens if the subcontractor is delayed? What if the subcontractor can't start the work because of the actions of the property owner or general contractor?

▌ What are the payment terms? Are there draw amounts for materials? Labor? What triggers payments: completion of a percentage of the work, or inspections?

▌ How will change orders be handled? Who authorizes them?

▌ Does the subcontractor carry liability insurance? Workers' compensation?

▌ Who is responsible for cleanup?

▌ What are the warranty terms? Who is responsible for warranties?

▌ What are the subcontractors' lien rights? Have they been waived?

▌ Is an arbitration clause necessary?

someone who's going to be looking around for someone to sue, that's the sub's problem too. So some employers "misunderstand" the rules and claim that people who are really employees are subcontractors. And it usually gets them in all kinds of trouble.

An Employee or an Independent Contractor?

Sam the plumber works for several companies, puts in bids for the work, gets Form 1099 from the general contractors he works for, sets his own hours, owns his own vehicles and tools, and has employees of his own — well, that's easy. He's an independent contractor.

If Sam comes and goes entirely at the direction of the general contractor, does everything under supervision, and gets paid by the hour, not the job, that's another easy call. He's an employee.

The problem is that often it isn't that clear just who is, and who isn't, an employee. For example, suppose Joe is a casual laborer, but one who only works during the summer months. If Better Builders tells Joe when to come in, supplies his tools, directs him about where to work and how, and pays him by the hour — Joe's an employee, right?

But suppose Better Builders had contracted with Temp Labor Inc. for casual labor, and Temp Labor sent Joe over. Nothing is different on the job site. Better Builders treats Joe exactly the same, but Temp Labor writes Joe's check, pays his withholding and carries insurance for him. Joe is an employee, all right, but he's Temp Labor's employee, and Temp Labor is Better Builders' subcontractor.

Making the call about who's an employee and who's a subcontractor can be difficult. It requires looking at the whole relationship. Suppose Sam the plumber never works anywhere but on Better Builders' job sites? Suppose Joe doesn't work for Temp Labor. He just comes in when Better Builders calls him, and they only call him once in a while. To make the call about their employee status, there are two factors that are critical:

1. Who controls the workers?

2. Do the workers act like independent businesspersons?

Who Controls the Workers?

The first factor is *control*. How much control does the general contractor exercise over those workers? Does the general contractor set their hours and tasks? Are they paid by the hour? How closely supervised are the workers? Who makes the decisions about how to do the work? Who owns the tools?

Do These Workers Act Like Independent Businesspersons?

The other factor is whether these workers actually *behave* like someone who owns their own business. Do they have their own tools? A vehicle? A business phone? A federal ID number? Do they ever work for other contractors? Do they keep records, submit bids, bill by the job? Finally, are they insured?

The IRS Form SS-8

If you're not sure, you can ask the IRS to decide if a particular worker is an employee or an independent contractor. Just file a Form SS-8 asking for a determination. If you get back an opinion that the worker is an independent contractor, you're protected from suffering penalties if the IRS later decides that it was wrong and that your independent contractor is really an employee. You'll still owe the money that you should have withheld from that worker's wages, but at least you'll be spared the backbreaking penalties. To get a Form SS-8, call the IRS at 1-800-TAX-FORM or fill out an IRS publication request form.

The IRS "Safe Harbor" Rule

The IRS has some killer penalties if you classify someone who's really an employee as an independent contractor. The problem with those penalties is that sometimes it's an honest mistake, because it's not always easy to tell who's an employee and who's not.

For example, suppose Better Builders has Ed the electrician on the job. Ed has come in every day all day long for months, and gets paid on a time-and-materials basis. Ed sets his own hours and owns his own tools. When Ed arrives on the job site, the site superintendent tells Ed what Better Builders needs, and Ed gives the super an estimate of the job cost. The site superintendent keeps Better Builders informed about Ed's estimates. Ed doesn't ask for, or accept, supervision. Better Builders tells him what they want done, but they don't tell him how to do it.

The time-and-materials method of payment and the regular ongoing hours tend to make Ed look like an employee, but he probably isn't.

If Ed occasionally left Better Builders' job site and did some work during the week for somebody else, there would be no question at all that Ed is an independent contractor. But if Ed only worked for other people on the weekend, that could be used as evidence that Ed's really an employee.

In an effort to be fair to people who don't intend to violate the law, the IRS now uses the safe harbor rule. It allows people who have honestly misclassified employees to avoid some or all of the penalties. To avoid *all* of those penalties, the employer has to pass all three tests, but there's some limited relief available even if the employer can only pass one or two of these tests.

The Threshold Test

To be even considered for relief from these penalties, the employer must have filed a Form 1099 with the IRS for every independent contractor who earned more than $600 during the year. If you've filed those 1099s, you may be able to get some limited relief even if you fail the next two tests.

The Consistency Test

The second test requires you to show that you treat all the workers doing the same job in the same way. For example, you can't claim you honestly believed that one painter was an independent contractor when you treated another painter, who was doing exactly the same job under the same conditions, as an employee. That's not "honestly believing." That's wishful thinking. And the IRS will make you wish you hadn't!

The Reasonable Belief Test

The third test is that you must have had some honest reason for believing you could treat that worker as an independent contractor. Perhaps you were relying upon an industry manual, or maybe your accountant or attorney assured you that the worker was an independent contractor.

For example, Better Builders might have a plumber that they mistakenly classified as an independent contractor. Better Builders had made some phone calls to other employers in the area and were told that licensed plumbers are always classified as independent contractors. The point is that Better Builders made an effort to find out how their plumber should be classified. When they incorrectly classified that plumber as an independent contractor, they honestly believed they were doing it correctly.

The best "reasonable belief" would be a belief based on the IRS's own information, such as a response to an SS-8 request or a prior audit of that employer.

If an Independent Contractor Is Injured on the Job

Subcontractors are independent contractors, so they're not covered by the workers' compensation laws. In theory, the contractor isn't liable for a subcontractor's injuries, or the injuries of his employees, unless the contractor was negligent *and* that negligence caused the subcontractor's injury.

Why did I use those words *in theory*? Because in reality the courts don't like to see workers who are injured on the job left out in the cold without benefits. There are two different legal ways you might be required to pay for an injury to an independent contractor. Which way you get caught makes a difference, because one way you'll have to pay out some money, and the other way you might have to pay out *a whole lot* of money.

The first way is that a court might decide the independent contractor was really an employee so you'll have to pay for part of his lost wages and his medical costs. The second way you could get caught here is that a court might decide your negligence caused the injury. For example, you have a duty to provide every worker on the job, whether they're employees or independent contractors, with a safe place to work. If you fail that duty, you're negligent — and negligence lawsuits can cost you huge amounts of money.

What If Employees of Subcontractors Are Injured on the Job?

The employees of subcontractors are supposed to get their workers' compensation from their employer, the subcontractor. But if that subcontractor doesn't carry workers' compensation insurance, his employees have a big problem. It's not that the subcontractor isn't liable for workers' compensation obligations — it's that he's probably not collectible. He didn't buy the insurance because he didn't have the money. In that case, the injured worker's attorney will probably be looking at you, the general contractor, or the property owner.

Is the Injured Worker Really Your Employee?

The injured worker could argue that he or she is *your* employee because the subcontractor was really your employee. If the subcontractor is your employee, then so is everyone in his crew.

This is not as difficult an argument to make as you might think, because the thrust of the law is to protect workers injured on the job site. That's why insurance companies audit contractors to make sure that they're getting (and keeping) copies of their subcontractors' current workers' compensation insurance certificates. If this argument is successful, the injured worker will collect workers' compensation damages from your policy. That's limited to a portion of their lost wages, and medical costs.

Were You Negligent?

The injured worker may not make the argument that he is an employee instead of an independent contractor. Instead, he may sue on the grounds that the general contractor was negligent. In some states, one of the ways the general contractor could have been negligent was when he didn't make sure his subcontractor carried workers' compensation insurance.

If the injured worker is successful with this argument, then, unlike workers' compensation claims, the sky's the limit on damages. A successful negligence lawsuit can include pain and suffering, even punitive damages.

The kind of insurance that would protect a general contractor from a negligence claim is liability insurance. Workers' compensation insurance doesn't apply to this situation.

Did You Provide a Safe Place to Work?

There's another way the general contractor could be negligent. Both the property owner and the general contractor have a duty to provide a safe place to work for their own employees, their subcontractors, and the employees of their subcontractors. If the general contractor or property owner *or both* failed to do that, then the injured worker could sue for negligence.

Since this would be a negligence lawsuit, the worker could sue for lost wages, medical costs, pain and suffering, and even punitive damages. If you wind up losing in a negligence lawsuit, you'll wish that worker *had* been an employee.

Who Has to Pay in a Successful Negligence Lawsuit?

If negligence caused the plaintiff's injury, sometimes more than one person could be successfully sued. For example, both the property owner and the contractor have a duty to provide a safe place to work. Both may be liable if it isn't safe. However, the injured person can pick and choose his defendants. He doesn't have to sue every single person who might be liable for his injury.

What if a general contractor or a property owner is the sole defendant in a lawsuit, and believes that someone else is also responsible and should help pay off some of this claim? If the plaintiff hasn't sued that person, then the defendant has to sue that other person for contribution. To sue for contribution means that the defendant sues someone else, saying, in effect, that person was also negligent and ought to be helping to pay this judgment. Just how much help the defendant is entitled to from that person, whom we can think of as "the other defendant," is a question of fact that's decided on a case-by-case basis.

For example, suppose Joe, who works for the subcontractor, has been injured on the job site. He can only sue his employer for workers' compensation damages: a portion of his lost wages and the cost of his medical treatment. But if his employer doesn't have insurance and isn't

---

Insurance for Subcontractors

Subcontractors should always ask if the insurance coverage on a project protects them—because sometimes it doesn't. Work that a subcontractor has completed, but hasn't yet been paid for, is not considered to belong to the contractor *or* the project owner. If there's a fire or damaging storm before payment, the amount owed may not be protected by the contractor's or project owner's builders' risk policy.

If you're a subcontractor, here's my advice. Either:

▌ Get an *installation* floater from your own insurer, or

▌ Negotiate a deal that requires the contractor or project owner to carry insurance that also protects you.

If you don't, you're taking a chance, because policies held by the project owner almost never insure a subcontractor's potential loss. Policies carried by the contractor are also often silent about coverage for subcontractors. Even when those polices *do* cover subcontractors, there's usually a limit on the amount of coverage, which might not be enough to cover the actual loss.

---

collectible, then Joe will probably want to sue somebody who either has insurance or deeper pockets than his employer (who apparently can't even afford insurance).

If you're the general contractor and Joe sues you on a negligence claim (instead of arguing that he's really your employee), then you need liability insurance to pay the judgment. Workers' compensation won't cover this kind of claim.

If There's Trouble Between the General Contractor and the Property Owner

Suppose there's a falling out between the general contractor and the property owner. What happens to the subcontractor? The law says that the subcontractor is entitled to the benefit of the contract rights that the general had under the contract, but the subcontractor doesn't have any more rights than the general had. In some situations, he may have less. If he isn't paid, the subcontractor should contact his attorney and make certain he takes every step necessary to protect his lien rights.

If the Owner Breached the Contract

If the owner breaches the contract, that excuses the general contractor from his obligations under that contract. Since he's excused from his obligations under the contract by the property owner's breach, in some states that also excuses the general from performance of his contract with the subcontractor. The general contractor's *performance* in this situation is allowing the sub to do his work, and then paying the sub for that work.

Does that mean that the subcontractor is just out of luck? No, not necessarily.

The Subcontractor May Be Able to Sue the Contractor

The outcome of this particular problem often depends upon what state the parties are in. Some states allow the contractor to get off the hook when the customer has breached the contract. The customer's breach gives the contractor a legal excuse to breach his contract with the subcontractor.

However, if it was the contractor who breached the contract with the owner, then the contractor cannot defend against a lawsuit by the sub.

In those states where the subcontractor can sue the contractor regardless of the situation between the contractor and the customer, if the contractor has to pay the sub, the contractor can then turn around and sue the customer for reimbursement. However, in the few states where the subcontractor can sue the general contractor regardless of what the customer has done, the sub isn't allowed to actually collect from the general contractor until the general contractor has collected from the property owner.

The Subcontractor's Lien Rights

If the subcontractor has actually performed work on the property, his *best* protection will be his lien rights. A subcontractor doesn't need to have a direct legal relationship with the property owner to enforce a lien on property. If the subcontractor has done work on the property *and* has exactly followed the Construction Lien Act in their state to enforce a lien, then the subcontractor will have a security interest — something like a mortgage — that can be sued to pay off the debt. Lien rights are set by statute, so it's critical that subcontractors follow their state's lien statute *exactly*.

Pass-Through Claims

Usually subcontractors don't sue the property owner themselves even in states where they can. What often happens instead is that the general contractor sues the property owner for breach of contract, and the general contractor includes a claim on behalf of the subcontractors.

The general contractor can include the subcontractors' claims as part of his requested damages in his own lawsuit, because the subs could have sued the general contractor for payment. But the general contractor isn't required to wait until they actually do, before he can sue and collect on their behalf.

If the General Contractor Breached the Contract With the Owner

The subcontractor can run into a real problem when it was the general contractor who breached the contract, not the property owner. If the general contractor breaches his contract with the property owner, that breach excuses the property owner from his performance under the contract. As a general rule, the subcontractor can't sue the property owner for breach of contract, because the general contractor couldn't successfully sue.

This isn't true every time. If the subcontractor performed his part of the contract, he may have a claim against the owner under the contract anyway. But the property owner may have a counterclaim, because of the actions of the general contractor. In a case like this, there are two reasons why it's important for the subcontractor to seek legal help. First, because the subcontractor rights under the contract are so dependent upon exactly what the facts of the situation are. For example, the subcontractors' rights could depend upon exactly when the general contractor breached the contract with the property owner: Did the breach occur before, or after, the subcontractor did his work? Did the breach negate the value of the entire contract or just a portion of the contract, and, if so, was it a portion that involved what that sub was doing?

Second, the sub should get legal help because there are other ways the subcontractor could collect his money. For example, he may have lien rights he could enforce.

There are also other ways the subcontractor could sue and collect. The subcontractor may be able to sue the property owner for unjust enrichment, or for what the law calls *quantum meruit*. (That's about the same thing as unjust enrichment.) The damages may not be precisely the same as the damages in a contract lawsuit, because unjust enrichment damages are based on the value of the work, but it still may be a way to get paid. Enforcing lien rights would be a better way to go, but this is an alternative for a sub who let his lien rights expire or failed to use them.

In the next chapter, we'll look at other contract problems subcontractors can face.

What Contract Problems Do Subcontractors Have?

Subcontractors have extra problems on top of the usual construction contract problems, because a subcontracting arrangement actually involves *two* contracts.

There's the contract between the general contractor and the subcontractor. In that contract, Sam the subcontractor promises to do certain work for Jim the general contractor, and Jim agrees to pay Sam for that work. This contract looks very much and works very much like any other construction contract. Sam promises to do the work, and if he doesn't, Jim can sue him for breach of contract. Jim promises to pay for that work, and if he doesn't, Sam can go to court and make Jim pay.

So far, so good — but Jim the general contractor doesn't actually *own* the property Sam will be working on, so there's another contract that's important to this deal. That's the contract between Jim and Mrs. Smith, the property owner. This contract doesn't have to be called the *prime* contract, but it often is. In the prime contract, Mrs. Smith promised to pay Jim for doing the work that he has just hired Sam to do. With us so far? When Sam promised Jim to do Jim's work for Mrs. Smith, Sam got certain rights in the contract between Jim and Mrs. Smith. However, Sam is still not a party to that contract, so Sam can't get more rights than Jim had — not from that contract anyway.

The legal word for Sam's rights in the contract between Jim and Mrs. Smith is *derivative*. Derivative means that Sam the subcontractor has legal rights in a contract that he wasn't a party to. That may not sound like such a big deal to you, but legally it is a very big deal, because the basic rule is that people who weren't a party to a contract have no rights in that contract. If you contract to buy a car from Al's Used Autos, you don't expect your banker to be able to go over and demand that Al give him the car. Nor would you expect Al to call up your son and demand payment for the car you bought. That's true even though the banker is financing the car's purchase, and your son will be driving it.

But in some construction industry situations, a subcontractor can require that the customer pay him directly even though that customer never promised him anything — in fact probably never even met him. Also, the customer can sometimes require the subcontractor to do certain things even though the sub never actually promised anything to the customer.

The Contract Between the General Contractor and the Customer

Subcontractors have problems general contractors don't. That's because the subcontractor doesn't just have derivative rights in the prime contract between the property owner and the general contractor, he also has some obligations in that contract. But often the subcontractor doesn't even see the prime contract between the general contractor and the customer, let alone read it, until after the project has started.

Here's what usually happens: During the negotiations between the general contractor and the subcontractor, the subcontractor is shown a set of bidding documents that refer to the prime contract between the general contractor and the property owner as the "standard contract form" — but there's no actual copy of the contract between the general contractor and the property owner attached to the bidding documents. This isn't intended to deceive anybody. It's common industry practice. Construction is an industry where time is money, and no one wants to wait while somebody carefully reads that contract.

But standard practice or not, if you're a subcontractor and you don't know what's in the prime contract between the general contractor and the owner, that can put you at risk. You are, after all, agreeing to terms and obligations in a contract you've never actually seen. There may be something in it you don't expect, and what you don't expect, rarely works to your advantage. To avoid unpleasant and expensive surprises, you should always ask for, and read, the contract between the property owner and the general contractor.

What if the general contractor won't open his records to you? Should you be headed for the door? Not necessarily. There are many reasons a general contractor could be reluctant to reveal contract terms to a subcontractor. At the end of this chapter, I'll describe how to do an addendum, and what language you could put into that addendum to protect your posterior to the extent that's possible.

In this section, we'll go through some examples of contract clauses that you should worry about. Then you'll have to consider if you're willing to take the risk embodied in these clauses.

Do Subcontractors Have Construction Lien Rights?

Yes, they do. Anyone who does construction work on real property has a right to claim a lien for the value of that work. However, it would be more accurate to say the subs have lien rights *if* they haven't given them away by signing a lien waiver, or by letting the general contractor waive them in the prime contract, or if the subs haven't lost them by not following the exact letter of the state lien law.

To enforce their liens, the subs must claim their lien in *exactly* the way that their state statute requires. Contact the Registrar of Deeds or the Tract Index in your county and ask about the procedure.

What also sometimes happens to subs is that the general contractor brings around a lien waiver and says, "Just as soon as you sign this, I'll get payment for you from the property owner." In fact, a smart property owner won't make a payment to the general contractor until he gets lien waivers from the subcontractors who have already worked on the property.

However, a sub who signs a lien waiver and then has to deal with a bouncing check or a disappearing general contractor has a problem. To protect himself, the sub should sign the lien waiver like this: "I hereby waive all liens upon the receipt of actual payment."

The No-Lien Contract

As a subcontractor, you should watch for a "no-lien" clause in the contract between the general contractor and the customer. In a no-lien clause, the general contractor waives all construction liens in advance. In other words, the general contractor waives your construction lien rights before you're even in the picture.

Fortunately, most states don't enforce this kind of blanket "no-lien" provision in the general contract. They recognize that it's inherently unfair to eliminate the protection that construction lien rights give a subcontractor without that subcontractor's consent. Even in the states that do enforce a blanket "no-lien" clause, most of them require that the subcontractor at least get written notice of the clause.

If you find a "no-lien" clause in the contract between the general contractor and the property owner, you can't assume you're in a state that won't enforce the clause. And remember that sometimes you don't actually read words like "no lien" in the contract. Instead the red flag words are "waive" or "waiver of liens" or "release."

Dispute Resolution

Often a prime contract will include a way to settle disputes. It might be arbitration, which is generally a good idea because hardly anyone but the lawyer wins when they go to court to settle contract disputes. In fact, it's just about impossible to win in court (in the sense of coming out ahead financially) when you have to pay out hundreds — even thousands — of dollars in legal fees, to say nothing of how long it all takes. With arbitration, you can usually establish what the language in a contract means, or what's the best way of doing the job much more quickly and cheaply than in a lawsuit.

However, the subcontractor should take a hard look at the dispute resolution method in the contract, because sometimes it's the architect or the project owner who resolves disputes. That may not be acceptable to you — especially if your dispute is *with* that person.

There's another trap in many dispute clauses for an unwary subcontractor. Because of procedural requirements, you may not win even if you were right in the dispute. In many contracts (and under the new AIA contracts), subcontractors lose a lot of arguments, not because they were wrong, but because they didn't follow the contract procedures for giving notice about the dispute.

In the event of a dispute, you should carefully follow the requirements in the contract for giving notice of a dispute. This usually requires you to mail notice of the dispute, by first class mail or by certified mail, within a certain number of days to the property owner and/or the architect.

Change Order Procedures

Getting paid for change orders can also be a problem. Watch out for a clause in the contract between the general contractor and the property owner that says change orders aren't binding on the property owner unless certain people (such as the property owner and/or the architect) get notice of those change orders and agree to them. To protect yourself, read the prime contract carefully to make sure you understand the change order procedures. Then follow those procedures to the letter before you do the work. Get change orders in writing, and get them signed by everyone who's supposed to sign them. Then make sure that everyone who's supposed to have a copy of change orders gets their copy within the time limit in the contract.

Sometimes the problem isn't just that certain people are supposed to have notice, it's that they are supposed to have that notice within a certain number of days so they can object to the change orders if they want to. Of course, even if you can't collect from the property owner, you can still collect from your general contractor — if you can find him, and if he's collectible.

Retention Provisions

Most prime contracts allow the property owner to retain a certain percentage or amount of the general contractor's payment for the work. Some states have specific statutory rules about retained amounts, but those rules usually relate to consumer rights.

The subcontractor can negotiate payment terms with the general contractor that don't include the retained amount or that involve a smaller amount of retainage. However, if the subcontractor has to pursue the property owner because the general contractor didn't pay, then the subcontractor will be bound by the payment terms in that contract.

For example, suppose Jim the general contractor had agreed to pay Sam the plumbing subcontractor $5000 as soon as Sam finished installing the plumbing — then Jim doesn't pay. If Sam goes after the property owner instead of Jim, and there's a clause in the prime contract that allows the property owner to hold back 10 percent of the payment until the job is completed, Sam's going to have to wait on 10 percent of his money. (Of course, it depends on the exact wording of the contract.) That's because no matter what the agreement was between Sam and Jim, if Sam has to go to the property owner for payment, Sam only has the payment rights that Jim had.

Considering this, the wise subcontractor would figure out exactly what triggers the obligation to pay those retained amounts before agreeing to do the work.

The Contract Between the General Contractor and Subcontractors

We've established that a subcontractor is subject to the terms in the prime contract between the property owner and the general contractor. The subcontractor is also subject to the contract between himself and the general contractor — and this is a contract. I don't care if every single word has been verbal. I don't care if the actual word "contract" has never been used. If the general contractor says, "I'll pay," and the subcontractor says, "Okay, I'll do the work," (or any other words to that effect), this is a contract between the sub and the general contractor.

If there's nothing specifically to the contrary between the subcontractor and the general contractor, then the subcontractor is simply accepting the prime contract as the contract between himself and the general contractor.

But for his own protection, there are certain kinds of clauses that a subcontractor should consider not accepting. And, yes, I do know that often subcontractors don't have much wiggle room. Usually the implication behind a contract offered to a subcontractor is "take it or leave it," but that's not always true. Sometimes these clauses aren't in a contract because the general contractor wants to take advantage of the subs. They are just part of the contract boilerplate and the general contractor doesn't even know what the clauses are there for. You'd be surprised what you can negotiate out of a contract. Often you don't have to physically rewrite the contract, either. A magic marker line through that particular clause in the contract on all the copies makes it clear that the subcontractor hasn't agreed to this clause. Or the subcontractor could write an *addendum*, which we'll explain at the end of this chapter.

In fact, considering the problems some of these clauses can cause, a sub who can't get the general contractor to agree to a change in the contract needs to remember that there are jobs you just can't afford to accept.

The Contingent Payment Clause

A contingent payment clause in the contract between the general contractor and the subcontractor means that the general contractor doesn't have to pay the subcontractor until some event, in addition to the sub

---

Attorney Fees

There's one clause in a contract that can help keep everybody honest: the losing party in a lawsuit gets to pay the winner's attorney fees.

A clause like this is something a subcontractor should want to see in the prime contract between the general contractor and the property owner. The subcontractor specifically wants the clause to say that the property owner must reimburse the attorney fees of *anyone* who successfully prosecutes a construction lien claim. That's because the lien right is one of the most useful weapons an unpaid subcontractor has. If there isn't such a clause, and the subcontractor has to pay a lawyer to enforce his lien rights, he will net much less in his recovery than he's entitled to. There's not much satisfaction in winning a $2000 lawsuit and then having to pay a $1500 legal bill, although some states automatically award attorney fees to a successful lien claimant.

The subcontractor should also get an attorney fee clause in his contract with the general contractor. If the general contractor has to pay the subcontractor's legal bills, that will cut down on the temptation to take advantage of the sub when cash flow is a little slow, and the general contractor is looking around for an invoice not to pay. The clause will also help in those situations where the general contractor wants to make the sub an offer he can't refuse, such as: "If you want to get paid for this job right away, just agree to do the electrical work on the ABC job for X amount of dollars." The subcontractor especially needs an attorney fee provision if he decides to agree to a retention clause or a contingent payment clause. That way if the subcontractor actually has to sue to collect those retained dollars, his attorney fees won't reduce the net gain on his winnings.

completing the work, occurs. Most often, that event is the owner paying the contractor. In other words, if Sam the subcontractor agrees to this kind of contingent clause in his contract with Jim the general contractor, Jim is saying that he will pay for Sam's work after Mrs. Smith pays Jim. Well, there are some small companies that don't have the cash flow to pay their subs until they get paid themselves. The problem is that not many subs, who are also small businesses, can afford to wait for the money.

This kind of contingent payment clause is called a "pay when paid" clause, but that's not the language that you'll see in the prime contract documents. The contract will specify that payment is "conditioned upon" or "contingent upon" or "due upon payment by" the owner.

There are big problems with "pay when paid" clauses. The first problem is figuring out exactly what the clause means. Does it mean the subcontractor is giving up the right to collect from the general contractor if the owner doesn't pay the general contractor?

The good news for subcontractors is that most states say that a "pay when paid" clause doesn't mean the subcontractor can *never* collect from the general contractor until the property owner pays up. In those states, the clause only means that the sub has to wait a reasonable amount of time before he's entitled to collect from the general contractor. He's just agreeing to give the general contractor a reasonable opportunity to get the money from the property owner before demanding payment.

The bad news is that there are a few states where a "pay when paid" clause means just that. If the owner doesn't pay the general contractor, the general contractor doesn't have to pay the sub — even for work already completed. Here's the real question: Who has the headache of collecting from a nonpaying property owner — the subcontractor or the general contractor? And the answer is: In those states that uphold the "pay when paid" clause, the general contractor has shifted the burden of collecting from a defaulting property owner from himself to his subcontractors.

For example, suppose Dan the drywaller agrees to a contingent pay clause. Then it turns out the property owner never pays the contractor. So the contractor says to Dan: "I don't have to pay you, because I never got paid."

So what's Dan going to do if he's in one of the states that say he can't collect from the general contractor unless or until the general contractor collects from the property owner? Dan's only choice is to try to collect for his work from the property owner. Of course, if the general contractor had no luck, Dan's chances probably aren't much better. Depending on the situation, Dan will be able to sue the property owner for payment - but he'll probably need a lawyer. Notice that under the "pay when paid" clause, it's Dan who's paying for the lawyer to sue the property owner, not the general contractor.

Be Careful to Protect Your Lien Rights

If Dan has his lien rights in place, he'll be able to use that lien as security for the money the property owner owes him. But there could be a problem with Dan's lien rights in a "pay when paid" situation: Usually, lien rights start running from the time the subcontractor completes his part of the work. That means that subs only have a limited number of days after they complete the work to claim a lien. Their time limit starts when their part of the work is done, but the job itself may not be finished for months. If the subcontractor waits to claim his lien until the general contractor is paid, he may not have a lien to enforce. His lien rights may have expired!

For example, suppose Dan the drywaller didn't give notice of his intent to claim a lien as soon as he finished with his part of the job, because he was waiting for the owner to pay the general contractor. Dan may lose his lien rights, because he didn't give the proper notice of lien rights soon enough. Or perhaps he didn't file his Claim of Lien within the 30 days, or whatever the statute in his state requires.

The moral here is to always give notice of the right to claim a construction lien in the way your state requires as soon as the work is done. Giving notice doesn't mean that you have to follow through on the lien and try to force the sale of the property. It simply protects one of your ways to collect for completed work.

Delay is a Problem for Subcontractors

Delay costs money. Consider this. Dan the drywaller based his bid to Better Builders on having his crew on-site for a week. Dan's five-man crew costs him $2000 a day in labor and benefits.

When Dan's crew arrives at the job site, they can't start because the framing sub isn't done, so they stand around all day drinking coffee and offering unsolicited advice to the framing guys. That will cost Dan at least an additional $2000 beyond his original bid.

Dan's probably out more than that extra $2000 because the increase in job time extends his overhead. It can also cause many different consequential damages. Suppose on Tuesday there's an increase in the cost of drywall mud that Dan hadn't factored into his bid. And what about that other job he was supposed to start the following Monday?

Delay is always about who's going to pay. If the bidder caused the delay, the rule is simple. When he agreed to do the job for a certain cost, he also agreed to take the risk if the job didn't go according to schedule. However, he didn't agree to take the risk of someone else's delay. Generally he can get reimbursed for those damages, but there are some problems.

What If the General Contractor Doesn't Pay the Sub?

You see this problem in every economic slowdown. Some contractors finance their costs on the current job with the advance money they get from the property owner for the next job. That works as long as business is good and there's lots of advance money coming in. It's illegal in most states and can cost a contractor his license — but plenty of contractors do it anyway.

It blows up if the jobs in the new-job pipeline dry up. Then the general contractor doesn't have the money to pay the subcontractors who are working on the current new job, because he's already spent their money on the old job.

So, what happens to the subs? They probably can't collect from the general contractor because he doesn't have any money. In fact, usually they're lucky if they can even find him. But when the sub tries to collect from the property owner, the property owner says "Hey, I already paid for that work."

Whether the subcontractor can collect from the property owner who has already paid the general contractor for the work, depends upon what state they're in:

1. **In a few states, the subcontractor loses**

    In a few states, if the property owner has paid the general contractor, then the property owner is all paid up. Period. That property owner doesn't have to pay twice. The property owner's payment to the general contractor effectively kills all the subcontractor's rights against the property owner, even the subcontractor's lien rights. The only hope the subcontractor has is to collect from the disappearing general contractor. But a subcontractor who finds himself in that situation should always check with the state licensing agency, because some states operate an insurance fund to protect unpaid subs.

2. **In a few states, the property owner still owes unpaid subcontractors**

    If the subcontractor has done the work, he's owed for it until he's paid. If he can't collect from the general contractor, he can collect from the property owner. Sometimes, the subcontractor is required to use a legal form called a *quantum meruit* action — or in English, *unjust enrichment* — instead of suing for breach of contract. The significance of this is that the subcontractor can't collect what the contract said he could. Instead the contractor collects the "value of his work," which may be, or may not be, the same dollar amount as the payment the contract called for.

3. **In most states, the subcontractor can collect if he has secured his lien rights**

    This is why those lien rights are so important. In most states a subcontractor who has followed the state procedure for securing a lien has not only protected himself against property owners who don't pay, he has also protected himself against absconding general contractors, because that lien cannot be taken off the property until the sub is paid. So if the property owner pays the general contractor, and the general contractor doesn't pay the subcontractor, then the subcontractor can get paid by enforcing his lien against the property owner.

What If the General Contractor Doesn't Pay the Sub? (continued)

Does this mean the property owner gets to pay twice for the same work? Yes, it does. Is this fair? We're not talking about fair here. Some comparatively-innocent person is going to be out some money, and we're talking about which innocent person it will be: the property owner or the sub. A well-informed property owner wouldn't make progress payments or a final payment until the general contractor shows him a Lien Waiver signed by the subs who've been working on the property.

Sometimes subcontractors sign Lien Waivers in advance of getting paid. This is common in commercial construction work where the financing agency often demands it. It's my opinion that any sub who signs a lien waiver in advance ought to be very sure of where his money is coming from in the event of a problem.

Remember that sometimes, especially if a financing agency is making progress payments directly to general contractor, an arrangement can be bargained for that will protect the subs better than the standard blanket draw arrangement.

No Damages for Delay

A No Damages for Delay clause in a contract means that somebody gives up their rights to be reimbursed for the money that a delay on the job site cost them.

So who gives up that right? Usually it's the contractor who agrees not to charge the property owner for the extra expenses caused by the delay. Sometimes it's a subcontractor who agrees not to charge the contractor for the extra costs of the delay. This isn't an issue of fault unless the contract says so. The contractor or the subcontractor agrees to give up getting reimbursed for the cost of delays *that were not his fault*.

There are cases where the general contractor waived his right to collect delay damages from the property owner, and the subcontractor just accepted the contract between the property owner and the contractor without any changes. In such cases, because he agreed to be bound by a contract that says no damages for delay, if he suffers job delay costs, he'll have trouble, in some states, getting reimbursed for those extra costs for delay.

The only good news for those subcontractors is that the waiver doesn't automatically eliminate their rights for a time extension.

Backcharges for Delay

Sometimes subcontractors will agree to be backcharged for the costs of delay that the contractor suffers. That's fine unless the contract spreads those costs among all the subs, including the ones who weren't at fault.

From the subcontractor's standpoint, he wants an agreement that doesn't charge the subcontractor for delay costs unless that subcontractor was at fault.

Liquidated Damages Clauses

Delay always costs money. It can make the difference between profit or loss on a job — everybody knows that. Another thing that everybody knows is that there's always delay. Builders often put in "no damages for delay" clauses because they know how difficult it can be to predict a delay or predict what it will cost, but there's a better way of dealing with this problem.

To solve the delay problem, sometimes the parties will agree in advance that whoever causes a delay will pay a certain amount of money for each day's delay. That money is intended to reimburse the injured party for the damages they suffered because of the delay.

The legal term for this kind of agreement is a "liquidated damages" clause. Sometimes in contracts, however, this kind of clause is called "damages for late performance."

It makes a lot of sense to agree in advance that if a delay occurs, the party causing the delay will have to pay a specific amount for the damage the delay causes. That way, the parties won't have to go to court to decide exactly what the damages were. Even if the amount agreed upon is not precisely the real cost, the claimant will usually still end up with more cash in hand than they would have recovered if they had to hire a lawyer to document and litigate every nickel and dime.

Don't Agree to Pay for Damages Somebody Else Caused

Sometimes there's a trap in the liquidated damages clause for subcontractors who didn't cause the problem. Some of these clauses say that the cost of damages for late performance will be divided among all the subcontractors on the project. The effect is that every subcontractor pays for the delay that only one of them caused. The general contractor will like this clause because it means that among all of the subcontractors, there ought to be at least one with money to pay.

If you're a subcontractor who's asked to agree to a contract with a liquidated damages clause in it, read that contract very carefully to see who is actually supposed to pay these damages. Are you agreeing to pay for a delay you caused, or are you agreeing to help pay for any delay — maybe even every delay? Watch for a contract that simply says that the subcontractors are responsible for meeting the liquidated payment clause, and doesn't say anything about who caused that delay. It would be worth your time to first ask your lawyer to read over that clause to see exactly what you're agreeing to, especially since these rules vary from state to state.

Scope of Work

If the general contractor offers the subcontractor a contract with a clause that limits the subcontractor to "the scope of work in the plans," that can create an unexpected trap when problems come up during the job that require extra work. If the subcontractor asks for a change order that includes additional payment for extra work, the general contractor might say: "You agreed to do the job for your bid. That means you agreed to do whatever is necessary to get the job done for that amount of money."

You can avoid this problem (before you sign the contract) by writing language into the clause on change orders, or into an addendum, that states that you'll charge an additional fee for any work not in the original specifications of the original contract.

Design Responsibility Clauses

Subcontractors should be wary of clauses that require the subcontractor to advise the architect and/or owner about design deficiencies.

There's a good reason for that caution. A clause that puts a responsibility for reporting all design flaws on the subcontractor can have the effect of making that subcontractor responsible for *finding* those flaws, not just reporting them if he happens to see them. This is a problem for subcontractors who aren't design professionals, who are required to exactly follow the contract specifications, and who don't typically carry design Error and Omissions insurance. The real purpose of a clause like this is to spread the liability for someone else's mistake onto the subcontractors so they can help pay for it.

If you, as a subcontractor, come across this phrase in a contract, you have two options. First, you can insist that it be removed. Or you can ask the general contractor to rephrase this clause to read that subcontractors have a duty to report all the deficiencies that they discover during the process of doing their work. That won't adversely impact anyone, because subcontractors already have a duty to report any design flaws that they notice, whether or not the contract requires it. Rephrasing the clause just means that the subcontractor doesn't have to worry about being saddled with the cost for someone else's mistake.

Attorney Fees

As a subcontractor, you should always add a clause to the contract with the general contractor that you'll receive reimbursement of your attorney fees if you prevail in a claim. I mentioned this earlier in the chapter, but it can't be overstated. If you don't add this clause, you may not ever get that money back, because in most states court rules provide that each party, win or lose, pays their own attorney fees. Attorney fees cost so much that sometimes, without such a clause, you may have to give up the claim because you simply can't afford the cost of going to court — even if you win.

A Solution — The Subcontractor's Addendum

If you, as a subcontractor, aren't offered a specific contract, or if you have problems with the prime contract, you can ask your attorney to prepare an additional document that only addresses your role in the project. We don't have to call this a contract. It's usually just a short document called an addendum. You don't have to call it that, of course. You can call it anything you want to. Just get it written up, date it, leave a place at the bottom for the general contractor to sign it, and then add it to the construction documents.

All "addendum" means is that you have a few more words to say about this job than what is in the prime contract. Your addendum will not affect the contract between the property owner and the contractor, and it can't give you any more rights against the property owner than the general contractor had — but it will affect the terms of the contract between you and the general contractor. This is where you want to put an attorney fees clause, scheduling responsibilities, arbitration issues, delay issues, and responsibility for design errors. And this is where you want to say that, regardless of what the payment arrangements are in the prime contract, you are to be paid on a specific schedule.

You also want this addendum to say: "Notwithstanding anything to the contrary contained in the agreement between the general contractor and the property owner, the terms contained herein shall prevail over any such agreement and shall be controlling."

Blank Copy on CD-ROM

There's a blank copy of Figure 12-1 included on the disk in the back of the book.

This language won't give you any extra rights against the property owner, but it will improve your position if you have a dispute with the general contractor, because it will keep him from hiding behind the provisions of the prime contract. Figure 12-1 is a sample Addendum. There's a blank copy of this form on the disk in the back of the book.

Well, you've got your contract language set to provide you as much protection as possible. What do you have to worry about next? Express and implied warranties, that's what.

And that's the topic of the next chapter.

Bigger Builders Inc.
22 Commerce Drive •Lansing, MI 55555
Phone (555)555-1234 • Fax (555)555-6789
Website: www.biggerbuildersinc.com

ADDENDUM TO CONTRACT

(An addendum is an agreement between the subcontractor and the prime contractor. It's an addition to the prime contract between the contractor and the customer, and may contain terms which are different or inconsistent with those in the prime contract.)

Contractor Bigger Builders, Inc.
(Name the contractor here.)

Project Lone Tree Strip Mall, 44 West Park, Smalltown, MI
(Identify the project here by name, address, and any other identifying information for that project.)

Property Owner John Smith, Owner, 123 East St., Lansing, MI
(Insert property owner's name and address.)

Prime Contract Prime contract dated 5/2/00 and signed by Cal Irvin,President of Bigger Builders and John Smith.
(Identify the prime contract here by inserting the names of the parties signing the prime contract, and the date the prime contract was signed.)

Subcontractor Loral Drywallers, 88 West St., Lansing, MI
(Identify the subcontractor here by inserting his/her name and address here.)

1. The undersigned Subcontractor accepts the terms of the proposed subcontract subject to the Contractor's acceptance of this addendum. The Contractor may signify his acceptance by signing this addendum, or by permitting the Subcontractor to begin work.
(If the contractor doesn't actually sign this document, the subcontractor must at least deliver a copy of this addendum to the contractor before beginning work, or the addendum is unlikely to be enforceable. However, without the contractor's signature, in some states it won't be enforceable anyway.)

2. The scope of the work will include only the work described in the attached Subcontractor's proposal, which is hereby incorporated into and made a part of this addendum. The following documents are attached to this proposal:
(List all the relevant documents here, which will include a copy of the prime contract, a copy of the specifications for the subcontractor's work, as well as any other relevant documents. It's better to list it, than omit it. The following documents are for example purposes only. There could be other or additional items depending upon the project.)

3. If there are inconsistencies between this addendum and other contract documents, including the prime contract, this addendum will control the agreement. No con-

Figure 12-1 *Sample addendum*

tract document that impacts the Subcontractor will be binding upon the Subcontractor, unless a copy of that document has been furnished to the Subcontractor before the Subcontractor has signed this document, or unless the Subcontractor specifically accepted that document by signing that document.
(This language protects the subcontractor from unseen change orders, especially those that the subcontractor may not wish to consent to.)

4. The Subcontractor will have the same rights and remedies against the Contractor that the Contractor has against the Owner in the prime contract between the Contractor and the Owner.

5. If the Subcontractor requests it in writing, the Subcontractor will be provided with the legal description of the property, the name and address of the Owner, and evidence of adequate financing, and that information will be furnished to him by the Contractor within seven days.
(This is information the subcontractor will need if the subcontractor has to enforce a lien.)

6. Regardless of any higher standard stated elsewhere, the Subcontractor warrants that his work will be completed in a good and workmanlike manner and free from defects that are not inherent in the type of work. Contractor can reject the Subcontractor's work only if that work does not demonstrably comply with the subcontract documents. All Subcontractor warranties will be for a period of <u>one year</u> *(insert time period)* from the substantial completion of the Subcontractor's share of the project. The Subcontractor will not be subject to consequential damages without the prior written consent of the Subcontractor.
(This language is structured so that the year the warranty runs will start when the subcontractor is finished with the project, not when the builder is finished. The subcontractor should always try to avoid promising to pay consequential damages.)

7. The Subcontractor's duty to bring errors, defects, or other problems with the contract documents, project site, materials, or the work or design services of others is limited to only those things which the Subcontractor could discover by a reasonable sight examination.
(It is important to include this for the subcontractor's protection.)

8. The Subcontractor is entitled to rely upon the accuracy and completeness of plans, specifications, or permits furnished to the Subcontractor.
(If there is something wrong with the plans, that should not be the subcontractor's problem.)

9. The Contractor will obtain all necessary permits and will pay all necessary per-

Figure 12-1 *Sample addendum (Continued)*

mit fees in the absence of a specific agreement signed by the Subcontractor to the contrary.

10. The Contractor will supply all temporary site facilities, material storage facilities, and utilities without cost to the Subcontractor, unless specifically agreed otherwise in writing by the Subcontractor. The Subcontractor is not responsible for erecting project site safety barriers unless this is an express term of the subcontract.

11. The Subcontractor will take all reasonable safety precautions in the performance of the work, and will conform to the Contractor's safety programs except as provided otherwise in this document, and will report all hazardous material exposures and all job-related injuries to the Contractor.

12. The Contractor will cooperate with the Subcontractor to avoid scheduling conflicts or interference with the Subcontractor's work. The project schedule, and any modification of that schedule, shall allow the Subcontractor reasonable time to complete the Subcontractor's work in an efficient manner.

13. If there is a change in the project schedule, or if there is any delay not caused by the Subcontractor, the Subcontractor will be entitled to reimbursement for any increased costs of materials and for any increased cost of labor, including overtime. The Subcontractor's entitlement to increased costs is not limited to the amounts that the Contractor may receive from the Customer under the prime contract.

14. The Subcontractor will not be required to commence or continue work until the project site is in an adequate condition for his work to begin. If the project site is not in an adequate condition for the Subcontractor to start work, that is a delay under the terms of this contract.

15. The Contractor will give instructions or orders only to the Subcontractor or the Subcontractor's named representatives, not to the workers or sub-subcontractors used by the Subcontractor.

16. The Contractor may make no claim for liquidated or actual damages caused by the Subcontractor's delay beyond the money which the Contractor has to pay to the Owner for that delay under the terms of the prime contract.

17. The Contractor will pay the Subcontractor the amount of $15,000 *(the job total for labor and materials)* subject to the additions or deductions as may be described

Figure 12-1 *Sample addendum (Continued)*

in the attached contract documents.

(Or this payment language could be used: The Subcontractor will be paid based on the following terms: (then language for time and materials, or cost plus, or similar payment structures should be inserted here. Specific language for these terms is in the sample remodeling contract.)

18. Payment is due to the Subcontractor in full no later than <u>on the last day of each calendar month</u> *(Or any other payment date that the contractor and the subcontractor agree to.)* for all properly performed work and for all materials delivered to the job site during that month. Payments that are not made according to this schedule are overdue. Interest in the amount of <u>6</u>% will be owed on all overdue amounts. Such payments are due from the Contractor to the Subcontractor and are not dependent upon payments being received by the Contractor from the Owner. If payments become overdue, the Subcontractor may elect to suspend work until payment, or to terminate the contract.

(There is no provision in this sample contract for the contractor to terminate the subcontractor. The contractor may wish to include a clause that allows the contractor to terminate for nonperformance by the subcontractor.)

19. Money received by the Contractor from the Owner, or from the project developer or from a financing body for subcontract work will be held in trust and used solely for payments to the Subcontractor, its employees, and its sub-subcontractors.

20. Any form, document or contract wherein the Subcontractor releases a lien or bond is hereby qualified by the following language: "This release will apply only to work for which payment has been received in full by the Subcontractor, and said payment has been accepted for credit into Subcontractor's account."

(This language is to avoid giving up lien rights for a check that turns out to be bad.)

21. The Subcontractor may take all steps reasonably necessary to preserve and enforce its lien and bond rights.

22. If the Owner terminates the Contractor, the Contractor is liable to the Subcontractor for all work performed to the date of suspension, and all costs incurred by the Subcontractor for which the Subcontractor has not received payment, including, but not limited to, reasonable overhead and profit, damages, attorney fees, reasonable interest, and lost profit on unperformed work.

23. All claims, disputes, and matters rising out of this agreement will be submitted to arbitration by the American Arbitration Association. All such claims, disputes, and matters will be decided in accordance with the Construction Industry Arbitration Rules of the American Arbitration Association and the laws of the state where the

Figure 12-1 *Sample addendum (Continued)*

project is located. The arbitration will be conducted in the state where the project is located.

24. The Subcontractor will purchase and maintain the following types of insurance <u>Workers' Compensation insurance and General Liablility insurance</u> *(Name the kinds of insurance which the subcontractor agrees to obtain. Remember that this clause only includes those kinds of insurance that protect the prime contractor from possible loss. This does not include other kinds of insurance, such as Builder's Risk, which the subcontractor would need to protect himself from property loss.)* and will provide a certificate of insurance to the Contractor before beginning work. The Contractor will, if the Owner does not, purchase and maintain all risk insurance upon the full value of the work performed and materials delivered to the job site, which will include the interest of the Subcontractor. The Contractor must provide a certificate of insurance to the Subcontractor before the Subcontractor begins the work.

25. If Owner and Contractor fail to provide Builder's Risk insurance (unless the Subcontractor agrees otherwise) for the full value of subcontracted work, including any stored material and unpaid labor, the Subcontractor will be entitled to reimbursement of any insurance premium paid by Subcontractor for Builder's Risk insurance to protect the value of the Subcontractor's unpaid for work and materials. *(The contractor's builder's standard risk insurance may not cover unpaid demands for materials and work. The subcontractor should either require the contractor to obtain a rider protecting the subcontractor, or the subcontractor should get such a rider for himself. The language in this clause will allow the subcontractor to demand reimbursement for the premium cost of the extra insurance rider.)*

26. Any indemnification or hold harmless obligation of the Subcontractor will extend only to claims relating to property damage or bodily injury, and only to the extent that the property damage or bodily injury was caused by the negligence or intentional act of the Subcontractor, its employees, or its sub-subcontractors.

27. No back charge by the Contractor will be valid unless the Subcontractor has been given written notice of the Contractor's claim, has been allowed reasonable time to correct any deficiency, and has failed to do so. Further, any back charge will not exceed an amount reasonably calculated to cover the cost of the anticipated liability or claim. All remaining amounts due the Subcontractor will be promptly paid.

28. The Contractor will not require any contract closeout procedures or any forms that have not been provided to, and specifically accepted by, the Subcontractor prior to signing this addendum.

Figure 12-1 *Sample addendum (Continued)*

29. The Contractor is liable to the Subcontractor for any expenses incurred by the Subcontractor in enforcing the terms of this addendum, including, but not limited to, reasonable interest, attorney fees, and lost profits.

Subcontractor <u>Loral Drywallers</u>
(Company name)
By <u>*John Loral*</u>
Address <u>88 West St</u>
<u>Lansing, MI, 55555</u>
Title <u>Owner</u>

Date <u>10-1-00</u>

Contractor <u>Bigger Builders, Inc.</u>
(Company name)
By <u>*Bill Bigger*</u>
Address <u>22 Commerce Dr,</u>
<u>Lansing, MI, 55555</u>
Title <u>President of Bigger</u>
<u>Builders, Inc.</u>

Date <u>10-1-00</u>

Figure 12-1 *Sample addendum (Continued)*

Part Five: Legal Issues in the Construction Industry

Chapter 13

What Warranties Affect the Construction Industry?

Chapter 14

What Consumer Protection Laws Affect Your Business?

Chapter 15

What Legal Protection Is Available for a Company in Financial Trouble?

Chapter 16

What About Retirement, Disability or Death?

Chapter 17

A Few Last Words About You and Your Lawyer

What Warranties Affect the Construction Industry?

A warranty is a promise to your customer about the work you do. When you breach a warranty to your customer, you have to pay to fix it. In most situations, you cannot charge that cost back to your customer.

Warranties are a 20th century reform of an old legal rule that used to work, but fell apart in the modern world. The rule was *caveat emptor* — let the buyer beware — which worked fine in a less complicated world.

After all, Mr. 19th Century's bathroom was usually a privy that was outside and down the path. It didn't take much special knowledge to design or build, and it didn't come with warranties. If Mr. 19th Century realized there was a problem with his new privy after he paid his builder, there wasn't much he could do to get his money back or to make that builder fix it. That wasn't unfair, because there wasn't much that could be wrong with a privy that Mr. 19th Century couldn't have seen for himself *before* he paid his builder if he'd taken the time to look.

Times change. When Mr. 21st Century hires a builder to install a bathroom, and he discovers, after paying the builder, that his bathroom doesn't work in the way it's supposed to, he can do something about it. That's because Mr. 21st Century got warranties about the usefulness of that bathroom from his builder. That's fair, because Mr. 21st Century doesn't have the expertise to evaluate the work his builder has done until after the problems develop.

The warranties that Mr. 21st Century has can be *express* or *implied* — or both.

Express warranties are promises that the builder actually said or wrote. Implied warranties are promises that don't need to be spoken or written. The builder might not even realize he's making implied warranties. It doesn't matter. The idea behind an implied warranty is that when someone pays for something, it automatically comes with certain promises: the car will run, the toaster will brown the bread, the new roof will keep out the rain, and the toilet will flush into the waste pipe.

Express Warranties

Express warranties are easy to understand. Those are the actual spoken or written promises that the builder made.

For example, if the builder said, or wrote into the specifications "handicapped-accessible bathroom fixtures," that's a promise to use handicapped-accessible fixtures. It's part of the contract and it's also an express warranty.

Is It a Warranty or Sales Puffery?

Luckily for the loose-lipped, not every single word a builder says is an express warranty. That's good news — but how do you tell the difference between words that amount to an express warranty and words that are just sales talk. If a builder tells his customer that this will be "the nicest bathroom in town," is that a warranty that it will be the "nicest" in town?

The word "nicest" is not an express warranty because it's too vague. It's not possible to figure out exactly what is being promised. "Nicest" is a matter of opinion. It's just hype — words that people generally understand

Can "Best" Get You Into Trouble?

Until recently, I was confident sales personnel could freely use words like *nicest, best* and *greatest.* Every modern consumer, I felt, understood that the job of a salesman is to talk up the product. I was confident the law on the subject agreed with me, even about written statements such as "the greatest car on the road," "the nicest sweater" or "the best pizza in town." I assumed people who read such language understood this is just sales talk. What do you expect advertisers to write? "An okay car," "a miniskirt your friends may or may not admire" or "a pizza as good as anybody else's?"

Yes, I understand about the Truth in Advertising laws, but I thought the truth to which those laws refer is the specific details in advertising—like *red, 18 ounces,* or *equipped with ground fault interrupters.* Statements like these are representations of specific facts.

I may be out of date. In this state, we recently had a court decision (now on appeal) relating to pizzas. A local pizzeria was sued for calling itself the "best" pizza in town, even though its pizza wasn't any different from the pizzas produced elsewhere in the community.

I don't know what the outcome of this particular case will ultimately be after the appeal process, but I think it's a harbinger of changes to come. In the meantime, it's probably a good idea to be discreet with the superlatives in your advertising. Stick to adjectives that are not comparatives, such as *terrific, lovely* or *outstanding.* Be careful about using words like *best, nicest* or *greatest.*

as only sales talk. After all, what's the builder going to say to a potential customer: "I'm going to build a bathroom that will be almost the nicest?"

But builders have to be careful with sales talk, because sometimes it isn't as vague as the builder might have intended. If a builder talks about an "Art Deco" bathroom, that alone probably isn't an express warranty. Exactly what is Art Deco? Every time you open a decorating magazine and see something with curves on it, the magazine calls it Art Deco. But it is possible for sales talk about Art Deco to become a warranty.

The difference between sales talk and actual warranties depends on the details and on the customer's reasonable expectations. If the sales talk is vague effusive language that's difficult to pin down, it probably doesn't amount to a warranty. However, if it's possible for the customer to reasonably distinguish what was promised from something that wasn't promised, then we're probably talking about an express warranty.

For example, the words "Art Deco" would be an express warranty if the builder said he would use the Giant Plumbing Company's Better Art Deco line of fixtures. That's not vague at all. It's an express warranty about fixtures. The builder knows exactly how to keep that warranty: Buy that line of fixtures.

There's another way that throwing Art Deco words around could become an express warranty. Suppose the builder promises to build an Art Deco bathroom in a historic house, because that's what was there when the house was new. It's possible to find out what an Art Deco bathroom of that era would have looked like. So, in those circumstances, that could be an express warranty to make the bathroom look as authentically Art Deco as it's reasonably possible to make it.

Reasonable doesn't mean the builder has to go out and look for antique fixtures — unless that's what he said he'd do. But it does mean the standard tub and sink he puts in every other house won't do. The builder had better get on the phone to Giant Plumbing Fixtures to ask about their Art Deco line. If the builder can't find fixtures in an Art Deco style, then he should talk to his customer and the two of them should come to an agreement to use something else. Here's what the builder should *not* do: order Victorian-style fixtures without first discussing it with his client.

Limitations on Express Warranties

When you make express warranties, the best way to limit those warranties is to say exactly what you mean: how long, how much, and how often. *Limiting* a warranty is how you keep yourself from promising more than you intended to promise.

For example, if you promise that the house you will build won't cost the customer more than $600 a year to heat, what do you mean by that? Do you intend to promise that it won't *ever* cost more than $600? I'll bet you don't. You could avoid an open-ended promise with language like this: *This house will have no more than $600 in heating costs during its first year of occupancy.* That language clearly limits the life of that express warranty about heating costs. Or, you could include language in your express warranty like this: *This house will have no more than $600 per year in heating costs at the present cost of utilities.*

Implied Warranties

Implied warranties are based on the idea that taking someone's money and building something for that person automatically implies certain promises about the usefulness of that structure. Implied warranties don't need a spoken or a written promise to exist, because implied warranties are based on what people reasonably expect to get when they pay for something. That includes a garage door that's wide enough to get your car through; lights that come on when you flip the switch; water that flows when you turn the taps; stairs that will carry your weight when you walk on them. That sort of thing.

There are two implied warranties in construction law: the warranty of habitability and the warranty of good workmanship. Not every state and court uses exactly those words, but no matter what words are used, they boil down to those same two warranties.

Habitability

Habitability means that the structure can be used in the way it was intended to be used. If the structure is an office, it's wired for office machines and there's room for a desk, files, and so forth. If the structure is a garage, it will hold cars. If it's a house, people can safely live in it.

If you build a house and can't get a certificate of occupancy for that house, that house isn't habitable. No matter how great it is otherwise, or how small the problem, nobody can live in the house. If you don't take steps to correct the problem and get a certificate, you've violated your warranty of habitability, because people can't live in a house for which they can't get an occupancy permit. And it was their reasonable expectation that they would be able to live in that house.

Here's an example of a violation of the implied warranty of habitability. Say your customer moved into the house, and then afterwards discovered you had neglected to connect the soil pipe to the septic system or sewer. That house isn't habitable, *even though the customer is living in it.* If the regulatory agency finds out about the health hazard, they'll move those people out. Your failure, as the builder, to connect that soil pipe is a breach of the warranty of habitability. The customer can force you to fix that problem, and also to pay for any direct damages the customer suffered, such as the cost of moving into a motel while you're doing the repairs.

Good Workmanship

The implied warranty of "good workmanship" doesn't mean what you might think it does. It's not a promise of good craftsmanlike work or a promise of the best work you could do. It's a promise of *good enough* work. The warranty of good workmanship means the work is good enough to meet the standard of what's acceptable in the trade. Many people who have a custom home built have a hard time with this, because they expect perfection and you're providing work that meets *trade standards*.

Trade Standards

For example, suppose you install a kitchen and the cupboards are a little out of plumb and the trim work isn't totally aligned. That's sloppy work, right? That customer probably won't call you to do any more work for them, though they may call for you to come redo it. But sloppy work isn't, by itself, a violation of the warranty of good workmanship, because the trade standards don't call for perfectly hung cupboards or perfectly mitered corners. That's because we all know some people do neater work than other people.

Trade standards involve questions like these: Do the cabinet doors open? Are the cupboards level enough to stack dishes on? Is the trim attached or does it hang loose in some places?

However, suppose you put on a new roof for your customer. The roof was very difficult to install, because it had lots of peaks and valleys, but you did a great job except for one tiny leak around the chimney. Even if the roof is absolutely perfect in every other way, that tiny leak is a violation of your warranty of good workmanship. The trade standard of good workmanship in the roofing industry is a roof that doesn't leak.

Limitations on Implied Warranties

The law does let you get out from under implied warranties, but it's not easy. You have to do it with clear blunt language that everybody understands. Words like AS IS printed in big letters across an item for sale is clear. Everybody knows that means: no warranties. None. You need to aim for that level of communication if you want to avoid giving your customer an implied warranty.

For example, suppose you install a new steel entry door, and the customer insists that you reinstall his old screen/storm door over it. You recommend against it, but he insists. If you don't want to pay for the damage when that new steel door is ruined by the heat the storm door traps, you have to say that very clearly and very specifically. Words like this would work: *The contractor disclaims all implied warranties of usability on this door.* Or, you could say: *The contractor makes no express or implied warranties of usability on this door or its installation.*

To protect you the way you want it to, your disclaimer needs to be as precise and as exact as you can make it. Suppose the customer or architect asks you to install shingles on a roof with such a low pitch that you know there will be a problem with ice dams, but the customer or architect doesn't want a rolled roof because they like the look of shingles. That's up to them, but if there's a problem with ice dams, it shouldn't be your problem. Write language like this into your contract: *The contractor does not warrant this roof against damage caused by ice or weather.*

Disclaimer of Warranties

The law on warranties is something like a default mode on a computer. If you don't include what you need to about warranties in your contract, the law will do it for you. For example, if you don't limit your express war-

---

What Are Limitations and Disclaimers?

A *disclaimer is* language that means you aren't making a warranty. You disclaim a warranty by simply saying—in writing—you aren't giving a warranty. You should explain what kind of warranty you aren't giving: express, implied or both.

For example, a roofer makes an implied warranty (whether he realizes it or not) that the shingles he installed are fit for their purpose. But suppose they aren't? Suppose there was a problem in the manufacturing process and the shingles curl in the sun? The roofer should disclaim his liability for defects in the manufacturing process with language like this: *"The contractor disclaims all warranties against manufacturing defects in the roof shingles."*

A *limitation* is language that means you are making a warranty, but you're putting some limiting language into it so your warranty doesn't cover things you don't want it to cover and isn't open-ended. You do that by explaining in detail what you are and are not covering.

Suppose an electrician makes this express warranty: "The wiring in the home office addition will be adequate for business equipment." Then, two years later, the homeowner installs bigger, better, and more electricity-greedy equipment that didn't even exist at the time of the original warranty. The customer may want to file a claim against the electrician when he discovers he needs more wiring. That electrician should have limited the warranty to a specific time period, or limited it to *"the business equipment presently in use."*

ranties to one year, and you wind up in court arguing how long that warranty was supposed to last, the law will fill in that blank, and it might decide on a longer period, such as two, three or six years.

Unless the state law specifically prohibits it, usually you and your customer can agree to something different. For example, suppose you're concerned about the presence of an underground stream, but your customer and his architect don't think it will be a problem. You're willing to build there, but you don't want to accept any responsibility if there's a problem caused by soil shifting. You and your customer can agree to put a disclaimer into the contract.

However, there are state laws and federal laws that limit how far you can go with a disclaimer, and exactly what you have to say in that disclaimer to make it effective. For example, the law on warranties makes it very difficult to disclaim safety issues. If you build a deck that has no support, and it collapses the first time someone steps on it, you'll find that contract language that said you make no warranties about the safety of this structure won't get you off the hook in most states.

Why Disclaim or Limit Warranties

There are three reasons you would want to disclaim or limit your warranties. The first reason is that sometimes warranty damages can cost you more money than the profit you made on that job. The second reason is that you don't want to pay for damage caused by things beyond your control. The third reason is that you don't want those warranties, even the express ones that you voluntarily gave the client, hanging over your head indefinitely.

The Amount of Damages

If you've violated your warranties, you may have also breached your contract. In most cases, it's the customer's choice whether to sue you for breach of contract or breach of warranty — and that choice could make a *big* difference in what it might cost you. In a breach of contract lawsuit, the general rule is that the customer can't win more money than the contract amount, except for direct, consequential damages.

But warranty lawsuits are different. Your customer could win much more money in a warranty lawsuit than just the contract amount. That's because a warranty claim is *not* a breach of contract suit. It's a tort action. The customer could win money for fixing the problem, and also win tort damages.

So what would tort damages include? Everything that happened because of the breach of warranty, and *more besides*. For example, suppose you didn't hook up the soil pipe to the sewer connection. If the owner sues you for breach of warranty, he could win the cost of hooking up the soil pipe. Fair enough. But he could also win the cost of things like living in a motel until the soil pipe was connected, medical bills, and possibly even punitive damages and damages for the pain and suffering caused by discovering his soil pipe was unconnected. Who knows what previously-undiscovered illnesses that unconnected soil pipe brought on? He may never be able to work again!

You want to limit these kinds of damages, but you can only do that if you do it in advance. You can limit your warranty obligations to pay for this kind of thing by putting language like this into your contract: *Contractor's warranties are limited to labor and materials only.*

Exclusions of Things You Can't Control

One of the problems with warranties is that sometimes you can find yourself responsible for damages that have been made worse by people or events after you finished the job.

For example, suppose you install a roof. A month later the homeowner gets up on the roof and installs a skylight. While he's up there, he cleans out his gutters and then tromps all over the roof admiring the view. If a leak is discovered soon afterwards, you don't want to pay to fix that, because maybe it wasn't there when you left the job site. Or maybe it was, but wasn't as big a leak.

You can exclude things the homeowner did with language like this: *The contractor's warranties do not cover ordinary wear and tear, or damages caused by the owner's actions or abuse.* Or, you could simply write: *The contractor's warranties exclude damages for abuse by others.*

There's another way you could be responsible for things outside your control. Suppose, for example, you installed a roof and it turns out the shingles were defective. Obviously, you can't do anything about quality control in the manufacturer's factory, yet you could be held responsible

---

Maintaining the Manufacturer's Warranties

If there's a problem with the product, the homeowner gets the benefit of the manufacturer's product warranties - if the product has been installed according to the manufacturer's directions. Since the contractor has a duty to maintain the manufacturer's warranties, it follows that he has a duty to follow those directions exactly.

Sometimes the contractor actually knows a better way of installing the product than the manufacturer's recommendations. But he'd be foolish to do so. If there were a problem with the product, the contractor would find that it's his problem unless that product was installed exactly according to the manufacturer's instructions.

to the homeowner when that roof fails. You could turn around and possibly sue the manufacturer for reimbursement. But since you aren't in the business of suing people, and since a lawsuit will probably end up costing you money even if you win, you'd rather not be left in that position. You can avoid most of these kinds of problems with language like this: *The contractor warrants that he will select new materials of good quality. The contractor will maintain all manufacturers' warranties. The customer is limited to the manufacturer's warranties for defects in the manufacture of materials.*

This language doesn't let you off the hook if you didn't install the shingles according to the manufacturer's directions, but if the problem is that the shingles are defective, this language makes that a problem between the homeowner and the manufacturer.

The Life of the Warranty

After you've retired to Florida, you don't want to hear from unhappy customers. You can solve that problem with language like this: *All contractor warranties are limited to a period of no more than one year* — or six months or one month or whatever you and your customer agree to.

A Word of Caution

There are situations where a contractor has acted outside the law or has placed the homeowner or others in jeopardy in such a reckless way that the best disclaimer or limitations in the world won't avoid that liability. See Chapters 9 and 10 about safety and injuries on the job site.

And warranties aren't the whole story. You also need to know how other consumer protection laws affect your business. Keep reading.

14

What Consumer Protection Laws Affect Your Business?

In this chapter we're talking about the rights of your customers who are *consumers*, not your commerical customers. Almost everyone would agree that some consumer protection laws are necessary. But there are honest contractors who feel like they're innocent bystanders who got hit by a consumer protection shotgun blast aimed at the dishonest contractors.

Those contractors agree that consumers need protection from dishonest practices. "But I'm an honest guy," they say. "I never cheated anybody. Why do these laws make it so hard for me to do business?"

The problem is the law doesn't have a legal laser gun. When the law sets out to regulate consumer rip-offs, it has to take the shotgun approach. When Rip-off Roofing goes around browbeating old ladies into signing roofing contracts for six or seven times what they should be paying, the legislature can't pass a law saying we aren't going to let Rip-off Roofing do that any more. Any law aimed at a particular person or company is unconstitutional. If something is illegal, it has to be illegal no matter who does it. So if the legislators want to stop Rip-off Roofing, they have to regulate what he's *doing*, not him. Then, after they pass the law, they can stop Rip-off Roofing.

I hear a contractor asking: "Why don't they just take Rip-off Roofing's license away instead of writing a law that makes it more complicated for me to write contracts? That puts me in a position where a dishonest consumer could take advantage of me!"

Why not just pull Rip-off Roofing's license? Think about it for a minute. The state can't take Rip-off Roofing's license away for doing something that isn't illegal. Besides, Rip-off Roofing probably never bothered to get a license in the first place.

State Consumer Protection Laws

There are a number of consumer protection laws at the state level, and some are tougher than the federal laws. When there's a difference between the state and federal requirements, the general rule is that the contractor must meet whichever is the higher standard.

The Right of Cancellation — Cooling-Off Periods

Many states protect consumers by providing homeowners with a Right of Cancellation. That's a legal shotgun aimed at construction salesmen who go into people's homes and pressure them into signing construction contracts. You know the kind of contract I mean: "I was in the neighborhood, and saw your roof needed replacing. If you sign this roofing contract right this second, I'll do it for half-price."

The right to cancel that contract exists because the contract was signed in the consumer's home, after the contractor or his agent persuaded the consumer to sign. If the consumer had signed that contract in the contractor's office or in a showroom — anyplace outside the consumer's home — then there would be no right of cancellation.

The issue of the consumer's home is the key here. Once an elderly person (or even some not-so-old consumer) has let someone into their house, there's the possibility of intimidation. How do they get this guy out of their house without signing something? His mere presence and persistence could be intimidating, even if that's not his intention.

But when the customer walks into the contractor's office, it's unlikely that they'd be badgered or intimidated into signing something they didn't want. When they're in the contractor's office or showroom, the consumers have an easy solution if they're feeling intimidated. They can walk out the door.

The consumer may not be entirely happy with the contract they've signed in the contractor's showroom, but it's clear that they did want some kind of contract. There's an element of consent in this situation that sometimes isn't present in some door-to-door selling. The customer is talking to the contractor (or salesperson) because that's what they want to do.

Required Notice for the Right of Cancellation

In most states, when the customer has the right to cancel the contract, the contractor has to tell the customer about that right in writing. If the contractor doesn't give the customer written notice of the customer's right to cancel, then that customer's right to cancel just goes on and on, instead ending when a certain period of time expires. The customer could cancel the contract at any time before job completion. Any contractor who doesn't give notice of the right to cancel is taking the chance that he could do the work and not get paid.

How to Give Notice

The notice of the right to cancel can be part of the contract — it doesn't have to be on a separate page, like the right of rescission. The notice should tell the customer how and where to cancel, usually by mail at the contractor's business address.

If the customer wants to cancel, all they have to do is follow the procedure described in the notice of the right to cancel. It doesn't matter if the mailed notice doesn't get to the contractor until after the cancellation period has expired. It only matters that the customer mailed it within that time period. The customer doesn't need a good reason to cancel. He or she can just change their mind. The deal is off. End of discussion.

The customer has the right to cancel even if the contractor was foolish enough to start the work immediately. But if they do cancel, the customer has to let the contractor remove any materials and tools the contractor already brought to the job site. As a general rule, the contractor can remove already-installed materials, provided that the contractor can return the structure to its original state. And if the customer has already paid money, the contractor has to return the money.

Are There Any Exceptions to the Right of Cancellation?

Obviously a contractor shouldn't take the chance of starting work until the right to cancel has expired. That's a problem when there's work that needs to be done immediately, such as a board-up after a fire. Work like that can't wait, so there's an exception in the law for emergency repairs. Generally, in most states, a contractor doesn't need a specific or written contract to be entitled to payment for emergency work done to protect the health, welfare and safety of the general public — such as children who might be drawn to a fire site or the safety of the customers.

Limitations on Payments

Some states limit the amount of money a contractor can collect in advance of doing the work. This kind of limitation can have the effect of putting contractors into the financing business.

For example, suppose Contractor Cal is hired to build a deck. If he's limited in how much money he can collect in advance, he might not get enough to buy all the materials, or to pay for the hours that his crew puts in before the next payment is due. For practical purposes, Cal is financing the job. If he has to wait for some of the money he puts into the job through his labor and material, he's lending front money to the customer. If he's a small contractor who needs the money to pay his crew — and it turns out that his customer is a slow pay — that's a big problem for Cal.

This is more of a problem in some states than others. In Connecticut, for example, advance payments are limited to 10 percent, and the contractor has to put in a certain amount of work before he can collect any more money after the initial payment.

To make this kind of problem more manageable, I'd suggest a contract that requires the customers to make small, frequent payments tied to specific parts of the job. For example, if you were building an addition, you could trigger payments when you finish digging the foundation, pouring the foundation, framing the addition, wiring, drywalling, and so on. Or you can require the customer to get financing from a bank or other professional lending institution in advance. That way, at least you know the money is there.

Licensing Laws

Many states use license laws as a way to protect consumers from dishonest and unskilled contractors that doesn't cost the state much money. Typically, the state's license laws require contractors to complete construction contracts in a workmanlike manner for the stated price, and to build in accordance with the building codes. Contractors who don't meet these requirements can be disciplined by the licensing board. They may lose their license after a hearing before the proper officials, who are usually part of the licensing board.

But to make that work, these states need to rigorously enforce their license laws. When they don't, it puts a real burden on the licensed contractors. What if you, after paying for your license and insurance, have to compete with a contractor who doesn't spend money on stuff like that? You're at a competitive disadvantage. It costs you more money to be in business than it costs him.

There are other ways of enforcing the license laws besides waiting for the licensing board to pull someone's license. The most common (and cheapest) way for states to enforce their licensing laws is to prevent unlicensed contractors from suing their customers for payment. A few states even allow customers to recover money already paid to unlicensed contractors.

You can make the argument that this policy unjustly enriches certain consumers who take advantage of unlicensed contractors — and it's true. There are people who use that law to get something for nothing. Because of that, a few states have allowed unlicensed contractors to erode that law by collecting payment in certain limited situations. However, the state has a big stake in making contractors get a license. And the simple fact is that people in the construction industry, after discovering they may not be paid for the unlicensed work they've done, will usually go out and get a license. See Chapter 1 for more information about licensing requirements.

Restrictions on Arbitration Clauses

There are a lot of advantages in arbitration for a contractor: usually the arbitrator is familiar with the industry, the process is quicker, and it's usually cheaper. That's why most contractors prefer arbitration to going into court.

Arbitration isn't necessarily such a good deal for the customer, however, because the arbitrator may not be as familiar with, or as sympathetic to, complex legal issues. Also, the truth is that some sophisticated consumers can use a lawsuit as a kind of legal blackmail against the contractor: Settle the lawsuit for something less than the contract price to avoid the expense and time involved in protracted legal action, or see all your profits eaten up in legal fees.

Many contractors include a clause in their contract requiring customers to give up their right to sue over disputes and instead enter arbitration, but some states put restrictions on contract clauses that limit the customers' rights to go to court. Those states require, for example, that a clause in a contract that requires the customer to go into arbitration instead of suing in court must be in bold face. You must also include an explanation with your arbitration language that clearly explains to the customer that they're giving up the right to go to court. Some states require the arbitration clause to be countersigned by the customer. If it isn't, the state won't enforce that clause.

Mandatory Writing Clauses

Many states require construction contracts to be in writing to protect consumers from misunderstandings or outright fraud. However, the problem that regularly pops up in the construction business is change orders. You can count on something like this: After you've installed the framing for the kitchen island exactly according to the customer's specs, the customer will look at it and say: "I need more space between the island and the sink." So you tear out the framing you've already done and do it over.

This is a change to the contract. Change orders have a lot of built-in problems. What happens when the customer gets the final bill that's higher than the stated price in the contract because of the extra framing and tearout time? What happens if it's the husband who ordered the change, and when the wife sees the new framing, she says: "What did you do? That's not how it's supposed to be." What happens if the customer looks at your now-higher bill, and says, "What change? That's how it was always supposed to be."

As your lawyer, I would tell you to always, *always* get those change orders in writing and signed by someone who's authorized in the contract to sign change orders. But I'm a realist. I know that out in the field that's often not what happens. What happens is the customer is standing at the lead carpenter's elbow as he's swinging his hammer, saying, "Move it just a little bit over there."

Does a Change Order Have to Be in Writing?

If you're in a state where the original contract has to be in writing, does the change order also have to be in writing? It won't be a problem unless there's a disagreement with your customer or your customer is uncollectible. But let's assume you didn't put in writing. Can you enforce the additional costs of a change order where your state law requires that your construction contract be in writing?

The answer to that depends on what state you're in. Connecticut, for example, requires that all change orders be in writing. If they're not in writing, the law says, the contractor can't collect for the work done under the change order. In most other states, the contractor can successfully argue that the change order doesn't have to be in writing — only the original contract has to be in writing. Regardless, I still recommend that you *never* start work on a change until you've got a signed change order, no matter what your state law requires. A document describing work to be done, with the customer's signature, holds a whole lot more weight in court than two people's conflicting memories.

Special Notices

Some states require contractors to put a notice into their contract with the homeowners that contractors are required by law to be licensed, and that dissatisfied customers can complain to the licensing agency.

Special Requirements About Construction Liens

Some states require the contractor to inform the homeowner in the construction contract about the potential for a construction lien, and to explain that if a construction lien is enforced, the customer could lose his home.

Some states require the contractor to put into the remodeling or building contract a promise that the contractor will provide a signed release of liens in exchange for the final payment. In those states, usually the contractor can't lawfully collect the final payment without such a lien release. To protect themselves, contractors in those states sometimes write into the mandatory lien waiver that it's *good* only upon the bank's honoring the customer's check. Then if the final payment check bounces, the contractor's lien rights are resurrected.

The Building Code

Building codes and certificates of occupancy requirements are intended to ensure that the building is safe and that it can be used as intended. If a building doesn't conform to the building code, the customer can't get a certificate of occupancy. If a customer can't get a certificate of occupancy, that's a violation of the implied warranty of fitness of purpose. It's also a violation of the contract.

That's what that boilerplate language about *applicable laws* that you see in some contracts is about. It's an agreement that the contractor has to build in a lawful way — in other words, to meet the requirements of the local building code. However, even if the contract doesn't have a single word in it about applicable laws or the building code, meeting the building code is still an implied condition of the contract. The builder doesn't have any right *not* to meet the local laws. Failure to meet the building code standards is a breach of contract *and* a warranty violation.

If, for example, a remodeler opens up a wall to start putting on the new addition and discovers noncompliant wiring, he'd better fix that wiring. He has a duty to deliver an addition that meets code requirements. Well, I can hear you asking, what if the wiring has nothing to do with the addition? What if the addition will have its own wiring? All I can say is, once he opens up that wall and discovers the problem, it becomes his problem.

That's why, when that remodeler writes his contract, he should explain to the customer that it's impossible to know exactly what the exact cost of the job will be. It depends on the possibility of discovering things like bad wiring, dry rot, termites, water damage, shifted foundations and so on. If the remodeler has already agreed to a fixed price contract, when he discovers the bad wiring, that bad wiring will reduce his profit margin.

State Warranty Requirements

Several states regulate implied warranties and the way warranty disclaimers, especially implied warranty disclaimers, should be written. If you're using a disclaimer, you should check to see if it will work in your state — especially if you're disclaiming implied warranties. If you're using a disclaimer or a limitation that doesn't meet your state standards, the court will simply ignore your disclaimer or limitation if you wind up in court.

If you try to limit an express warranty where the state law doesn't let you, the court will use what you might think of as the state's default standards to define that warranty. For example, suppose you limited your warranty about no leaks in the roof to six months, but your state law says a contractor can't limit building warranties to less than a year. If you're dragged into court because the roof started leaking after eight months, the court will determine the length of your warranty based on the state law. If there's no specific state law on roofs, the court will use trade standards and other decisions in similar lawsuits.

As another example, suppose you were trying to disclaim a warranty of habitability and your state says that's illegal. Your disclaimer is then unenforceable. Your project has to meet the legal warranty standards of habitability that your state imposes.

Also check Chapter 13 on warranties.

The Federal Consumer Protection Laws

There aren't very many federal laws that impact contractors. Well, let me rephrase that. There aren't many federal consumer protection laws that directly impact construction contracts. Of the ones that do, the most important to the construction industry are the Right of Rescission and the Magnuson-Moss Warranty Act.

The Right of Rescission

The Truth In Lending Act applies when the contract involves a security interest or a lien on the customer's home. It gives construction customers a right of rescission for 72 hours after the contract is signed — or for 72 hours after the homeowner is given notice of the right of rescission, whichever comes later. *Rescission* means to put the parties to the contract back in the position they were before there was a contract. The phrase you sometimes see that means the same thing is "rescind the contract." Figure 14-1 shows a Notice of Right to Rescission.

In most states, rescission and cancellation work very much in the same way, although rescission is a federal right and cancellation is a state right. Each gives customers time to change their mind. Each requires that the contractor give a notice of that right to the customer that tells the customer how to rescind. If the contractor doesn't give the customer the proper notice, then the right to rescind or cancel extends to the end of the job. Each requires the contractor to return any money the customer has given the contractor if the customer rescinds or cancels.

But there are some ways the right of rescission is different from the right of cancellation. The most significant is that the right of rescission doesn't exist unless the project involves a *security interest* in the customer's home, such as a mortgage.

There are some procedural differences, too. The notice of the right of rescission must describe the kind of security interest that could attach to the customer's house. The notice must be on a separate document, and

NOTICE OF RIGHT TO RESCISSION

Your Right to Cancel This Contract:

You are entering into a contract that will result in a lien on, or a security interest in, your home. Federal law gives you the legal right to rescind or cancel this contract without cost to you, but you must give notice of your decision to cancel within three (3) business days from whichever of the following events occurs last:

1. The date you signed the contract, which is _____.

2. The date you received this notice of your right to cancel.

Payments made by you under the contract and any negotiable instrument executed by you will be returned within 10 business days following receipt of the seller of your cancellation notice.

If you chose to cancel the contract, the lien or security interest is also canceled. Within 20 calendar days after we receive your notice to cancel, we must take the necessary steps to cancel any lien or security interest we have created in your home in conjunction with the contract.

Although you may keep any money or property which we have given you until we have done the things described in the previous paragraph, you must then offer to return the money or property. If returning the property is impractical or unfair, you must compensate us for its fair market value. You may offer to return the property at your home or at the location of the address below. If we do not take possession of the money or property within 20 calendar days of your offer, you may keep it without further obligation.

How to Cancel

If you decide to cancel this transaction, you may do so by notifying us in writing at:

Bigger Builders, Inc.
(Remodeler's or Builder's Name)

22 Commerce Drive
(Street or Post Office Box)

Lansing, MI 55555
(City, State, ZIP)

You may use any written statement signed and dated by you that states your intention to cancel, or you may use this notice by dating and signing it below. If you cancel by mail or telegram, you must send the notice no later than midnight of_____(or midnight of the third business day of the events listed above). If you send or deliver your notice in some other way, it must be delivered to the above address not later than that time.

I Wish to Cancel

_____

(Consumer's Name)   *(Date)*

Figure 14-1 *Notice of Right to Rescission*

Required Notices

If there's any doubt in your mind about whether or not notice is required, just go ahead and give notice. The risk is serious if you're supposed to and don't, while the likelihood that the customer will cancel or rescind the deal is small. If the customer actually does cancel or rescind, the deal probably wouldn't have worked out anyway.

Here's a summary of your requirements under the right of cancellation and right of rescission laws.

Notice of the Right of Cancellation

▋ If the contract was signed in the customer's home, the customer has a right to cancel the contract without a penalty and to have his money returned to him. This right expires 72 hours after signing the contract or delivery of notice of the right of cancellation, whichever comes last.

▋ The notice of the right to cancel can be written into the contract.

▋ The notice must tell the customer how and where to give notice of the decision to rescind the contract.

▋ The notice must tell the customer that he has 72 hours to rescind, and must tell him when the 72 hours end.

▋ The customer must be told that he or she will get their money back if the contract is canceled.

You can give notice of the right to cancellation by including the following language in your contract:

A consumer who has signed a contract for consumer services in his or her home has three days during which the consumer may cancel that contract. The consumer may cancel the contract by personal delivery or by mailing notice of cancellation to the contractor's place of business no later than midnight of the third day. If the consumer cancels the contract, the contractor will return all money or other goods advanced to the contractor by the consumer. The consumer must return the contractor's tools and any materials which the contractor may have brought to the job site. The consumer may do this by making the tools and materials available to the contractor at the consumer's home.

(In Michigan, where the author practices law, the time period for cancellation is 72 hours. Your state may have a different time period, or may not provide a right of cancellation at all.)

Notice of the Right of Rescission

▋ If the contract involves, or may result in, a security interest or a lien on the customer's home, the customer has 72 hours after signing or delivery of the notice of the right of rescission, whichever comes last, to rescind the contract.

Required Notices (cont.)

▌ Each customer is entitled to two copies of the notice of the right of rescission. If husband and wife both sign, each gets two copies, for a total of four.

▌ The notice of the right of rescission must be on a separate document.

▌ The notice of the right of rescission must contain a form that the customer can fill out as notice of the customer's intention to rescind.

▌ The notice must describe the lien or the security interest that could be placed on the customer's home.

▌ The customer must be told that he or she will get their money back if the contract is rescinded.

▌ The customer must be told exactly when the right to rescind expires.

---

each customer must get two copies. If both a husband and wife sign the contract, that means they get a total of four pages.

The 72-hour time limit starts running from the signing of the contract or delivery of the notices of the right of rescission, whichever comes later. The notice of the right of rescission must include a form for the customer to sign and mail should the customer wish to rescind. If the customer mails the notice within the 72-hour time limit, it doesn't matter when the contractor actually receives the notice.

The Magnuson-Moss Warranty Act

The Magnuson-Moss Act only covers consumer products and manufactured items. It doesn't require remodelers to give their customers warranties about their work, although you should be aware that there might be other laws that do. See Chapter 13.

What Magnuson-Moss does is regulate what a warranty — or a disclaimer of a warranty — on consumer products or manufactured equipment should look like. It doesn't have to be on a separate document; it can be in the contract itself.

I can hear you saying you're in the construction business, not the consumer products business, so Magnuson-Moss doesn't have anything to do with you. But that's not as true as you might think. For example, suppose Cal the contractor signs a contract to install a new kitchen for Harry the homeowner. The kitchen specs call for a new stove, refrigerator, dishwasher and garbage disposal. Those are all consumer products. If Cal orders these appliances and installs them, he has probably bought them and resold them to Harry (depending on the circumstances of the contract). That triggers the Magnuson-Moss Act.

Unless the customer goes out and buys the products himself, assume you're selling consumer products. And if you're selling consumer products, Magnuson-Moss gives you three choices:

1. You could give no written warranty at all by including a statement in your contract that says you disclaim all implied and written warranties. But you might find your customers don't like that too much.

2. You could give your customer a warranty on your work, but exclude consumer products from that warranty. Because Magnuson-Moss only covers consumer products, excluding those products from your warranties will avoid triggering the Magnuson-Moss requirements. The customers will still have their manufacturers' warranties, and it's worth reminding them of that. You can do that with this language:

    > This warranty does not cover any appliance, piece of equipment, or other item which is a consumer product for purposes of the Magnuson-Moss Warranty Act. The contractor guarantees to take all necessary steps to maintain the manufacturers' warranties for those products.

3. You can give a warranty that conforms to the Magnuson-Moss requirements. See the sidebar with the requirements for a limited or full Magnuson-Moss warranty.

Other Federal Laws

There are other federal laws, such as the Americans With Disabilities Act, which impact certain consumers. Those topics are covered in other chapters.

In this chapter we took a look at laws intended to protect the poor innocent consumer from the big bad contractor. In the next chapter, we'll cover laws that protect you, the contractor, from some of those consumers.

Magnuson-Moss Act Requirements in a Limited Warranty

▮ The name of the person receiving the warranty, and whether or not that person can transfer that warranty to subsequent purchasers.

▮ Exactly what the warranty covers and what it does not.

▮ What the builder or remodeler will do to fix a warranty violation.

▮ Will fixing the warranty violation cost the customer money? For example, the warranty might cover parts only, and labor would be a charge to the customer.

▮ How the customer has to give notice of a warranty problem to the contractor. For example, the warranty might require the customer to give notice in writing and mail it to the contractor's place of business. Include that address.

▮ Does the warranty require arbitration? If so, does the arbitration requirement conform to the dispute resolution standards outlined in the Magnuson-Moss Act?

▮ Does the warranty exclude consequential damages? Consequential damages are those damages caused by the warranty violation, which can't be fixed by fixing the product, For example, suppose the contractor installed an outlet for the customer's business machines and when the outlet failed the customer lost thousands of dollars because he couldn't process his business orders.

▮ If the warranty the contractor gives the customer excludes consequential damages, the contractor must insert the following words after the exclusion:

Some states do not allow the exclusion or limitation of incidental or consequential damages, so the above limitation may not apply to you.

▮ The warranty must also include the words:

This warranty gives you specific legal rights, and you may also have other rights which vary from state to state.

Magnuson-Moss Act Requirements in a Full Warranty

▮ A full warranty (that's one without any limitations on it) must provide for remedies within a reasonable time.

▮ A full warranty can't put any limitation on the duration of implied warranties.

▮ The full warranty, like the limited warranty, must state whether consequential damages are limited or excluded, and, if they are, must include this language after the limitation:

Some states do not allow the exclusion or limitation of incidental or consequential damages, so the above limitation may not apply to you.

▮ If the item can't be repaired, a full warranty must allow the customer to decide to either take a refund or a free replacement.

15

What Legal Protection Is Available for a Company in Financial Trouble?

There are several ways small construction companies get into money trouble.

First, of course, they get in trouble when business is bad. Like most small businesses, the construction industry is susceptible to economic cycles. When the economy looks iffy, even people who are in good financial shape will put off buying that new house or remodeling that kitchen.

But too much business can be even worse. I was once told that no construction business ever failed because it didn't have enough work — rather, construction businesses fail when they have *too much* work. At the time I thought that sounded stupid, although I've come to understand it's true. When business is good, you get lots of calls for more work than you can really manage — but when you own a small construction company, turning away business is just about the hardest thing you can do. So you don't turn it away; you figure you'll do it all somehow. Of course, the truth is that accepting more business than you have the crews, equipment or time to handle gets you in over your head in a hurry.

This is the same sort of problem subcontractors run into. Afraid all of their bids won't be accepted and they'll be left without enough work, they put bids on more jobs than they can handle. They assume that only some of those bids will come through, and they can get into real trouble if too many bids are accepted.

Sometimes it's not how many jobs you've accepted, it's one particular job that creates the problem. Everybody has had the Client From Hell who just won't let you make any money. They tie up your resources, your time, and your crews until the first thing you know, you aren't taking care of your other customers. Or maybe the project itself was bad. It might have had problems no one anticipated that affected the scheduling or the cost of the project.

Another common way I've seen construction companies get into trouble is when they start financing their current project with the advance money from the next, as yet unstarted, project. Maybe it's because of bad bookkeeping, slow-paying customers, or inadequate company capitalization. Whatever the cause, that's a ball that you can only keep in the air as long as business is good, and you have plenty of projects and lots of advance money in the pipeline.

So there are lots of ways to get into trouble — but what can you do to get back out? There's one appealing prospect that probably won't work: just quietly going out of business. That *won't* solve all your business's financial or legal problems (although if you're a corporation, it could get very close).

Protecting Your Personal Assets

The problem with just folding up your tent and stealing silently away is that, unless you're a corporation, you can still be sued even when you aren't in business anymore. You're vulnerable if you've breached your contracts, still owe money, or if there are customers with outstanding warranty claims.

Even if your company was a corporation, you may still have some leftover problems. Remember, that corporate shield doesn't protect you from problems with the IRS. And your lenders, not being dummies, may have required the corporate officers (and even their spouses) to co-sign the corporation's debts.

For example, suppose John owns and runs John's Bigger Kitchens, Incorporated. He wants to open up a new line of credit with Home Town Bank, which is willing to extend the credit only if John co-signs with his company on the loan. That means that John signs twice, first as the President of John's Bigger Kitchens, Inc. and then again as an individual. That way, if John's Bigger Kitchens goes down the tube, Home Town Bank can still collect from John.

Another problem with just folding your corporate tent is that you probably won't be able to salvage the assets of the corporation, like accounts receivable or tools and equipment.

Unless your business was incorporated and you did *not* cosign any of the debts, your business creditors or customers can sue you successfully even after your business is history. Those creditors can seize personal assets such as your car, your earnings or salaries from your new jobs, or tools and equipment that you may own — even things you bought after you went out of business. They can seize your bank accounts, even if you're trying to set up a new business and the money in those accounts represent advance money from new clients. It doesn't matter. If the money's in an account in your name, they can seize it to satisfy debts unless you have already successfully protected that money, or your other assets, from your creditors.

Do You Have Any Property That Creditors Can't Reach?

If your creditors have judgments against you, they can even summon you into court, where they can ask you questions about what kinds of property you own and where it is. Then they can get an attachment order to seize that property. Unless your business was incorporated, there's not much of your property that your creditors can't reach unless it's protected in a bankruptcy proceeding.

State Law Protection

Some states have what's called a homestead exemption law that can protect at least part of the value of your home from creditors (except your mortgage holder). It doesn't protect you against a mortgage foreclosure.

What About Your Spouse's Property?

As a general rule, unless you're in a community property state, property that belongs to your husband or wife is mostly safe from your business creditors.

In the states that don't have community property laws, a creditor can sue, get a judgment against you and attach your property — but not the property of your spouse. Of course, that's not the case if your spouse is one of the business owners, or has signed as a guarantor on the debt. However, if your spouse doesn't fall into one of these exceptions, your business creditors can't reach your spouse's property.

For example, suppose Harold's Trucks sues Cal the carpenter for several thousand dollars — and wins. In most states, when Harold tries to collect on that judgment, he can't get Mrs. Cal's property, because it's hers, not Cal's although Harold might be able to reach Cal's share of jointly-owned property.

None of this is true, however, in the nine community property states. In those states, Harold's Trucks could garnish or attach jointly-owned property even if Mrs. Cal wasn't a part owner or co-signer of any business debt. The only property that would be safe would be property Mrs. Cal owned before the marriage, or that for some reason wouldn't be considered community property under the laws of that state.

Be Careful about Transferring Business Property or Cash

However, suppose Cal thought things were looking iffy in the business, and he deposited a big hunk of cash into a personal bank account belonging to him and his wife so his creditors couldn't get it. That's an entirely different situation. Harold's Trucks can claim that this transfer was fraudulent, because Cal made it specifically to keep Harold from collecting on his judgment.

In this situation Harold's Trucks can reach money in Mr. and Mrs. Cal's bank account. But he still can't reach Mrs. Cal's regular monthly salary deposits in that account.

It's fraud to transfer assets to friends or relatives in an effort to hide those assets from your creditors. The idea is that your creditors relied on you having certain assets or a certain income from your business. If you're going to transfer assets or cash to, say, your wife, do it *before* you apply for a loan or incur the debt. But even then, there's a complication.

If you file for bankruptcy within a year of transferring money or another asset to a wife or friend, the court can force the return of that asset if the court believes that transfer was made to put the money out of reach of your creditors.

Payments in the Ordinary Course of Business

You can pay your bills and do the ordinary financial things that you need to do with your money even if you're facing bankruptcy. Money you pay out in the ordinary course of business or use to pay your debts or living expenses are exempt from the fraudulent transfer rule, even if you made those payments the day you filed for bankruptcy.

Be Careful with Your Bank Account

If you're having problems with your creditors, and one of those creditors is your bank, consider moving your account to a different bank. Otherwise your bank might seize the account. If you read the very fine print on your deposit agreement, you'll find the bank can do this through its right of "offset."

Be Careful About a Home Equity Line of Credit

Many small business owners use their home as a source of business capital. Keep in mind, that line of credit is really a mortgage on your home. It's bad enough to lose your business: it's worse to lose your home, too.

What You Should Do When Your Business Is in Trouble

If you're having serious and pressing problems with creditors and cash flow, especially if you're facing lawsuits, there are some steps you can take to ease some of these problems.

Make Your Employees' IRS Withholding Payments

When your business is in trouble, cash flow is usually a big problem and it may be really difficult to send in those quarterly withholding payments, but believe me, it's a big mistake to let those payments slide. The IRS can, and will, close your business if you don't make those payments. If you're trying to work out something with your creditors, or asking for additional credit, they probably won't be much interested in working with you if they discover your employee withholding hasn't been paid. They know the IRS gets first pick on anything you have, and they'll get a share of any scrap that may be left.

Also, you can't discharge employee-withholding payments in bankruptcy. That's true even for corporations. If you think you might be headed for bankruptcy, pay the employee withholding payments even if you have to let your other debts slide. You can discharge those other debts in bankruptcy.

Look for Professional Help

The things you need to know in construction — how to pour a foundation, site a building, wire a house — are *not* the things you need to know to run a business. But you can hire people who do know those things, or you can just learn from them.

If you decide to get business advice from a financial consultant, an accountant or an attorney, check their credentials. Get the names of their other clients and talk to those clients. You're looking for assurance that your professional has good experience in *your kind of industry*. If you're building strip malls, a financial consultant who works with Internet companies probably won't be as much help to you as someone with specific experience in commercial construction.

You can learn how to do the office stuff. If you can pass a contractor's license exam, you can learn the business management techniques you need to know. And there are lots of places that teach them. For example, here in Michigan, some of the community colleges run excellent programs that teach business management to local small business owners. Your local Chamber of Commerce or your builders' association can probably recommend educational resources.

Try to Save Your Business Without Bankruptcy

If your business is viable, but better financial management doesn't work — or hasn't yet had a chance to work — consider approaching your creditors with a private workout proposal.

A nonbankruptcy workout is a private agreement between you and your major creditors. They agree to hold off suing you, or collecting on judgments they may already have, or forcing you into bankruptcy. The goal of this workout is to keep you in business. The workout could be an arrangement where you don't have to pay off 100 percent of your debts, or may simply give you more time to pay them.

Begin by finding an accountant or a lawyer to help you negotiate a workout. Get one who can give you the names of other people in your situation that he or she has helped. Call those people and talk to them about their experience with that lawyer or accountant. When you've found someone you believe you can work with, use their advice to help you develop a workout plan that will keep your business alive.

Be sure your workout plan is *realistic* before you present it to your creditors. Remember that you'll not only be paying off old debts, you'll also be paying new ones as they come along, so this plan has to be something that can really happen. Don't base it on the most optimistic forecast for your business. Put some wiggle room in your workout plan so that if an emergency comes up, you can deal with it. Be absolutely honest with your creditors about your situation. If you deceive them, that's fraud.

Some workouts even include a plan for getting more credit from your creditors. A lot of this depends on how much they need you to stay in business. Remember, your best argument is that they'll get more out of you in the long run if they keep you in business. A lumberyard, for example, doesn't want to put you out of business to collect a $5,000 debt if they do $10,000 worth of business a year with you.

The agreement doesn't need the participation of every creditor. In fact, no creditor has to participate unless they're willing to. A workout is entirely voluntary, but you'll have more luck getting your other creditors to agree if as many as possible are included. In fact, some of your creditors may say that they'll agree only if certain other creditors also agree.

Get as many of your creditors to agree as possible, and then get their signature on a written contract. Once the contract is signed, it becomes an enforceable contract with your consenting creditors. Your creditors can't change their mind after they sign, as long as you keep your part of the bargain.

Bankruptcy May Be the Only Solution

If nothing else works, it's time to consider bankruptcy. But many people don't realize that there's more than one kind of bankruptcy. There's the Chapter 7 straight bankruptcy — that's the kind most people think of when they think of bankruptcy. You go into court, declare that you're bankrupt, list all your debts, pass out your assets, and then the court discharges you so that you can start over again.

But there are two sections of the federal bankruptcy act that aren't aimed at liquidating the bankrupt's debt. They're called reorganization and they're intended to give the bankrupt person or business some protection while they get back on their feet. You could call it legal breathing space.

General Bankruptcy Regulations

At this time, Congress is discussing an overhaul of the bankruptcy laws, so exactly what your options are will depend on what Congress might do. If you do decide to go further, you will need to consult a local bankruptcy attorney.

Automatic Stays

As soon as you file a bankruptcy petition, whether it's a straight bankruptcy or bankruptcy reorganization, you get instant protection from your creditors. That happens automatically. Your creditors can't take any action against you without the permission of the Bankruptcy Court.

Secured and Unsecured Creditors

There are two different classes of creditors in bankruptcy: secured and unsecured. Secured creditors are creditors who have some sort of security interest in your property, like a note on your car or a mortgage on your house. They're not treated in the same way as unsecured creditors. Bankruptcy will eliminate the right of a secured creditor to collect on the debt, but in a straight bankruptcy, that creditor could still foreclose on the house or the car or whatever property they have a security interest in.

Chapter 7 Bankruptcy

A bankruptcy brought under Chapter 7 of the bankruptcy code is a straight bankruptcy; the bankrupt person simply declares his debts and assets, and takes his exemptions (like the exemption for his home and his personal tools). Then the Trustee in Bankruptcy distributes the bankrupt's nonexempt assets to his creditors and declares the bankrupt's debts discharged. *Discharged* means that the creditor no long has the right to go to court and sue to collect that money.

In most states, the bankrupt's creditors that can be discharged in bankruptcy include customers whose contracts he may have breached. However, a Chapter 7 bankruptcy does *not* discharge most security interests such as mortgages or liens. Nor does it protect other people who may have co-signed on the bankrupt's debt or who are liable in some other way. A creditor who has been discharged in the bankruptcy can still go after a co-signer.

Chapter 11 Bankruptcy

There's another kind of bankruptcy proceeding that offers a business the protection of the Bankruptcy Court while still letting them stay in business. It's called Chapter 11 bankruptcy reorganization, and it's a kind of financial workout.

Any business, partnership, or corporation can use Chapter 11. It allows the business to retain its assets and remain in business while the business repays as many of its business debts as possible. To qualify, the business must identify its creditors and then put together a realistic repayment plan for at least part of the bankrupt business's debts. That payment plan may involve a partial discharge of the bankrupt business's unsecured debts and an extension of time to pay off the rest. The majority (51 percent) of each of the two classes of creditors (secured and unsecured) must agree to the business's repayment plan. If a majority of the creditors accept the plan, even creditors who didn't consent are bound by it.

If the majority of the creditors will not agree, and the bankruptcy judge does not use his power to order them to agree, then the business has no choice but to go into straight bankruptcy. However, it's usually much better for creditors to agree to a plan that will allow the debtor to stay in business, so that the creditor can keep doing business with the bankrupt business.

For example, suppose Better Builders asks for the protection of the bankruptcy court because they can't pay their debts. Suppose Better Builders typically does $100,000 worth of business a year with the Wood Lumberyard, and currently owes Wood Lumberyard $20,000 in back charges. If Better Builders offers to pay half of the $20,000 if Wood Lumberyard will vote to let Better Builders stay in business under a Chapter 11 reorganization, Wood Lumberyard would be foolish not to agree. Losing $10,000 won't be as painful as losing a customer from whom they usually make more than that in a year. Remember that the alternative to agreeing to the reorganization is for Wood Lumberyard to see a valuable customer go out of business.

Also, when Better Builders' attorney negotiates with Wood Lumberyard, he should remind Wood that they probably wouldn't collect much of their $20,000 in a Chapter 7 bankruptcy. Typically, creditors in a straight bankruptcy only collect about 10 cents on the dollar. Sometimes they don't get that much. That kind of argument can be a powerful incentive for Wood Lumberyard to agree to a plan to keep Better Builders in business, and, hopefully, earning some money.

Unlike what happens in a non-bankruptcy workout, bankruptcy judges have a power that can make the difference in the success or failure of Chapter 11 reorganization: they have the power to terminate a lease or a contract.

For example, suppose Cal's repayment plan would work out better if he could cancel his very expensive lease on a piece of earthmoving equipment. Or suppose that one of Cal's financial problems is that he contracted to build a strip mall and it turns out he doesn't have enough crew or resources. The bankruptcy judge can cancel that contract or that lease without exposing Cal to a breach of contract lawsuit.

Chapter 13 Bankruptcy

Chapter 13 is somewhat similar to Chapter 11, but is simpler and more user-friendly. It allows what you might think of as a partial bankruptcy. Chapter 13 is supposed to be restricted to individuals, not businesses, but a sole proprietorship can use it.

Under the current laws, a debtor using Chapter 13 can keep most of his or her assets and can take up to five years to repay as much of his outstanding debts as possible at a rate established by the bankruptcy court. To determine how much of the debt will be repaid and at what rate, the bankruptcy court looks at each debtor's situation to decide what's reasonable. The bankruptcy court may reduce or discharge the debtor's unsecured debts.

A major advantage for Chapter 13 is that the bankruptcy judge can order creditors to stop action against a co-signer or guarantor. It's a way to protect your friends and relatives who have tried to help your business.

16

What About Retirement, Disability or Death?

It's time to look at those things everybody puts off looking at — partly because nobody wants to think about becoming disabled or dying, and partly because everybody believes there's plenty of time for that later. Today, they want to concentrate on today's problems.

In a way, I agree. I'm a believer in concentrating on the problems at hand. However, some day your family and your business associates may pay the price if you never take care of these things. Every day, someone like you gets in his car to drive home — and doesn't make it. Today it could be your turn. It's a morbid thought, but pretending it doesn't exist doesn't make it so. And if some inattentive driver runs a red light and just disables you instead of killing you, you'll be the one wishing you hadn't put it off.

Your retirement could be harder than you think, too. If you wait till you're 45 before you start saving for your retirement, you'll have to take much more money out of your annual income stream than you would have had to if you'd started sooner — say, when you were 25. If you start young enough, you can build up significant amounts of money even though you only save tiny amounts. Of course, don't we all wish we had done that? You could mention it to your children, however.

Retirement Plans

If you own a business, in a way that is your retirement plan. As your business goes up in value, your future looks more secure, but putting all your eggs in one basket is risky. You don't have to do that — not when the tax laws give you so many ways to build up pensions and avoid taxes at the same time.

People think tax-deductible pension plans are complicated, and they are. That's not really a problem, though. There are people working in banks, insurance companies, or stock brokerages who earn their living managing small pension funds. They're ready to do it all for you. Of course, they will charge you for this service, but those charges are deductible expenses.

Before these companies can act as a custodian for your tax-deductible pension, they must first be authorized to manage small pension funds by the IRS. When a would-be pension manager uses the word "qualified," that means authorized by the IRS. Once you've found an authorized manager to work with, you just deposit your money. They set up your pension plan and keep the records for you. They'll also invest the money for you if you want them to, although you can make investment decisions yourself if you set up a self-directed account.

IRA

An Individual Retirement Account (IRA) is a relatively simple and popular way to save for your retirement. And they're a pretty good deal for most people. If you're single, you can contribute up to $2,000 each year. If you're married, you can contribute up to $4,000 for you and your spouse, even if your spouse isn't employed. Congress is presently considering a bill to expand those limits.

Anyone who isn't an active participant in another pension plan and who doesn't exceed the income limits can deduct the money they pay into their IRA from their income taxes. For example, if you earned $30,000 in 1999 and contributed $2,000 to your IRA, you'll only be taxed on $28,000 of your income. Then suppose you retire in, say, 2010, when you're only earning $15,000. If you withdraw $2,000 that year, it will be taxed at a much lower rate than it would have been in 1999.

The current income limits for year 2001 are $33,000 adjusted gross income if you're single, and $52,000 adjusted gross income if you're married and filing jointly. However, it's a stepped-down sort of disqualification, so you may still be able to contribute some tax-deductible money into your IRA even if you do exceed the income limits.

The rule used to be that you couldn't have an IRA if your spouse was a participant in another pension plan. That rule was changed in 1998. You'll still be disqualified from having an IRA of your own if you and your spouse have an adjusted gross income of more than $160,000, but if you have that kind of income, you probably don't care.

Other Kinds of IRAs

There's a new kind of IRA called a Roth IRA. Your contributions to a Roth IRA aren't deductible, but the earnings on the money in the Roth IRA aren't taxed. You pay the taxes up front, then don't have to pay income tax when you withdraw funds during your retirement.

An Educational IRA offers a tax-free way to save for a child's education.

There is also what's called the SIMPLE IRA. This is a retirement plan intended for small businesses (20 or more employees), which is easier to set up and manage than a 401(k), but requires the employers to match their employee's contributions. The employer and the employees can deduct the money they pay into the SIMPLE IRA. The employees won't pay income tax on that money until it's distributed for their retirement. There's a $6,000 limit on the total annual contribution.

Simplified Employee Pension Plans

These are called SEP pension plans. They work much like an IRA, except that you can put a lot more money into a SEP. They're very useful because they allow a self-employed person to put in as much as 15 percent of their income, up to $24,000. You can set it up so that each year you decide how much money you want to put into your SEP, and there's no minimum contribution. You can make your contributions during profitable years, and just skip them during a bad year. All the money you contribute comes right off the top of your taxable income, so you don't pay any taxes on it or the money that your SEP plan earns until you retire.

So, you ask, if this is so great, why isn't everybody doing it? What's the catch? The catch is that if you have employees, they're participants in your pension plan. You can't make a contribution for yourself unless you make contributions for them, also.

Keogh Plans

Only a self-employed person can set up a Keogh Plan. You can contribute up to 20 percent of your self-employment income up to $30,000 dollars to your Keogh for your own benefit.

Your Employees Are Entitled to Participate

Once the Keogh Plan is set up, your employees can contribute towards their own retirement by participating in the plan. You must also make contributions for them. The IRS monitors private pension plans that include employees, and has some nasty penalties for employers who don't manage those funds carefully or contribute according to the rules.

Keogh Plans Allow Vesting Schedules for Employees

If you have employees, a Keogh plan may be better than a SEP, because a Keogh allows you to put vesting requirements on your employee's pension benefits. Vesting means that the employee doesn't get property rights to the money until a certain event occurs — usually something like working for you for awhile. After all, one of the reasons you want to invest in a pension plan for employees is to encourage the good ones to stay with you.

For example, suppose you hired Curly, Moe and Larry. You would be better off if they didn't become vested in their pension funds until, and unless, they had worked for you for at least a year. When they're vested, the funds in their pension funds become their property, and they can take with them if they leave (or if you fire them).

You Can Treat Some Workers Differently in a Keogh Plan

Most of the different tax-deductible pension plans that include employees require that all employees must be treated the same. If you decide to match the first 3 percent of the employee's contribution, then you have to match a 3 percent contribution for every employee. However, it's possible to structure a Keogh plan so that some employees in the company can contribute more and thus eventually collect more.

It's called *social security integration,* and it allows the company to contribute more money to the Keogh plan on behalf of higher paid employees (usually the company owners) by including social security payments into the calculation of how much the contribution will be. This allows higher paid earners to contribute more in both actual dollar amounts and in the percentage of their income than employees who aren't so highly paid.

For example, suppose Bigger Kitchens is owned by John, who makes $100,000 a year from it. His only employee is Jane, his administrative aide, who earns $20,000 a year. John sets up a Keogh contribution formula that pays 15 percent of their annual earnings into the Bigger Kitchens plan. By including social security contributions into that 15 percent, John will wind up with a much bigger contribution than Jane, because John has about $30,000 a year in excess income above the social security ceiling.

Anyone who handles pensions for small companies will be able to explain all the options open to your company, and make recommendations about which kind will work best for you.

Health and Disability

Ill health and disability are subjects nobody wants to dwell on — but the price for avoiding them may be much higher than you can afford.

Health Insurance Plans

Although the new tax laws allow self-employed people to deduct a greater part of their health insurance premiums than ever before, it's still not a 100 percent deduction — unless your company is incorporated. An incorporated company can purchase health insurance and disability insurance for its employees (including you) and deduct every dime of the premiums.

Disability

Too many self-employed people forget how critical they are to their own success. What would happen to your business if you weren't available for a while? What would happen to your family if your income was interrupted? Unfortunately, that's something that's statistically likely to happen. Three out of five workers in the U.S. between the ages of 35 and 65 will be disabled for a total of 90 days during their career. And a worker under the age of 45 is seven times more likely to be disabled than to die.

That's where disability insurance can help, although no disability policy will replace 100 percent of your income. Usually the payout is about 60 percent of what you were earning before your health problems. There are disadvantages: The premiums are expensive and unless the company is incorporated, the premiums aren't deductible. But disability insurance is the kind of thing that when you need it, you really need it.

There are two types of disability policies.

Short-Term Disability

These are policies that are only intended to help you until you get back to work. Think of it as something like sick pay for the self-employed. Short-term disability benefits don't usually start until you've been disabled or sick for a certain period of time. What that period of time is depends on the terms of your policy. Short-term benefits don't pay for a long-term disability, so if you're so disabled you can never work again, this policy won't be what you need. Exactly how long the short-term policy will pay depends on the terms of your particular policy, although this kind of policy typically only pays for a few months at the most.

For example, suppose Sam the self-employed carpenter (usually a subcontractor) falls off a roof. For at least the first week, his short-term disability policy won't pay a penny, but once he's been too disabled to work for the required number of days, his short-term disability will kick in and he'll get some help with his lost income. However, if Sam broke his back and is never be able to work again, once the payout period of his short-term disability runs out, that policy won't pay Sam another dime.

Long-Term Disability

Long-term disability insurance policies are for income protection if you're permanently disabled. A typical policy will pay if you can no longer work in the field for which you were employed and trained. That's a better deal than social security disability, which will not pay you unless there is no field or position in which you could work.

Death

Think about these things when you consider the possibility of your own death: What will happen to your assets? What will happen to your business? What will happen to your family?

Insurance

You can use insurance to keep your business alive after the death of a critical person, or use the insurance settlement to fund a buyout. Suppose John and Sam own Ajax Roofing as a partnership and they're worried about what happens if one of them dies. Sam and John could buy term life insurance policies that could be used in several ways.

For example, say John dies and his wife intends to participate in running his half of the business. The insurance policy would provide money so that the business can keep functioning while the taxes and funeral expenses are paid. She won't have to raise money by trying to sell her part the business.

Or suppose that John's wife doesn't actually want his half of the business. After all, John and Sam are roofing subcontractors, and she doesn't want to help nail shingles. With a life insurance policy in place, the policy can pay John's wife the value of John's share of the business. That way everyone wins. Sam winds up owning the whole business, while John's wife winds up with money for the value of John's half. The insurance provides the money to do that.

Wills

Many people manage without a will. They simply own their assets jointly with their spouses or their partners. If they die, the surviving spouse, or whoever the survivor is, just presents a death certificate and takes over the asset.

It's my opinion that they ought to have a will anyway — just in case. Suppose you die with assets you didn't expect to have when you decided to do without a will? Suppose you and your joint owner both die in the same car crash or house fire? If you die without a will, the state will appoint an administrator and distribute your assets according to state law. That may be the way you wanted it, and it may not. What is certain is that the costs to your estate will be much greater than they would have been otherwise. I've seen estates with nothing left in them after administration and legal fees were paid.

You definitely should have a will if you have minor children. That way, you can nominate a guardian for your children. You can also offer some direction for the management of your estate for their benefit.

Also, I'd recommend a will if you have a "blended" family. For example, if you have a stepson along with three natural children, you may find that the state intestacy laws cut your stepson completely out of your estate — which may not be what you would want to happen. By failing to write a will in that situation, you may be sending your stepchildren a message you did not intend. Or suppose you have children from a previous marriage who are now in a better financial position than the children from your current marriage, who are still dependant minors. Under most intestacy laws, all of those children will share equally. It doesn't matter that some may need the money more than others. Unless you have a very large estate, this may not be what you want to happen.

There are a number of kits and do-it-yourself books available about writing your own will. I don't have a big problem with those kits, but there are situations in which I would recommend seeking professional help.

For example, if you have a number of different kinds of assets, or if you're trying to provide for minor children, or if you have only a few assets but the value of those assets will exceed the federal estate tax exemption, you should hire an attorney to help write your will. A professional can help minimize the impact of estate taxes on a large estate.

Finally, once you have a will, keep track of it. Put it in your safety deposit box or somewhere similar so that your survivors can find it. It helps if you tell them in advance where to look.

17

A Few Last Words About You and Your Lawyer

I'm often asked how to decide when to pick up the phone and call a lawyer. That's a judgment call, but let me suggest some guidelines.

How to Choose a Lawyer

If you need a lawyer, you need one who does a lot of work in your field. Otherwise, it's quite possible you'll know more about the law in your field than the lawyer does. So look for a lawyer with experience in the kind of problem you have. Ask for references. Call those references and ask them about that lawyer.

When you're making these calls, remember the goal is to find out if that lawyer has the experience you need, *not* how those clients feel about that lawyer. Often clients don't actually know whether their lawyer did a good job or not, because it's difficult for a client to identify the trouble that he or she avoided because of good legal advice. Just watch for red flags such as missed deadlines (happens more often than you would think) or problems that had to be fixed by someone else.

Once you've picked out a lawyer, remember one truth that all law students are taught: The only thing a lawyer has to sell is *time*. So they charge for every contact and every phone call, no matter how short. The end result is that you hardly dare say Hello to them if you see them at the mall!

When to Call a Lawyer

So with all that expense in mind, when should you call your lawyer?

Always call your lawyer when you're in a situation where, if something goes wrong, it could put you out of business. For example, suppose you're a foundation subcontractor and the largest job you've ever done was a $40,000 residential concrete pour. You're offered a million-dollar commercial job. You need someone to take a look at that contract before you sign it. Yes, I know time is money, but the agreement you're signing may not be exactly what you think it is. Spending a few hundred dollars in advance to spot potential problems could save your business.

If you're sued, pick up the phone and call your lawyer. Even if the lawsuit is in small claims court, you should give your lawyer a heads-up about it. You may not need your lawyer with you. The small claims court rules may not even allow you to take your lawyer, but he or she should still know about it.

You should also give your lawyer a heads-up if you're involved in arbitration. It used to be that arbitration was a quick, simple and cheap way to settle things. Often that's still true. However, sometimes arbitration gets to look and cost an awful lot like a regular trial. Call your lawyer and let him or her know if you give notice — or are given notice — of intent to arbitrate. At a minimum, keep your lawyer posted on what's going on.

When to Call Another Professional

However, sometimes it's not *your* lawyer you should call when you pick up that phone. For example, if you're served with a lawsuit in which someone claims they were injured and it was your fault, call your liability insurance carrier immediately. They keep platoons of lawyers on retainer to deal with this kind of problem. In fact, if you read the fine print on your liability policy, you'll probably find that you're not *allowed* to take care of this kind of problem yourself.

If your employee is injured, call your workers' compensation insurance company. They'll tell you what to do. If you need a lawyer, they'll provide one. Like your liability insurance company, they also have platoons of experienced lawyers on call.

If you're being audited, think about calling in a professional accountant. I'm not talking about the person who keeps your payroll. Call a tax professional who's a CPA and has experience with the IRS, preferably one who is "enrolled" with the IRS. That means he or she can represent you in front of the IRS.

Getting Ready

If you get into legal sorts of trouble with a job, what will you need - besides money — for your lawyer, your accountant, or yourself if you're acting without your lawyer? You'll need the following items:

- your logbook
- all of your contract papers

▌ all of your material records

▌ all of your labor records

▌ any other related reports or records — even if you don't actually use them.

If you're talking to your lawyer or accountant, these records will give your professional representative the full picture of what actually happened. If you're going into court or arbitration, a piece of paper that backs up what you're saying has an almost magical power to convince people.

Your Logbook

First, I hope you've been keeping a running log of all your business contacts and your business phone calls. A spiral notebook works just fine as a logbook. Just keep track of any business calls or contacts you make or receive and your response to those contacts.

For example, under the day's date of June 6, 2000, Cal the Carpenter's logbook could have three notes in it: the first describing a phone call from a customer who's complaining about the trim work on his new shelves; the second note describing a conversation Cal had that morning at the lumberyard when the lumberyard guy said, "We're sorry, but your clear pine is on back order, and we don't expect it in until maybe late July;" and a third note saying that Cal called the customer and told him about the delay.

None of these notes needs to be more than a few lines, nor do these notes have to contain magic legal words or be especially neat. A few coffee stains or grease marks aren't important as long as the logbook is still legible. What's important is that the notes are made when the contact, phone call or incident happens. The notes must be dated (very important), and kept on a regular basis. The notes in this type of running log are called *Contemporaneous Notes,* and you can use them as evidence.

Those of you who watch Court TV will be saying, " . . . but this is hearsay." Yes, but it's an exception to the rule that you can't use hearsay. Regular records kept in the ordinary course of business are admissible. However, even if these records wouldn't be allowed into your lawsuit as evidence, is that a reason not to keep a logbook? *No!* (That's me screaming.) Even if, for some strange reason, you aren't allowed to use your logbook as evidence, keeping your running log will help you enormously when it comes time to remember what happened and when exactly it happened. If you're in court or arbitration, you'll need that help — the best of memories fades or becomes confused over time. Consider this scenario:

"And Mr. Contractor, when were you first made aware that the lumber delivery would be delayed?"

"I dunno."

Who was it, at the lumberyard, that told you this?"

"I dunno."

"How long was it, after you were made aware of this delay, that you notified the plaintiff?"

"I dunno."

I think you get my drift. Keep a running log of everything.

All of Your Contract Papers

You need to take every single piece of contract documentation about the particular project that's in question with you to your lawyer, accountant, arbitrator, or to court. Contract documentation includes original contracts, change orders (you *are* getting those change orders in writing, aren't you?), shop drawings, architectural drawings, draw schedules, and so forth.

All of Your Material and Labor Records

You'll need every single scrap of paper that relates to the job in question. That includes material receipts, subcontractor bids and receipts, and salary records.

Your Required Reports

Any records that you keep as a matter of law such as injury reports, immigration reports, safety records, etc — anything that pertains to the problem — should be with you. This includes your personnel records if the problem involves an employee.

I include personnel records as required records, even though there may be no specific law in your state that requires you to use and keep them. This includes personnel records such as employment applications, and written records of employee-employer conferences on employment issues and safety issues. The law is such that you should treat keeping these records as a legal requirement, even if it isn't.

A Note of Caution

I don't like to sound paranoid here, but I've learned this lesson the hard way: *Don't ever give up your records.* Pass out copies, but don't pass out your original records, not even to your lawyer. What if he has a heart attack and dies on the way to court and you don't know where he put your originals? What if the two of you have a falling out and you accuse him of malpractice? Give him copies and take the originals with you. If you're not going to be in court with him — okay, I understand there are exceptions to every rule. But I'm very serious about this: If you're in legal trouble and you're pinning your hopes on an injury report from 1997, if you let that report out of your control, you're taking a chance.

What to Expect

Once you've called your lawyer and screamed for help, what should you expect from him or her? Well, to begin with, you don't want a lawyer whose first impulse is to run into court and do battle there. That may be what ultimately happens, but the best lawyer's first response will be to try to keep you out of court — or if it's too late for that — to get you out of court. I'm not saying, however, that your lawyer shouldn't ever decide to fight it out, but that choice ought to be a last resort, not the first.

When your attorney advises you about the best course of action, unless you have an awfully good reason to the contrary, follow that attorney's advice. That's what you're paying all that money for.

If you do have to go into court, especially as a defendant, remember that in addition to being one of life's major expenses, getting involved in a lawsuit is also one of life's major stresses. You concentrate on dealing with the stress. That's *your* job. It's your attorney's job to deal with the legal problems.

Glossary

A

Abandonment A legal term describing a construction project where there have been so many changes to the contract, that for practical purposes it no longer exists.

Accelerated Depreciation Section 179 of the tax code allows personal property items that don't exceed a certain value, such as a nail gun or a table saw, or sometimes even a truck, to be written off in the year they're purchased regardless of their life expectancy. It's called *expensing* the item, rather than *depreciating* the item.

Acceleration When the date for the contract completion remains the same, but so many change orders have piled up that there's now more work than time. It's the same as if the property owner had demanded that the contractor finish ahead of schedule. This gives the contractor the right to damages for disruption.

Acceptance If two parties agree to the terms of a contract, their acceptance, whether verbal or written, turns it into an enforceable contract.

Addendum A supplement added to a contract, such as an agreement between a subcontractor and the prime contractor, which is added to the prime contract between the contractor and the customer.

Allowance A specific dollar range given to the customer by the contractor for the selection of items that the customer hasn't decided on at the time of the contract signing. For example, since there's such a wide range of choices and prices for kitchen faucets, the contractor doing a kitchen remodel may allow the customer $100 for the kitchen faucet of his choice. If the customer decides a $59 faucet suits him, he'll have a $41 credit, to be either taken off the total contract price, or used on an upgrade of another item. If the customer decides on a gold and brass designer faucet at $295 — they can have it, but have to add the $195 difference to the contract cost.

Arbitration A way of settling disputes without going into court. The parties agree during the contracting stage on a person to be their arbitrator. There are associations of arbitrators who offer a list of qualified and experienced arbitrators. The arbitrator listens to both sides and makes a decision according to the construction industry standards adopted by that association. It's usually faster than waiting for a court date, and in most cases, saves on attorney fees.

Articles of Incorporation A document that must be filed with the state in order to form a corporation. The Articles of Incorporation states the name of the corporation, its purpose, its initial agent, its directors and the number and type of shares it's authorized to issue.

Assumed Name Registry See *Fictitious Business Name Statement*. Most states regulate what you can call your business. At a minimum they require you to register the name so that the State or other interested parties can find out who, for example, actually owns Better Builders and where they can find that person.

"At Will" Employee An employee who doesn't have an employment contract is called an "at will" employee, meaning that the employer can fire that person at any time. Of course, an "at will" employee also has the right to quit at any time.

B

Back Charge The term used when a contractor withholds some money from his subs to compensate himself for money the customer has withheld from the final payment to the contractor because of delays or problems with the work. What the contractor wants to do is charge the sub who caused the problem. Sometimes, the contractor spreads back charges among *all* the subcontractors on a *pro rata* basis. He figures that more than one sub probably contributed to the problem, and doesn't want to try to figure out exactly who did what. Obviously, subs who believe they're innocent will object. Then it comes down to whether the terms of the contract allow the contractor to spread back charges among all the subcontractors.

Bid A bid is a proposal, based on the plans and specifications for a project, to complete a job for a certain amount of money. Some bid proposals are written as contract offers. But as a general rule, a bid without language that doesn't clearly create a contract isn't a contract unless it's accepted. However, subcontractors sometimes find that their bids are treated as a binding contract even if the bid isn't actually accepted, because the prime contractor relied on his sub's bids when he made his bid to the property owner.

BOCA The Building Officials and Code Administrators International, Inc. This organization publishes a building code that's used in many communities, mostly in the North East.

Bona Fide Occupational Qualifications A genuine requirement of a particular job position. If an employer makes a decision not to hire a person who falls into a class of people protected by the anti-discrimination laws, that employer can defend his or her hiring decision by demonstrating a *bona fide* occupational qualification that the applicant didn't meet. For example, if typing is a requirement of the job, an employer can defend his decision not to hire someone who can't pass a typing test, as long as all applicants are given the same test.

Breach of Contract The failure of one party to a contract to meet the obligations under the contract in a serious and substantial way. For example, if the contractor starts work, but then walks off the job site and doesn't return within a reasonable time, that's a breach of contract. Conversely, if the property owner doesn't pay a progress payment on time, that's a breach of contract.

Building Permit A building permit is issued by the local housing authority, and is a permit to start the work. It isn't a guarantee that the plan meets the building code. That's the purpose of the Code-mandated inspections made as the work progresses.

Buy Out Plan A plan set up in a partnership agreement that allows the remaining partners to buy out the interest of a partner who wishes to quit the partnership, or who dies.

C

Certificate of Acceptance A form the contractor can ask the property owner to sign that acknowledges that the work has been finished by the contractor.

Certificate of Occupancy A document obtained from the local authorities that certifies that the building under construction conforms to the building code and can be used as intended. The building code requires it before the building may be occupied. It's also evidence that the contractor has substantially performed his part of the contract, because he has built a building that can be used as intended — that is, occupied.

Change Order A change to the original contract. Typically a construction contract will be changed in several ways before the work is finished. That's partly because of the problem with concealed conditions, but more often with property owners who decide as the work progresses that they want something different or extra.

Closely-Held Corporation A privately-owned business whose stock isn't sold in the open market. There are often only a few stockholders — sometimes only one.

Consideration Both parties to a contract must make a promise of value to the other, or there isn't a legally binding contract. Typically consideration is the promise to pay money, the promise to perform services or the promise to deliver goods.

Construction Documents All of the papers that make up the entire construction contract. Although some construction contracts can be entirely written on a few blank lines on a preprinted form, contracts for larger jobs may take many different documents to describe the entire deal, including separate specifications, plans, work schedules, and change orders. A hundred pages plus blueprints aren't uncommon. When many documents have been used in the planning stages of a construction project, the contract document that's signed by the parties should identify exactly which documents are intended to be part of the contract. If possible, copies of those documents should be attached to the contract document.

Construction Lien A security interest in real property that's something like a mortgage. A construction lien can be obtained by a person who has supplied goods or labor for construction work on that property and seeks reimbursement. Even if a person has had no direct contact with the property owner and may not even know him, he can still file a lien if he's owed. The lien claimant must follow the regulations for filing a lien *exactly* as required in his state. Lien laws vary from state to state, so contractors, subcontractors and suppliers must make themselves aware of the regulations in every state where they do business.

Constructive Change Directives Written orders prepared by the architect and signed by the owner, directing a change in the contract and stating a proposed basis for contract adjustment. Because these are actually change orders, the contractor's consent is necessary, but they typically give the contractor only a limited time to object to the proposed changes before those changes become a binding part of the contract. The idea is that if the contractor doesn't promptly object, he accepts.

Contract A legally binding agreement between two or more parties.

Coordinate The owner has a duty to the contractor to coordinate the engineering and architectural plans, so that they're functional. For example, the space for the ductwork must be adequate in the final plans.

Corporation A business that is, in the eyes of the law, an independent person. That person isn't a real person, of course, but that doesn't matter in the eyes of the law. See also *Subchapter S Corporation* and *Limited Liability Corporation.*

Cost Plus Contract A contract in which the contractor charges for the actual labor and material costs of the job, then adds onto those charges either a fixed fee or a percentage of those charges to cover overhead and profit.

Critical Path Critical path is a term that refers to those work items which must be completed before the next work item can begin. This is a contract term that's used to limit time extensions for the contractor to finish the work to only those items that are on the critical path.

D

Depreciation Under the tax laws, businesses can recover the cost of purchasing qualified capital assets by writing off the value of the capital expenditure in small increments over the estimated life of the item. The IRS publishes extensive tables showing the recovery periods and the amount of depreciation that can be claimed each year for various types of assets. Most small businesses prefer to write off some items in the year of their purchase, and that's possible using Section 179 of the IRS code. Of course, it requires a special IRS form, and there are some restrictions.

Derivative Rights This is the term that describes the legal rights in a contract a person who wasn't a party to that contract may have. For example, a subcontractor working for a general contractor has those same legal rights in the contract between the general contractor and the homeowner even though that subcontractor hasn't signed that contract. However, because these are derivative rights, the subcontractor in theory has no greater rights than the general contractor. This can get to be a problem if the general contractor waived his lien rights, but most states don't extend that lien waiver to the subcontractors working on the job site.

Design/Build Contract A contract in which the contractor is both designing and building the structure. Contractors who do this must be careful about the effects of licensing laws and design warranties on this kind of contract. Some states, for example, don't allow unlicensed architects, which is what a design/build contractor is, to design structures.

Disclaimer Words that limit the life of a warranty, exclude a warranty, or put a dollar maximum on the amount the customer can collect for a warranty violation.

Disruption A property owner or a contractor's failure to schedule the permits, or the various subcontractors, so they can work according to their contractual commitment. This failure gives the subcontractor or the contractor whose schedule has been disrupted the right to demand disruption damages.

Doing Business As Statement See *Fictitious Business Name Statement* or *Assumed Names Register*.

E

Economic Loss The legal term for the damages sought by one person who sues another for breach of warranty or negligence when no one has been physically injured.

Eichley Formula A legal formula that courts use to calculate the amount of money that would have been available to pay the contractor's home office overhead costs if he had been allowed to finish the project on time. Home office refers to the contractor's principal place of doing business.

Estimated Payment Vouchers Forms used by the IRS for self-employed people to report their earnings each quarter. It's a device that allows the self-employed to do their own income and social security tax withholding.

Estoppel This is a legal bar to alleging or denying a fact because of one's own previous actions or words to the contrary. For example, suppose the homeowner never actually signed the contract for his new kitchen. When the contractor finishes the work and goes to collect, the homeowner says, too bad, we didn't have a contract, because I never signed it. The contractor can say, you knew what I was doing and you stood there and watched without saying a word. You're "estopped" from saying we had no contract.

Express Warranty A warranty or guarantee of the quality or integrity of materials or labor given to a customer in addition to, or instead of, the implied warranties. An express warranty is a specific statement or action such as: "You can safely use this wiring for your brand-new high-tech electronics that consume as much power as the average small town."

F

FICA The social security contribution deducted from employees' wages which employers must match with company funds.

Fictitious Business Name Statement Most states require anyone running a business under a name other than the owner's name to file a statement, usually with the County Clerk or Secretary of State, reporting who actually owns the business and where they may be found. This is called an *Assumed Name Statement*, *Doing Business As Statement* or *DBA Statement*.

Float This term is sometimes used to describe a contractor's right to schedule according to the way he wants to. For example, the contractor decides to put off pouring an outside patio until so close to the completion date that, when a problem such as bad weather occurs, he's unable to complete that work on time. He then requests a time extension. Is he entitled to a time extension, given that if he had scheduled in a more efficient way he would have been able to complete the job according to the contract? In most jurisdictions he is.

FUTA Payments Federal unemployment taxes paid by the employer for the benefit of the employee.

H

Hostile Working Environment This is a phrase used to describe certain working conditions that can lead to liability under the anti-discrimination laws. The phrase indicates a situation where, because of an employee's particular race, sex or age, that employee is subjected to harassment, which makes it particularly difficult to continue working in that setting. For example, allowing lewd pictures to be posted on the company walls where women work can be construed as a hostile working environment.

I

Illusory Contract A legal term referring to a contract or an agreement that isn't a real contract, and isn't enforceable because one of the parties to the contract has given themselves the right to cancel the contract at any time.

Implied Warranty A warranty that's imposed on a product or services by law. For example, if you build a garage, you're giving the property owner an implied warranty that the building entrance will be large enough to allow a typical passenger car to come through it. If you promised the property owner that he could get his oversized RV through that door, it would be an express warranty.

Indemnification The right to be reimbursed for losses caused by someone else's errors, omissions, or negligent acts. For example, suppose the drywaller did such a bad job that the homeowner retained part of his final payment so he could hire someone else to fix it. The contractor can't collect the money from the homeowner because the drywall wasn't correctly installed, but he can sue the drywaller.

J

Joint Venture A partnership formed for one particular purpose and for only a certain period of time. An example of this would be a partnership set up to develop a particular subdivision. When that subdivision is completed, the partnership will expire.

Judgment A judicial decision or a court act creating or affirming an obligation, such as a debt. It's important to remember that a judgment isn't a check. To actually collect money from that judgment will require further legal action.

L

Land Use A planning term referring to how a particular piece of land may be used in the zoning laws. For example, some land can only be used for farming, so it's zoned agriculturally. Other land might be determined to be more useful as commercial, so the land use that the zoning will reflect will be commercial. Imposing a zoning on property for a different kind of use will not affect the right of the existing owner, for example, a farmer whose property was zoned for a commercial use could continue to farm, but if he wanted to build a barn or to sell the land to someone else, he could have a problem because of the zoning on the property.

Letter of Credit Financial institutions can open up a certain amount of credit, which the holder can draw upon as needed. This is sometimes referred to as a *line of credit*. It's in the nature of a loan, but, for example, if you borrowed $50,000, that's how much you owe whether or not you used the entire $50,000. If you get a line of credit for $50,000 and you only use $25,000, then you would only owe $25,000.

Liability Insurance A type of insurance that protects the insured when the insured may be liable because of negligence, either his own, his employee's or agent's.

Lien Money can be collected for certain kinds of unpaid debts by putting a charge upon real or personal property as security for that debt, and then selling that property. See also *Construction Lien* or *Mechanic's Lien*.

Lien Claimant Someone claiming the right to a lien against real property. See also *Construction Lien*.

Lien Release A document that a contractor, subcontractor or supplier signs that releases his or her right to place a lien on property where they have worked, or supplied materials to others who have made improvements to that property. See also *Lien Waiver*.

Lien Waiver This is the same thing as a Lien Release. A contractor, subcontractor, material man or laborer is giving up his right to get a lien on the property where the work was done.

Limitation A legal term that puts some *limiting language* into a warranty, so that the warranty doesn't cover things it isn't intended to cover. As a contractor, you can prevent your warranty from being open-ended by explaining in detail what you are and are not covering.

Limited Liability Corporation Some states allow a form of incorporation called *limited liability*. It's a hybrid partnership/corporation that allows some protection from liability for company debts and wrongdoing.

Limited Partnership If one person's only an investor, and if there's a written agreement to that effect, then that investor is called a *limited partner* and isn't (depending on state law) liable for the partnership debts. State laws heavily regulate limited partnerships. Always consult with a local attorney before agreeing to become a limited partner or before setting up a limited partnership. If there are enough investors and enough money involved, extensive state and federal securities laws will apply. *Failure to comply with securities law requirements may be a criminal offense.*

Liquidated Damages A specific amount of money that the parties to a contract agree would be adequate compensation for problems that may occur during construction, such as delay. This kind of contract clause is enforceable when the amount of money represents a good faith effort to calculate what would actually be adequate compensation.

Lump Sum Contract A contract for a specific task to be completed for a specific dollar amount.

M

Magnuson-Moss Act A federal act that regulates how consumer product warranties — or the disclaimer of those warranties — should be phrased. A contractor falls under this act when the contractor buys the product himself, adds a markup, and then installs it. The contractor is then selling that product to the customer. If the customer is a homeowner, he or she falls into the "consumer" category under this act.

Material Man A common law term that referred to anyone who supplied goods to a construction site. The term still appears in many mechanic's lien or construction lien statutes.

Mechanic's Lien The term "mechanic's lien" means any lien that a laborer can put on real or personal property if he isn't paid for the work that he did on that property. That includes a construction lien, which is a form of mechanic's lien. It isn't possible to get a mechanic's lien — or a construction lien — on other property the debtor may own. It can only be the property that the laborer actually did the work on.

N

No Damages for Delay Clause Contract language that means one or more of the parties is giving up, in advance, their right to claim damages for losses caused by the other party's delay.

Notice of Commencement As part of their construction lien process, some states require a property owner to post a notice on the property, and also record it with the Registrar of Deeds, that tells subcontractors and suppliers how to let the property owner know that they have worked on the property or supplied material to it, and that they may be entitled to a lien.

Notice of Completion A notice that's typically given to property owners by contractors, subcontractors or suppliers that tells the property owner that payment is due for work completed. It also informs the owner that the contractor, subcontractor or a supplier has the right to claim a lien on the property if payment isn't received for work done on the property, or for construction materials that were delivered to that property for improvements made to the property.

Notice of Furnishing Some states require a subcontractor or supplier who has had no direct contact with the property owner to give written notice to a property owner of what they're doing. If the subcontractor or supplier doesn't give the property owner a Notice of Furnishing, that subcontractor or supplier will not be able to put a construction lien on the property. The purpose of the notice is to let the property owner know that there's someone on this job site who could put a lien on the property if he isn't paid.

O

Occupancy Permit A release issued by the building inspector when the work started by the building permit is completed. The occupancy permit means that the structure can now be used.

OSHA 200 Log A record of injuries and work loss that companies of a certain size, or companies who have had particular kinds of difficulties with work-related injuries, are required to keep.

P

Partnership An association of two or more people to operate a business for profit; in other words, a business with more than one owner. The owners don't need to have equal shares. See also *Limited Partnership*.

Pay When Paid Clause A contingent payment clause in a contract that says the prime contractor doesn't have an obligation to pay the subcontractors until he's paid by the property owner. Many states will not enforce this.

Peculiar Risk Doctrine A legal term used in situations where the property owner may be liable for injuries to the contractor's employees or to the subcontractor's employees. As a general rule, the owner isn't liable for injuries to the employees of independent subcontractors. However, the owner may be held liable for his own negligence in failing to control the work, negligent hiring, or the maintenance of a dangerous condition on the premises. Some states have held that the owner is negligent when he fails to require his contractors to carry workers' compensation insurance.

Perfecting a Lien The process used to secure a lien against property, and giving that lien priority over other security interests, such as mortgages, which may follow. It usually requires notice to the property owners and filing a Claim of Lien with the local Deed Recorder.

Performance Bond A promise from a surety that if a contractor or a subcontractor doesn't perform their contractual obligations, the surety will protect the property owner from the damage caused by that failure to perform. A surety is the person who promises to pay if the contractor or subcontractor doesn't.

Perpetuity Lasting forever. For example, corporations exist in perpetuity, or forever, unless the shareholders vote to go out of business, or the required annual reports aren't filed with the state.

Personal Liability A legal term referring to a situation where somebody who would otherwise be protected by incorporation can be held personally liable. Shareholders in a corporation aren't, as a general rule, personally responsible for that corporation's wrongdoing. If the company can't pay for it, the shareholders don't have to reach into their own pockets, but sometimes it's possible to "pierce the corporate veil." For example, if the sole shareholder is also the company president and manager, and he conceals a hazardous materials situation and someone's injured because of that. The injured person may be able to sue the company and the company president for damages, and collect from his personal assets.

PPE An OSHA abbreviation for *personal protective equipment*, such as safety glasses or steel-toed boots. OSHA requires employees performing certain types of work to use this equipment.

Progress Payments Most larger construction contracts key in the due date of payments to specific dates or milestones in the construction process, such as pouring the foundation, getting the framing finished, etc.

Promissory Estoppel A legal term meaning that a person's right to do something — such as withdraw a bid — is diminished because someone else has relied upon his or her promise. For example, a subcontractor may give a contractor a bid and the contractor accepts it, but the contractor uses that bid as part of the basis for his own bid. When the sub knew the contractor was going to do that, he can't then say, "Oh, did I say $10,000, I meant $12,000."

Public Contract A contract with a public body, such as the federal government or a local municipality. These contracts are subject to different rules than contracts with private individuals or businesses.

Publicly-Held Corporation A corporation that sells their stock to the public, often on the large exchanges like the New York Securities Exchange.

Punch List This is the informal term for an inspection by the contractor and the property owner that produces a list of items of work that need to be completed or corrected by the contractor. Some contracts require this before final payment, or use it as part of collecting the amount of the homeowner's retention.

Q

Quantum Meruit A legal theory intended as a remedy in those situations where somebody would be unjustly enriched if the letter of the law were applied. See also *Unjust Enrichment*.

R

Reasonable Time The customary time that one party allows another to decide on the acceptance of a bid or contract. It may vary within the local industry. A well-advised contractor or subcontractor would put an expiration date, such as ten days, on his bid so that everyone involved knows that the reasonable time for acceptance is ten days.

Reliance A legal term meaning that sometimes a person's right to do something — such as withdraw a bid — is diminished because someone else has foreseeably relied upon it. See also *Promissory Estoppel*.

Rescission To put the parties to a contract back in the position they were in before there was a contract; in other words, to cancel the contract.

Responsible Managing Employee (RME) The person who must hold the license in a corporation or partnership when state law doesn't allow a corporation or partnership to be licensed as a contractor. California, for example, requires that the RME be an employee who's "permanently employed and is actively engaged in the operation of the business for at least 32 hours, or 80 percent of the total hours per week such business is in operation."

Retention A clause in a contract that allows the customer to withhold a percentage of the payment until the customer has completed an inspection of the work, and until any complaints the customer identifies in that inspection have been dealt with to the customer's satisfaction.

Right of Cancellation When a contract is signed in the consumer's home in the presence of the contractor or his agent, federal law requires that the contract include a notice of the customer's right to cancel the contract, and notice of when that right expires.

Right of Rescission The federal Truth-In-Lending Act gives construction customers a right of rescission (cancellation) if the contract involves a security interest on the customer's home. The act gives the customer 72 hours after the contract is signed to rescind the contract, or 72 hours after the homeowner is given notice of the right of rescission, whichever comes later.

S

Satisfaction Common language used in a contract that means the completed work must conform to the *standards of the trade* and be suitable for use or occupation for its intended purpose. It doesn't mean absolute perfection, as many customers seem to expect.

Set-Aside Letters When a construction loan is in danger of default, or has defaulted, a surety who has given performance bond guaranteeing the completion of the job can ask the lender for a "set-aside letter." This is a document in which the lender agrees to set aside a portion of the project loan, and advance that money to the surety for project completion. Set aside letters are typically used as part of a "workout" plan where there are concerns about the owner's ability to pay.

Sole Proprietorship A legal term that means a business is owned by one person, and hasn't assumed any other legal form, such as a corporation or a partnership.

Statute of Limitations A term for the legal rule that the right to sue doesn't last indefinitely. Different states set different time periods for various causes of action. In the construction field, there can be a problem establishing when the statute of limitations went into effect on a particular job. For example, on a roofing job, did it start when the flashing was installed incorrectly, or when the leak became visible to the owner after the first hard rain six months later?

Stop Notice Some states allow a substitute for a construction lien which allows a subcontractor or material supplier to give a "stop notice" to the lending institution. It orders the lending institution, the property owner or the public agency to hold money back from the contractor to pay a subcontractor or material supplier. Most of the states that have this procedure only allow it on public projects, but a few allow it on private projects.

Subchapter S Corporations Subchapter S refers to a section of the tax code that allows a corporation's taxable income, gains, losses, and deductions to be "passed through" the corporation straight to the shareholders in much the same way as a partnership would. But in every other way, a subchapter S corporation functions just like any other corporation.

Subcontractor A contractor (usually one specializing in a particular trade) who performs part of a contract for the prime contractor who actually has the contractual obligation to perform. A subcontractor isn't a party to that contract and, except for lien rights, has only the rights to payment and other contract benefits that are granted to the prime contractor.

Substantial Compliance A legal term that means that the construction project has been completed to the point that it can be used for its intended purpose. Also called *substantial completion* or *substantial performance*.

Surety A company or person that provides a bond, such as a payment or performance bond. The surety promises to make good on the bonded agreement if the contractor defaults. If the surety actually has to pay off on the bond, the surety has the right to sue the contractor for reimbursement.

T

Time and Materials A construction industry term used to describe a pricing method based upon the exact amount of time expended on the job and the exact cost of materials.

Time and Materials Contract An agreement in which the property owner pays a flat hourly rate for labor, plus the cost of all materials.

Tort Any wrongful act, damage, or injury done willfully, negligently or involving strict liability, but not involving breach of contract, for which a civil lawsuit for damages can be brought. For example, if the property owner brings his friend over to the job site and they wander around until the roofer drops a hammer on the friend's head, the friend would sue the contractor for the tort of negligence. Fortunately for the contractor, this isn't like workers' compensation. The contractor must be shown to have been negligent before the friend can actually collect on his tort.

U

Uniform Building Code A model building code, published by the International Conference of Building Officials, in California, which is used in many communities. It has recently been replaced by the *International Building Code* and the *International Residential Code*, though many communities have been slow in adopting these.

Unjust Enrichment A legal term for an equitable action that can be brought against someone who intended to benefit by someone else's actions, but didn't intend to pay for those actions because of a technicality in the law. An example would be a person who deliberately hires an unlicensed contractor to do work and then refuses to pay for that work knowing that an unlicensed contractor can't sue for payment. Anyone wishing to sue for unjust enrichment should consult with an attorney because it's a narrow action that's often not available.

V

Variance A waiver or a variation from the standards in the zoning laws. For example, if you want to build a church in a residential neighborhood, you must ask the local zoning board for a "variance" from the zoning, because churches aren't residential. In other words, you're asking the zoning board not to enforce the zoning laws against you.

W

Wage Base The base amount of money that an employee may earn before the employer must make federal unemployment payments (FUTA payments) for that employee. There may also be a state wage base for state unemployment payments.

Warranty An assurance by the seller of goods or services that the goods, property or services are as represented, or will be as promised. It guarantees the integrity of the product and the maker's responsibility to repair or replace defective parts.

Workout Plan An agreement between a company and its major creditors to pay off a portion of their debt or extend the payoff time. The creditors agree to hold off suing, or collecting on judgments they may already have, or forcing the company into bankruptcy. The goal of this workout is to keep the company in business.

Z

Zoning Local ordinances that restrict land use and may restrict building placement and architectural features.

Index

A

Addendum, subcontractors 201-207
Addendums, subcontractors 190
Advertising, zoning code restrictions 9
Affirmative Action Programs
    discrimination laws 112
Allowances, construction contracts 84
Americans With Disabilities,
    discrimination laws 105
Americans With Disabilities Act
    building access 159-160
    commercial buildings 159
    consulting an attorney 80
    existing buildings 160
    hiring issues 105
    implied warranties 80
Appeals, tax audits 122-123
Arbitration
    construction contracts 93
    consumer protection laws 225
    debt collection 126
    disputes 93
    in-writing requirements 225-226
    writing requirements 225
Architects
    building code 149
    copyrighted building plans 151
    fitness of purpose 150
    indemnification agreements 161
    Zoning Code 157
At Will Employees, employees 110
Attestation Form I-9
    employees 107
Attorney Consultation
    accessibility laws 161
    Americans With Disabilities Act 80
    bankruptcy 241
    breach of contract 91
    choosing a lawyer 253
    contracts that are not in writing 56
    corporate benefit packages 117
    debts 240
    drug tests 109
    getting the contract signed 62
    illegal aliens 107
    incorporating 50
    injuries on the job site 177
    joint ventures 41
    lien foreclosure 137
    limited partnerships 41
    married couples 94
    multiple classes of stock 43
    non-competition restrictions 111
    priority 138
    public projects 142-143
    selling stock 44
    statute of limitations 22
    Stop Notices 142-143
    subcontractors and their lien rights .186-188
    substantial performance 85
    tax audits 122-123
    threatened license 12
    what your lawyer will need 255
    when to call a lawyer 253-254
    wills 250
Attorney Consultations, indemnification
    agreements 161
Attorney fees 194
Attorney Fees, construction contracts 85

B

Bankruptcy 241-243
    automatic stays 241
    Chapter 11 242-243
    Chapter 7 241-242
    construction contracts 242-243
    employees withholding 239
    secured creditors 241
    staying in business 242-243
    unsecured creditors 241
Benefits
    attorney consultation 117
    corporations 46-47, 249
    health and disability benefits 249
Bids
    fraud.................................60
    mistakes 77
    public agencies 60
    subcontractor's mistakes 59
    subcontractors 57-59
    when binding? 57-60
Bona Fide Occupational Requirements,
    discrimination laws 104
Breach of Contract, explained 91
Breach of Contract Damages,
    subcontractors not performing 58-59
Building Access
    Americans With Disabilities Act 159-161
    handicapped persons 159-161
    The Fair Housing Act 159-161
Building Code
    inspections 149
    who is responsible for meeting it 150
Building Codes
    BOCA 148
    building permits 148
    design process 148
    engineers & architects 149
    model building codes 148
    other kinds of permits 161
    Uniform Building Code 148
    what is their impact 147
Building Plans
    copyrights 151
    license to use 151
Business, funding for buy-out plans 250
Business Name 18-20
Business Names 18-20
    assumed names 18
    corporations 20
    d-b-a- certificates 20
    trademark restraints 19-20
    unincorporated businesses 18
Business Use of Your Home,
    IRS publication 10

C

Cars or Trucks Tax Deductions,
    IRS Form 4526 119
Certificate of Occupancy, warranties 215
Change Orders
    construction contracts 88-90
    how enforceable 60
    in writing? 61
    in-writing requirements 225-226
    payment for 60-61
    performance bonds 144
    subcontractors 192
    waiving the writing requirement 90

Civil Rights Act, discrimination laws 105
Classification, workers' compensation 174
Concealed Conditions, construction
    contracts 80
Construction Business
    advantages of starting small 8
    office in home 8-9
Construction Contracts
    accepting a contract 62
    allowances 84
    arbitration clause 93
    attorney fees 85, 194
    change order procedure with
    subcontractors 192
    consumer protections in contracts 94
    contingent payment clauses 194-196
    cost plus 82
    counter offer 63
    definitions 53
    dispute resolution 191-192
    estimates 57
    expiration dates 95
    hidden or concealed conditions 80
    how binding is a fax 62
    in court 256
    liquidated damages 87
    mistakes 77
    must they be in writing? 54-55
    "no damages for delay" 196-198
    no-lien clauses 191
    offers 55
    owner keeps contract 62
    progress payments 83
    punch lists 85-86
    retention of payments due 85-86
    right of cancellation 222-223
    Right of Rescission 64
    scope of the work 76
    signed in the customer's home 63
    substantial completion 84-85
    time & materials payments 81
    time of the essence clauses 87
    vague or missing terms 64
    who is supposed to sign the contract 94
    who should be named 67
    with tenants 94
Construction Liens
    an unlicensed contractor 15
    Right of Rescission 64
Consumer, defined 64
Consumer Protection, construction
    contracts 94
Consumer Protection Laws
    arbitration restrictions 225
    change orders 225-226
    license requirements 224
    limits on advance payments 223
    Magnuson-Moss Act 231-232
    rescission 228-231
    right of cancellation 222-223
    special notices 226
    state laws about warranties 227
    written warning about possible liens 226
Consumer Protection Notices 63
Consumer Protection Rights, state laws 64
Contingent Payment, subcontractors .194-195
Contractors' Liability for Injuries
    consulting an attorney 177-178
    employees 174
    job site visitors 175-176

liability insurance 177
Contractors' Liability for injuries, negligence 174-178
Contractors' Liability for Injuries
"peculiar risk" doctrine 176-177
subcontractors or their employees 183
to children 178
trespassers 177-178
Contractors-License.org Web site 13
"Cooling-off Period," consumer protection-laws 222-223
Copyrights, building plans 151
Corporations
advantages of subchapter S 45
as a business partner 30
assumed names 20
benefits 46-47
Board of Directors 46
business debts 47
closely-held corporations 45
death of a shareholder 48
definition 42
disadvantages 48
employer identification number 11
health and disability benefits 249
how taxed 117
license requirements 14
management 46
owners co-signing debts 47
paperwork 48
"piercing the veil" 47
procedure 43
publicly-held corporations 44
qualifying for subchapter S 45
selling the business 48
state taxes 46
state taxes on subchapter S corporations .45
Subchapter C Corporation 117
Subchapter S corporation defined 117
Subchapter S Corporations 117
Subchapter S definition 45
taxation of corporate profits 42
Cost Plus, construction contracts 82
Counter Offer, construction contracts 63
Criminal Records, employees 108

D

Death
corporate shareholders 48
of a partner 38
Death of a Business Owner 25
sole owner 28
Death of an Employee, OSHA rules 166
Debt Collection
judgments 128
mediation & arbitration 126
punch lists 128
Small Claims Court 127
Debts
bank's right of off-set 238
bankruptcy 241-243
consulting an attorney 240
fraudulent transfers of money or property 238
money belonging to spouse 238
private workouts 240
Debts-Business 26
corporations 47
in general 26-27
personal assets of owners 26
sole owner 29
Definition
corporation 42
partnerships 30
sole owner 27
Delay
liquidated damages 87
owner-caused delay 88
subcontractors 196-199
time of the essence 87
Demolition, permits 149
Department of Health 161
Derivative Rights, subcontractors 190
Design, building codes 148
Design and Build, licensing requirements ..18
Disability 248-250
Disclaimers
effect of state laws 227
Magnuson-Moss Act 232
of warranties 216-219, 227
Discrimination Laws 102-105
affirmative action programs 112
Americans With Disabilities 105
avoiding the appearance of 103
bona fide occupational requirements ...104
Civil Rights Act 105
English-speaking job requirements 104
job interviews 103
reasonable accommodations 105, 160
The Federal Age Discrimination Act 105
wording job advertisements 103
Divorce
impact on a partnership 39
sole owner 29
Down Payments, state consumer protection laws 83
Drug Tests, employees 108

E

EIN 11
Employee Handbook
contents 109-111
firing employees 109-111
legal impact 109
"moonlighting" 111
Employee Negligence, employees 107
Employee Records 22
INS Form I-9 22
Employees
Americans With Disabilities 105
compared with independent contractors 181-183
contractors' liability for injuries 174
criminal records 108
death of an employee 166
drug tests 108
employee handbook 109-111
employee negligence 107
employees' OSHA obligations 169
Employer's Supplemental Tax Guide 100
Fair Labor Standards Act 106
FUTA payments 102
illegal aliens 103, 106-108
IRS Form 941 102
IRS Form SS-8 ....101, 182
job firing procedures 109-111
lie detector tests 106, 108
"moonlighting" 111
non-competition restrictions 111
OSHA employee rights 167-169
OSHA inspections 170
OSHA rules on employer retaliation 168
OSHA safety-training rules 166
pension plans 247-248
right to refuse a dangerous job 168-169
"safe harbor" rules 100, 182-183
Simple IRA 247
social security payments 101
The Federal Age Discrimination Act 105
unemployment insurance 102
unlawful discrimination 102-106
W-2 forms 121
W-4 forms 101, 121
with alcohol problems 107-108
withholding 101-102, 121, 239
workplace posters 106
Employer identification number (EIN) 11
Employer's Supplemental Tax Guide, employees 100
Employer's Tax Guide, IRS Circular E, employees 11
Engineers, building code 149
Estimated Quarterly Payments, self-employment 114
Estimates, how binding? 57
Estoppel
bids 58-60
failure to deliver contract 62
Existing Buildings, *Americans With Disabilities Act* 160
Expiration Dates, construction contracts ...95
Express Warranties, defined 93

F

Fair Labor Standards Act, employees 106
Faxes, construction contracts 62
Federal Projects, licensing requirements ...18
Fitness of Purpose
architects 150
warranties 150
Foreclosure
construction liens 135-138
proceeds 137

G

Good Workmanship, legal definition 215

H

Hazardous Materials, OSHA rules 167
Hidden Conditions, construction contracts .80
Home office 8-9
IRS rules 9-11
residential zoning codes 8-9
Home Office, tax deduction 9, 120

I

Illegal Aliens, employees 103, 106-108
Immigration and Naturalization Service, keeping copies of Form I-9 22
Immigration Reform and Control Act, employees 106
Implied Warranties, defined 93
Indemnification, construction contracts ...92
Indemnification Agreements
accessibility laws 161
defined 161
Independent Contractors
employees 181-183
"safe harbor" rules 100, 182-183
INS Form I-9
keeping copies of 22
Inspections 149-150
final inspection 149-150
occupancy permit 149, 214
Insurance
Errors and Omissions 200
gaps in subcontractor coverage 186
health and/or disability 249
help from insurance company lawyers ..254
liability insurance 175-178
life insurance 250
workers' compensation 174
IRS
phone numbers for 10-11
"safe harbor" rules 100, 182-183
subcontractors 115, 183
IRS 1040 Schedule E Part II, partnerships ..116
IRS Form 1040 Schedule C, self-employment 115
IRS Form 1040 Schedule SE, self-employment 115
IRS Form 1040-ES 114
IRS Form 1065
partnership tax return 37
partnerships 116
IRS Form 1065 K-1
partnerships 116
IRS Form 1099
"safe harbor" rules 100, 182-183
subcontractors 115, 183
IRS Form 1120-Schedule K-1
corporations 118

IRS Form 1120S, corporations 118
IRS Form 2210 114
IRS Form 2553
corporations 117-118
IRS Form 4562
deducting vehicles 119
IRS Form 8829
home offices 120
IRS Form 940
FUTA payments 102
IRS Form 941
employees 102
IRS Form SS-8
employees 101, 182
IRS Form W-2
employees 121
IRS Form W-4
employees 101, 120
IRS forms, *Form 8829* for home office 10
IRS Forms
IRS Form 1065 37
IRS Form Schedule K 38
payment vouchers 114
IRS forms
SS-4, employer identification number 11
taxpayer identification number 10-11
IRS Notice of Deficiency, tax audits 122-123
IRS Publication 15, Circular E, employee withholding 101
IRS publications, *Business Use of Your Home* 10
IRS Publications, *Employer's Supplemental Tax Guide* 100
IRS publications
Employer's Tax Guide 11
ordering by phone 10
IRS publications, *Tax Guide for Small Businesses* 10, 115
IRS regulations
employer identification number 11
home office 9-11
taxpayer identification number 10-11
IRS Reporting Requirements 26
sole owner 28
IRS Requirements, for self-employment ...114

J

Job Advertisements, discrimination laws ..103
Job Completion
satisfaction 86
substantial completion 85
substantial performance 85
Job Interviews, discrimination laws 103
Job Site
children coming onto the job site 178
injury to visitors 175-176
reasonable care to keep it safe 175
Joint Ventures 14, 41

L

Laborers, construction liens 131
Lawsuits 27
against a partnership 40
license requirement to sue 224
lien foreclosure 135-138
pretrial settlements 128
property owner suing an unlicensed contractor 15-16
Small Claims Court 127
sole owner 30
unlicensed contractor suing 17, 18
winning 128
Lawyers, knowing when you need one 7
Liability insurance, employee negligence ..107
Licenses 12-16
corporations 14
design and build projects 18
developers 14
homeowners 13
joint ventures 14
lawsuits 224
managing partner 14
on a federal project 18
partnerships 14
penalties for not having one 15
subcontractors 14
supplier to an unlicensed contractor 17
when an unlicensed contractor can sue 15-16
who must be licensed 13
written notices to customers 226
Lie Detector Tests, employees 106, 108
Lien Waivers 138-139
conditional waivers 139
subcontractors 138-139, 190
Liens 129-139
contractor's duty to protect the property owner 130
foreclosure 135
laborers 131
lien claimants defined 130
lien defined 129
lien waivers 138-139
material suppliers 130
payment bonds 143
payment to contractor 131
public projects 142
stop notices 142
subcontractor lien rights 187-188
subcontractors 130
tenants 138
written warnings about possible liens ...226
Limitations on Warranties 213-214
affect of state laws 227
Liquidated Damages, construction contracts 87
Liquidated Damages Clauses, subcontractors 199
Logbooks 254-256
in court 255-256

M

Magnuson-Moss Act
defined 63-64
warranties 231-232
Managing Partner
in a corporation 14
in a partnership 14
Manufacturer's Warranties, maintaining the manufacturer's warranties 218-219
Material suppliers, construction liens 130
Mediation 93
Mistakes
bids 77
in subcontractor bids 59
"Moonlighting" restrictions, employees ...111

N

Negligence
contractors' liability 174-178
subcontractors' liability 176
No Damages for Delay, construction contracts 88
No Damages for Delay Clauses, subcontractors 196-198
No-Lien Contract Clauses, subcontractors 191

O

Occupancy Permits, fitness of purpose 150, 214
Offers
can an offer be withdrawn 57
expiration dates 57-59
Office
home 8-9
writing off expenses 10-11
OSHA 163-173
dangerous jobs 164
employee obligations 169
employee's rights under the OSHA rules 167-169
employers' obligations 164-
"free of recognized hazards" 164
injury reporting requirements 173
inspections 170
legal impact of the OSHA rules 163
OSHA 200 Log 166-167
personal protective equipment (PPE's) ..169
required safety records 166
safety-training employees 165-166
statement of purpose 163-164
OSHA 200 Log, OSHA 166-167
OSHA Rules
employer retaliation 168, 170
hazardous materials 167

P

Partnerships 30
a partner's divorce 39
agreements between the partners 31
control of 37
corporation as partner 30
death of a partner 38
definition 30
employer identification number 11
IRS 1040 Schedule E Part II 116
IRS Form 1065 116
IRS Form 1065 K-1 116
IRS Form Schedule K 38
joint ventures 14, 41
lawsuits against the partnership 40
license requirements 14
limited partnerships 41
mutual wills 38
Partnership Planning Checklist 30
selling the business 40
tax deductions 37
taxes 37
Uniform Partnership Act 31
"Pay When Paid," impact on subcontractors 194-196
Payment Bonds 143-144
construction liens 143
Payment to Contractor, construction liens .131
Peculiar Risk Doctrine 176-177
Pension Plans for Employees 247-248
Performance Bonds
defined 144
"set aside" letters 144
the impact of change orders 144
Permits
building demolition 149
building permit 148
Department of Health requirements 161
environmental permits 161
final inspection 149, 214
home shows 150
homeowners 149
local permitting rules 161
occupancy permit 149, 214
other kinds of permits 161
starting work without one 148
Personal Protective Equipment, OSHA rules 169
Polygraph Protection Act, employees 106
Posters
employees 106
OSHA materials 166-167
PPE's, personal protective equipment 169
Professionals, knowing when you need one ..7
Progress Payments, construction contracts .83
Property Owner, hiring an unlicensed contractor 16
Public Agencies, bids 60
Public Projects
construction liens 142
Stop Notices 142-143
Punch List, payments 86

Punch Lists
and debt collection 128
construction contracts 85-86

R

Reasonable Accommodations
discrimination laws 105
The Fair Housing Act 160
Reasonable Care, job site 175
Records 20-23
as evidence 21
insurance company audits 21
keep your originals 256
tax audits 20
Reporting Requirements, OSHA 173
Rescission, consumer protection
laws 228-231
Residential zoning codes, home office 8-9
Retention, construction contracts 85-86
Retention Provisions, subcontractors 193
Retirement 245-248
IRAs 245-246
Simple IRA for employees 347
Retirements, SEP pension plans 247
Right of Cancellation
consumer protection laws 222-223
exceptions 223
Right of Rescission
construction liens 63
The Truth In Lending Act 63

S

"Safe harbor" rules
employees 100, 182-183
IRS 100, 182-183
Safe Job Site Standards, legal impact of
OSHA rules 163
Safety Records, required by OSHA 166
Sale of a Business, in general 26
Satisfaction, job completion 86
Scope of the Work Clauses
and implied warranties 78-79
how written 76
Section 179 Deduction, tax
deductions 119-120
Self-employment 113
IRS 115, 183
IRS Form 1040 Schedule C 115
IRS Form 1040 Schedule SE 115
IRS requirements 114
long-term disability 250
short-term disability 249
social security 115
tax deductions 118
Selling the Business
corporations 48
partnerships 40-41
sole owner 28
Set Aside Letters, performance bonds 144
Shareholders
corporate debts 47
death 48
Social security number, using as your TIN ..11
Sole Owner 27
and lawsuits 27
divorce 29
IRS Form 1040 Schedule C 115
IRS reporting requirements 28
license requirements 14
taxpayer identification number 11
Sole Proprietor, definition 27
State Law Requirements
consumer protection 64
consumer protection laws 222-227
down payments 83
licenses 12
state taxes on corporations 46
Statute of Limitations 22
Subcontract, defined 179
Subcontractors
addendums 190, 201-207
attorney fees 194, 200-201
bid mistakes 59
bids 57-59
breach of contract damages 58-59
change orders 192
compared with employees 180
construction lien rights 187-188
construction liens 130
consulting an attorney 186-188
contingent payments 194-196
derivative rights 190
design responsibility 200
dispute resolution 191-192
gaps in insurance coverage 186
injured employees of 184
insurance company audits 21
IRS Form 1099 ....115, 183
job delay 199
liability for negligence 176
lien waivers 138-139, 191
liquidated damages 199
no-lien contracts 191
"pay when paid" contracts 194-196
payment bonds 143
"peculiar risk" doctrine 176-177
"safe harbor" rules 100, 182-183
"safe place to work" 174, 185
"scope of work" clauses 200
standard contract form 190
suing an unlicensed contractor 17
taxes 180
workers' compensation 174-175
Subdivision Regulations 161
Substantial Completion
construction contracts 84-85
defined 84
Substantial Performance, consulting an
attorney 85
Supplier, to an unlicensed contractor 17

T

Tax Audits 122
business records 20
correspondence audits 122
field examinations 123
Notice of Deficiency 122-123
office audits 122
office tax audits 122
Tax deduction, home office 9-11
Tax Guide for Small Businesses, IRS
publication 10
Taxes
deduction for cars and trucks 119
FUTA payments 102
home offices 120
if you haven't filed 123
IRS enrolled accountants 254
Notice of Deficiency 122-123
personal use of business car or truck 119
qualifying for subchapter S 45
Section 179 Deductions 119-120
self-employment 118-120
standard deduction for mileage 119
subcontractors 180
tool depreciation 119-120
Taxpayer identification number (TIN) ...10-11
corporation 11
employees 11
partnership 11
Sole Owner 11
Tenants, getting a construction lien 138
The Fair Housing Act
building access 159-161
multiple unit buildings 159
reasonable accommodations 160
The Family Leave Act, employees 106
The Federal Age Discrimination Act
discrimination laws 105
employees 105
The Truth In Lending Act, Right of
Rescission 64
Time and Materials, construction
contracts 81
Time of the Essence, construction
contracts 87
TIN 10-11
Tool Depreciation, for tax purposes ...119-120
Tools, taxes 119-120
Trade Standards, good workmanship 215
Trespassers, contractors liability for
injuries 177

U

Unemployment Insurance
employees 102
FUTA payments 102

V

Variance, Zoning Code 155

W

Waivers, zoning laws 155
Warranties
after the job is finished 218
and problems with the specs 77
certificate of occupancy 214
disclaimers 216-219, 227
exclusions 217-219, 227
express warranties defined 212
fitness of purpose 150, 214
good workmanship warranty 215
habitability 214-215
implied warranties defined 214
limitations on express warranties ...213-219
limitations on implied
warranties 215-219, 227
Magnuson-Moss Act 63-64, 231-232
manufacturer's warranties 218-219
state laws about warranties 227
unlicensed contractors 16
Wills 250
Withholding Amounts, *IRS Publication 15, Circular E* 101
Workers' Compensation
classification 174
exclusive remedy 172
gross negligence 172-173
insurance companies 173
subcontractors 174-175
Writing Requirements
arbitration 225
notice of rescission 228-231
special notices 226
written warning about possible liens 226

Z

Zoning Board of Appeals, Zoning Code 155
Zoning Code
arbitrary and capricious zoning 158
architects 157
constitutional issues 157-158
existing buildings 155-156
non-compliance 156-157
the "set back" 155
variances 155
waivers 155
Zoning Board of Appeals 155
Zoning codes, home office 8-9
Zoning Codes, what is their impact 147
Zoning Laws 151

The CD-ROM in the back of the book

The CD inside the back cover has blank copies of all legal forms in this book plus eight other forms. All of these forms are saved in both Adobe's PDF and RTF (rich text format) format. All forms are listed below.

There are two ways to use these forms:

1. In Windows Explorer, double-click on the file name on the CD, or
2. Install the forms to the hard drive of your computer.

To use the PDF files, you'll need Adobe's Acrobat *Reader*. It's available at no charge on the Adobe Web site. http://www.adobe.com Most word processing programs (including WordPad) can open an RTF file. To start WordPad, click Start, Programs, Accessories, WordPad.

To install some or all of these forms on your hard drive, put the CD in your CD drive. After a few seconds, installation should begin. Follow instructions on the screen. If installation doesn't begin automatically, click Start, Settings, Control Panel, Add/Remove Programs and then Install.

By default, the installation program transfers all forms to your hard drive. Only about 1 Mb of disk space is required. When the installation program begins, click Install Forms, Next, Next, Next, Install and Finish. Other options allow you to install only the forms and formats you select.

The eight bonus forms are saved to disk in two formats. Forms with names ending with 1 include instructions. Equivalent blank forms have file names ending in 2.

By default, all forms are installed to the My Documents folder in a sub-folder, Contractor's Plain-English Legal Guide Forms. Once the forms are installed, they can be accessed from the Start button. Click Start, Programs, Contractor's Legal Guide, Legal Forms. Then double-click on the format and file name you want to open. For assistance, call Craftsman's technical support line, 760-438-7828.

LEGAL FORM BLANKS	File Name	Page
Addendum to Contract	ADDENDUM	202
Articles of Incorporation	INCORP	43
Claim of Lien	LIENCLM	134
Contract Change Order	CHANGORD	89
Copyright Notice	COPYRITE	152
General Partnership	GENPRTNR	32
Lien Waiver — Full Conditional	LIENWVCN	141
Lien Waiver — Full Unconditional	LIENWVUN	140
Notice of Furnishing	NOTEFURN	132
Notice of Right to Rescission	RESCISSN	229
Proof of Service	PROOFSRV	133
Remodeling Contract	REMODCON	68
Sell Copyright	COPYRSEL	154
Use Copyright	COPYRUSE	153

BONUS FORMS & INSTRUCTIONS	Instruction Form File Name	Blank Form File Name
Certificate of Acceptance After Final Inspection	CRTACPT1	CRTACPT2
Contract to Build a House At	BLDCON1	BLDCON2
Lien Waiver – Partial Conditional	LIENWVC1	LIENWVC2
Lien Waiver – Partial Unconditional	LIENWVU1	LIENWVU2
Notice of Delay on the Job Site	DLAYNTC1	DLAYNTC2
Notice of Intent to Stop Work	STOPNTC1	STOPNTC2
Notice of Commencement to Start Work	NOTECOM1	NOTECOM2
Sworn Statement	SWORNST1	SWORNST2

Practical References for Builders

Builder's Guide to Accounting Revised

Step-by-step, easy-to-follow guidelines for setting up and maintaining records for your building business. This practical, newly-revised guide to all accounting methods shows how to meet state and federal accounting requirements, explains the new depreciation rules, and describes how the Tax Reform Act can affect the way you keep records. Full of charts, diagrams, simple directions and examples, to help you keep track of where your money is going. Recommended reading for many state contractor's exams. Includes test questions for every chapter. **356 pages, 8½ x 11, $30.50**

Moving to Commercial Construction

In commercial work, a single job can keep you and your crews busy for a year or more. The profit percentages are higher, but so is the risk involved. This book takes you step-by-step through the process of setting up a successful commercial business; finding work, estimating and bidding, value engineering, getting through the submittal and shop drawing process, keeping a stable work force, controlling costs, and promoting your business. Explains the design/build and partnering business concepts and  their advantage over the competitive bid process. Includes sample letters, contracts, checklists and forms that you can use in your business, plus a CD-ROM with blank copies in several word-processing formats for both Mac and PC computers. **256 pages, 8½ x 11, $42.00**

The Contractor's Legal Kit

Stop "eating" the costs of bad designs, hidden conditions, and job surprises. Set ground rules that assign those costs to the rightful party ahead of time. And it's all in plain English, not "legalese." For less than the cost of an hour with a lawyer you'll learn the exclusions to put in your agreements, why your insurance company may pay for your legal defense, how to avoid liability for injuries to your sub and his employees or damages they cause, how to collect on lawsuits you win, and much more. It also includes a FREE computer disk with contracts and forms you can customize for your own use. **352 pages, 8½ x 11, $59.95**

Construction Forms & Contracts

125 forms you can copy and use — or load into your computer (from the FREE disk enclosed). Then you can customize the forms to fit your company, fill them out, and print. Loads into *Word* for *Windows*™, *Lotus 1-2-3*, *WordPerfect*, *Works*, or *Excel* programs. You'll find forms covering accounting, estimating, fieldwork, contracts, and general office. Each form comes with complete instructions on when to use it and how to fill it out. These forms were designed, tested and used by contractors, and will help keep your business organized, profitable and out of legal, accounting and collection troubles. Includes a CD-ROM for *Windows*™ and Mac. **400 pages, 8½ x 11, $41.75**

National Repair & Remodeling Estimator

The complete pricing guide for dwelling reconstruction costs. Reliable, specific data you can apply on every repair and remodeling job. Up-to-date material costs and labor figures based on thousands of jobs across the country. Provides recommended crew sizes; average production rates; exact material, equipment, and labor costs; a total unit cost and a total price including overhead and profit. Separate listings for high- and low-volume builders, so prices shown are specific for any size business. Estimating tips specific to repair and remodeling work to make your bids complete, realistic, and profitable. Includes a CD-ROM with an electronic version of the book with *National Estimator*, a stand-alone *Windows*™ estimating program, plus an interactive multimedia video that shows how to use the disk to compile construction cost estimates. **296 pages, 8½ x 11, $48.50. Revised annually**

Basic Lumber Engineering for Builders

Beam and lumber requirements for many jobs aren't always clear, especially with changing building codes and lumber products. Most of the time you rely on your own "rules of thumb" when figuring spans or lumber engineering. This book can help you fill the gap between what you can find in the building code span tables and what you need to pay a certified engineer to do. With its large, clear illustrations and examples, this book shows you how to figure stresses for pre-engineered wood or wood structural members, how to calculate loads, and how to design your own girders, joists and beams. Included FREE with the book — an easy-to-use limited version of NorthBridge Software's *Wood Beam Sizing* program. **272 pages, 8½ x 11, $38.00**

Markup & Profit: A Contractor's Guide

In order to succeed in a construction business, you have to be able to price your jobs to cover all labor, material and overhead expenses, and make a decent profit. The problem is knowing what markup to use. You don't want to lose jobs because you charge too much, and you don't want to work for free because you've charged too little. If you know how to calculate markup, you can apply it to your job costs to find the right sales price for your work. This book gives you tried and tested formulas, with step-by-step instructions and easy-to-follow examples, so you can easily figure the markup that's right for your business. Includes a CD-ROM with forms and checklists for your use. **320 pages, 8½ x 11, $32.50**

How to Succeed With Your Own Construction Business

Everything you need to start your own construction business: setting up the paperwork, finding the work, advertising, using contracts, dealing with lenders, estimating, scheduling, finding and keeping good employees, keeping the books, and coping with success. If you're considering starting your own construction business, all the knowledge, tips, and blank forms you need are here. **336 pages, 8½ x 11, $28.50**

Getting Financing & Developing Land

Developing land is a major leap for most builders — yet that's where the big money is made. This book gives you the practical knowledge you need to make that leap. Learn how to prepare a market study, select a building site, obtain financing, guide your plans through approval, then control your building costs so you can ensure yourself a good profit. Includes a CD-ROM with forms, checklists, and a sample business plan you can customize and use to help you sell your idea to lenders and investors. **232 pages, 8½ x 11, $39.00**

National Construction Estimator

Current building costs for residential, commercial, and industrial construction. Estimated prices for every common building material. Provides man-hours, recommended crew, and gives the labor cost for installation. Includes a CD-ROM with an electronic version of the book with *National Estimator*, a stand-alone *Windows*™ estimating program, plus an interactive multimedia video that shows how to use the disk to compile construction cost estimates. **616 pages, 8½ x 11, $47.50. Revised annually**

Contracting in All 50 States

Every state has its own licensing requirements that you must meet to do business there. These are usually written exams, financial requirements, and letters of reference. This book shows how to get a building, mechanical or specialty contractor's license, qualify for DOT work, and register as an out-of-state corporation, for every state in the U.S. It lists addresses, phone numbers, application fees, requirements, where an exam is required, what's covered on the exam and how much weight each area of construction is given on the exam. You'll find just about everything you need to know in order to apply for your out-of-state license. **416 pages, 8½ x 11, $36.00**

Contractor's Guide to QuickBooks Pro 2001

This user-friendly manual walks you through QuickBooks Pro's detailed setup procedure and explains step-by-step how to create a first-rate accounting system. You'll learn in days, rather than weeks, how to use QuickBooks Pro to get your contracting business organized, with simple, fast accounting procedures. On the CD included with the book you'll find a QuickBooks Pro file preconfigured for a construction company (you drag it over onto your computer and plug in your own company's data). You'll also get a complete estimating program, including a database, and a job costing program that lets you export your estimates to QuickBooks Pro. It even includes many useful construction forms to use in your business. **328 pages, 8½ x 11, $45.25**

Contractor's Guide to the Building Code Revised

This new edition was written in collaboration with the International Conference of Building Officials, writers of the code. It explains in plain English exactly what the latest edition of the *Uniform Building Code* requires. Based on the 1997 code, it explains the changes and what they mean for the builder. Also covers the *Uniform Mechanical Code* and the *Uniform Plumbing Code*. Shows how to design and construct residential and light commercial buildings that'll pass inspection the first time. Suggests how to work with an inspector to minimize construction costs, what common building shortcuts are likely to be cited, and where exceptions may be granted. **320 pages, 8½ x 11, $39.00**

CD Estimator

If your computer has *Windows*™ and a CD-ROM drive, *CD Estimator* puts at your fingertips 85,000 construction costs for new construction, remodeling, renovation & insurance repair, electrical, plumbing, HVAC and painting. Quarterly cost updates are available at no charge on the Internet. You'll also have the *National Estimator* program — a stand-alone estimating program for *Windows*™ that *Remodeling* magazine called a "computer wiz," and Job Cost Wizard, a program that  lets you export your estimates to QuickBooks Pro for actual job costing. A 40-minute interactive video teaches you how to use this CD-ROM to estimate construction costs. And to top it off, to help you create professional-looking estimates, the disk includes over 40 construction estimating and bidding forms in a format that's perfect for nearly any *Windows*™ word processing or spreadsheet program.
CD Estimator is $68.50

Working Alone

This unique book shows you how to become a dynamic one-man team as you handle nearly every aspect of house construction, including foundation layout, setting up scaffolding, framing floors, building and erecting walls, squaring up walls, installing sheathing, laying out rafters, raising the ridge, getting the roof square, installing rafters, subfascia, sheathing, finishing eaves, installing windows, hanging drywall, measuring trim, installing cabinets, and building decks. **152 pages, 5½ x 8½, $17.95**

Construction Estimating Reference Data

Provides the 300 most useful manhour tables for practically every item of construction. Labor requirements are listed for sitework, concrete work, masonry, steel, carpentry, thermal and moisture protection, doors and windows, finishes, mechanical and electrical. Each section details the work being estimated and gives appropriate crew size and equipment needed. Includes a CD-ROM with an electronic version of the book with *National Estimator*, a stand-alone *Windows*™ estimating program, plus an interactive multimedia video that shows how to use the disk to compile construction cost estimates. **432 pages, 11 x 8½, $39.50**

Craftsman's Illustrated Dictionary of Construction Terms

Almost everything you could possibly want to know about any word or technique in construction. Hundreds of up-to-date construction terms, materials, drawings and pictures with detailed, illustrated articles describing equipment and methods. Terms and techniques are explained or illustrated in vivid detail. Use this valuable reference to check spelling, find clear, concise definitions of construction terms used on plans and construction documents, or learn about little-known tools, equipment, tests and methods used in the building industry. It's all here.
416 pages, 8½ x 11, $36.00

Building Contractor's Exam Preparation Guide

Passing today's contractor's exams can be a major task. This book shows you how to study, how questions are likely to be worded, and the kinds of choices usually given for answers. Includes sample questions from actual state, county, and city examinations, plus a sample exam to practice on. This book isn't a substitute for the study material that your testing board recommends, but it will help prepare you for the types of questions — and their correct answers — that are likely to appear on the actual exam. Knowing how to answer these questions, as well as what to expect from the exam, can greatly increase your chances of passing.
320 pages, 8½ x 11, $35.00

Craftsman Book Company
6058 Corte del Cedro
P.O. Box 6500
Carlsbad, CA 92018

☎ 24 hour order line
1-800-829-8123
Fax (760) 438-0398

Name _____

e-mail address (for order tracking and special offers)

Company _____

Address _____

City/State/Zip _____
○ This is a residence
Total enclosed_____(In California add 7.25% tax)
We pay shipping when your check covers your order in full.

In A Hurry?
We accept phone orders charged to your
○ Visa, ○ MasterCard, ○ Discover or ○ American Express

Card#_____

Exp. date_____Initials_____

Tax Deductible: Treasury regulations make these references tax deductible when used
in your work. Save the canceled check or charge card statement as your receipt.

Order online http://www.craftsman-book.com
Free on the Internet! Download any of Craftsman's
estimating costbooks for a 30-day free trial! http://costbook.com

10-Day Money Back Guarantee

○ 38.00 Basic Lumber Engineering for Builders
○ 30.50 Builder's Guide to Accounting Revised
○ 35.00 Building Contractor's Exam Preparation Guide
○ 68.50 CD Estimator
○ 39.50 Construction Estimating Reference Data with FREE *National Estimator* on a CD-ROM.
○ 41.75 Construction Forms & Contracts with a CD-ROM for *Windows*™ and Macintosh.
○ 36.00 Contracting in All 50 States
○ 45.25 Contractor's Guide to QuickBooks Pro 2001
○ 39.00 Contractor's Guide to the Building Code Revised
○ 59.95 Contractor's Legal Kit
○ 36.00 Craftsman's Illustrated Dictionary of Construction Terms
○ 39.00 Getting Financing & Developing Land
○ 28.50 How to Succeed w/Your Own Construction Business
○ 32.50 Markup & Profit: A Contractor's Guide
○ 42.00 Moving to Commercial Construction
○ 47.50 National Construction Estimator with FREE *National Estimator* on a CD-ROM.
○ 48.50 National Repair & Remodeling Estimator with FREE *National Estimator* on a CD-ROM.
○ 17.95 Working Alone
○ 49.50 Contractor's Plain-English Legal Guide
○ FREE Full Color Catalog
Prices subject to change without notice

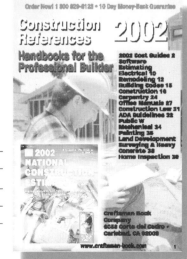